THE ELEGANT PROSTITUTE

A Social and Psychoanalytic Study

THE ELEGANT PROSTITUTE

A Social and Psychoanalytic Study

(A revised edition, with new material, of THE CALL GIRL)

Harold Greenwald

WALKER AND COMPANY
New York

This edition published in 1970 by Walker Publishing Company, Inc.
by arrangement with Ballantine Books, Inc.

Copyright © 1958 by Harold Greenwald
Revised Edition Copyright © 1970 by Harold Greenwald
Library of Congress Catalog Card Number: 70-109189
(Originally published under the title, *The Call Girl*
Library of Congress Catalog Card Number: 57-14679)

Published simultaneously in Canada by The Ryerson Press, Toronto.

Printed in the United States of America
ISBN: 0-8027-0093-4

To R. G.

CONTENTS

Acknowledgment

This book could not have been written without the assistance of many people. It would have been completely impossible without the cooperation of the call girls, whom I cannot thank publicly. But I do want to express my gratitude to the twenty who permitted themselves to be interviewed and most particularly to the three who helped with the interviewing, whom I call Beverly, Marie and Stella. In addition, I want to express my appreciation to Stella, Sandra, Barry and Henry for their permission to include their cases and for the helpful suggestions they made after reading the manuscript.

In the research effort I was greatly aided by a number of the members of the Social Psychology Program of Columbia University. Especially helpful were the contributions of Professors Goodwin Watson and Otto Klineberg, the co-chairmen of the program, Professors Herbert Hyman, Irving Lorge, Nathan W. Ackerman, and Charles M. Morris. Professor Hubert Bonner of Ohio Wesleyan University and Margaret Mead of the Museum of Natural History aided with encouragement and suggestions. A great deal of valuable insight was gained from consulting Drs. Ruth Berkeley and Theodor Reik about psycho-therapeutic problems.

A special debt of gratitude is due to Mr. Edward Jaffe, who made many facilities available. Stanley Kauffmann, editor at Ballantine Books, made me aware of how much a writer can be indebted to an excellent editor. Michael Fooner, my friend and agent, first suggested that I write this book and relentlessly pursued me until I did.

My wife, Ruth Greenwald, not only spared me many of the household burdens while I was working on the book, but in addition typed the manuscript, made literally hundreds of valuable suggestions, and showed a rare tolerance for the kind of research this book entailed.

—H. G.

Foreword

Most of the research on which this book was based was completed in the mid-fifties. However, since concluding actual research, I have maintained contact with the world of the prostitute through the number of call girls and other types of prostitutes who have sought out my services as a therapist after reading this book under its previous title, *The Call Girl*. I decided on the change of title because I wanted to emphasize the continuity in personality, if not in talents and education, between the call girl and her streetwalking sister. For while some of the specific facts have changed, i.e., minimum fees are now "half-a-hundred" (fifty dollars) and there are a larger number of semi-professionals and drug addicts in the field, the personality factors that influence the choice of prostitution as a profession at any level are still basically the same.

As I have continued my work with call girls, I have become more aware of the role of hostility in their behavior. However, as before, the hostility is usually expressed through self-attack. For example, a call girl who is angry with her lover-pimp for being unfaithful to her is much more likely to make a suicide attempt than to attack him or his new love (despite the hollow myth of Frankie and Johnny).

One major distinction has to be made at the present time. A large percentage of streetwalkers are drug addicts, but call girls are not. Because the addict cannot wait at home in the hope of "scoring" (getting money for a fix), few steady call girls are addicted, while more than 90% of female addicts have worked as prostitutes from time to time in order to earn the quick money they need to support their habit and the habit of the men with whom they live. In fact, the major reason for the proliferation of streetwalkers in our largest cities, most notably New York and Chicago, is the tremendous increase in the incidence of heroin addiction. Also, the

appearance of ever younger streetwalkers in the recent
past is owing to the spread of the use of heroin to girls
of high school and junior high school age.

One reason given by many authorities for the increase
in young addicts is the improvement in drug-marketing
techniques. Formerly, heroin was usually dispensed in
glassene bags for five dollars (a (nickel bag). Now it is
possible to purchase a $2.50 bag (half-a-nickel bag),
making it more available to younger people. Also the
vast increase in public attention to the problem of the
drug addict has made it a most attractive form of passive rebellion to many young people who find identification by joining the ranks of the hard-drug users.

Another change that has taken place since my original
research is the spread of semi-professionals. The spread
of group sex or orgies under a variety of names such as
"swinging," "partying," "freaking" or "scening," has
introduced an even more impersonal form of sex than
earlier promiscuity. In a typical group-sex experience,
it is quite common for men and women to indulge in the
most intimate relationships without even knowing each
other's names, or ever having seen each other before.

It becomes comparatively easy for a girl who has attended a number of such parties to accept an occasional
fee as either an additional "kick" or because she can use
the money. Sometimes the orgy may even be organized
by a host or hostess who charges some of the male
guests for attendance at the party. So it is quite possible
for a girl to become an unwitting prostitute. A very attractive, voluptuous girl of my acquaintance was quite
upset when she found out that the charming, friendly
hostess of the swing parties she would occasionally attend, was charging her male guests for the privilege of
attending. Being a shrewd businesswoman, my acquaintance demanded a percentage of the take before she
would agree to be a party to any further scenes. Also,
many call girls attend such parties as a leisure-time
activity and sometimes recruit enthusiastic amateurs
they encounter at such soirées. In general, there has
been some blurring of the lines that separate the professional from the amateur, but the professional call
girl still remains a distinct social and psychological type.

Perhaps the greatest single distinction is that of self-image. The professional identifies herself to herself as a call girl or a prostitute; the amateur usually does it chiefly for a thrill, and has to retain her amateur standing for the extra thrill of self-degradation it gives her.

An additional piece of rather informal research that I carried out was to compare the American call girl with some of her European colleagues. On three trips to Europe, I attempted to interview girls in London, Amsterdam, Paris, Rome and Moscow. In Moscow, I failed to locate any prostitutes despite enlisting the help of newspapermen, illegal money-changers and taxi-drivers. Whatever prostitution exists in Moscow and Leningrad is apparently so underground that it is impossible for the casual visitor to find; government officials of course claimed that the problem no longer exists.

In London I was fortunate enough to find a girl who wanted to improve her status by learning American know-how as it was practiced in her chosen profession. She arranged a meeting with several of her friends and I found myself in the dubious position of conducting a seminar on the techniques of elegant prostitution. However, being girls at a lower level of sophistication than most of the girls I knew in New York, they indignantly refused to resort to the flattery and blandishments that a skilled call girl customarily uses. They felt it would be a threat to their integrity!

Generally, I found more or less the same dynamics in the European prostitute as in her American counterpart. Suicide was still a major occupational hazard and one Italian streetwalker of fifty told me that almost all the girls with whom she had started out in life some thirty years before, were now dead. Homosexuality, depression and the pimp were also about as omnipresent in the lives of the European girls as in the girls studied in this book. Most described backgrounds of deprivation similar to those which girls in the United States described. It is true that during World War II and the post-war days of severe economic dislocation, many girls had drifted temporarily into prostitution. But when conditions improved and they found other ways of earning a living, they left the field unless the same severe

personality problems were present that had either encouraged the choice in the first place or were a result
of the choice of such a profession.

The major difference, if indeed it can be so described,
seemed to be related to national character and was most
graphically illustrated by the choice of language used in
attempting to entice me as a possible client. In all the
cities, I usually inquired of a cynical concierge where
the "girls" could be found, explaining my scientific interest in the subject. I must admit that they frequently
seemed most doubtful about my motives. I would then
go to the designated areas of the city and meet the girls
who solicited me, at which time I would explain my purpose and arrange to meet them for a drink.

In London, before the recent revolution in manners,
the girls would make their approach in typical Anglo-
Saxon fashion by saying, "Would you like to have a
quick time, dearie?" It was necessary to get such an
illicit matter over with posthaste. In Paris the girls
would say, "Would you like to come with me?" With
Gallic directness, it was understood that the only reason
a man would go with a woman was obvious and did not
need to be discussed. In Amsterdam, which is so petit
bourgeois, several girls approached me and asked, "Can
I make you comfy, dear?" While in Italy, where the
prose is still often as ornate as the decor, two girls approached me, a blonde and a brunette, and the blonde
started the conversation by saying, in Roman dialect,
*"Io so' bianca, ell 'e nera e tra tutt'e duc t'appriamo le
porte del paradiso."* ("She is black and I am white and
between the two of us we will open the gates of Para-
dise for you.")

Much of what I learned from studying the call girl has
been useful to me in treating other women patients both
directly and indirectly. This is not to indicate that I
consider all women prostitutes; rather that in our society, women other than prostitutes are frequently the
victim of exploitative relationships, as both Simone de
Beauvoir and Betty Friedan, among others, have pointed
out.

As an example of the direct way in which my research has helped, I can cite two examples from my practice. A young, strikingly attractive but depressed housewife became involved with a commercial artist. She was extremely secretive in discussing her lover, but did give enough information for me to be able to predict that sooner or later he would try to "turn her out" as a call girl. When I first mentioned this to her, she hooted in derision. However, I persisted and, because I was familiar with his style of operation, I told her that he would soon be in some serious financial difficulty and would need help.

In a few weeks she called, quite distressed, not only because he had made the request for her to become a call girl but because, as she explained, "I'm really tempted." Like so many of the other girls, she too experienced that sense of rejection by parents who are critical; she was frequently plagued by depression and feelings of worthlessness. However, unlike most of the other girls in my sample, she was married to a providing husband and had three charming daughters. Her husband, unfortunately, was one of those perpetual adolescents who preferred to go out with the boys and seemed incapable of meeting her emotional needs. He considered her therapy as the ultimate sign of insanity. Still, it is interesting to note that her lover did not try to get money from her except by sending her out as a call girl *even though* she had ample funds.

In another case a young and attractive psychiatrist I knew as a colleague called and asked if she could have lunch with me. At lunch, she told me that she had recently divorced her husband and was living with a man active in local politics. Recently he had confessed to her that he was in trouble. A few years earlier he had been involved with the Mafia as a distributor of heroin. At one time he had been arrested and twenty thousand dollars worth of drugs had been confiscated by the authorities. He then left the rackets and started a small business. Now he said that the Mafia was after him again and wanted him to go back to work for them until he could pay off the twenty thousand dollars he had lost as a result of arrest and confiscation. He also informed her that much as he hated to go back to his old way of life he had no choice and that he was starting back in the rackets. While I suspected the story, I was not certain it was false until my friend, who had always been a very independent, self-sufficient individual, asked me if I could lend her some money, while at the same time acting in a sexually seductive way (to me) for the first time since I had known her. It was only when she indignantly sent back the twenty dollars I had loaned her that I began to see the picture clearly.

Frequently, when a pimp decides that he needs a large sum of money—for a new car, a summer wardrobe, an expensive piece of jewelry or to refurnish his apartment—he will put operation "jackpot" into effect. He convinces his girl or girls that they must call all their steady Johns and old friends with a dramatic story of great danger and ask for immediate financial help. My psychiatric colleague was obviously carrying out her friend's suggestion, even to the indignant return of the money with the expectation of asking for more as the supposed crisis worsened. I called her and told her that her lover would soon be in worse trouble and would expect her to come to the rescue with much larger sums of money. I expected that either his "Mafia" creditors would demand immediate payment, or that he would be "arrested" and have to raise money to pay off the police or something else of the kind. My impression was strengthened when three mutual friends told me they, too, had heard the story and been asked for money. My friend was furious at my suspicions and hung up. Shortly thereafter, one of our mutual friends called to tell me she had received another importuning call. When I explained my estimate of the situation, she called our psychiatrist friend and made the circumstances once and for all clear enough for her to break with her lover. He had already begun to suggest that she have affairs with some wealthy friends to soften them up so they would provide the money he needed so desperately—for whatever purpose.

My knowledge of the call girl and her culture has also been helpful in treating psychopaths. The psychopath is usually described as a conscienceless manipulator who relates to everyone in an exploitative way. Armed with a keen sensitivity to the weaknesses of all with whom he comes in contact, and with complete ruthlessness, he attempts to satisfy his impulses and cravings immediately, no matter what the cost to his victims. The pimp is of course an excellent occupation for the psychopath. However, there are many who are not pimps who are also psychopathic, frequently at painful cost to their victims.

Actually, many psychopaths do suffer, particularly when their inability to manipulate people close to them becomes evident. Owing to a basic insecurity and an alternating feeling of inferiority and superiority to all others, they conceive a failure in manipulation as devastating and then often turn to alcohol, drugs, or sexual promiscuity or go into a depression that may even lead to impulsive suicide. Because of their conscienseless impulsivity and manipulativeness, psychopaths pose a grave social problem. Call girls are frequently the chosen companions of psychopaths because the psychopath is either incapable of or completely disinterested in warm, human relationships. The prostitute in her professional life makes no demand for warmth or intimacy, demanding only money; to the psychopath that is a bargain. However, even here he cannot drop his need to manipulate, and psychopaths often try to lower the price or, if possible, use some subterfuge to avoid paying anything at all. The pimp uses the relationship with the prostitute almost exclusively for exploitative reasons.

Since the first publication of this book, I find that my point of view has changed somewhat. While I still believe that the personality structure I first described holds true for all the girls I have seen since, there are certain qualifications to which I would give greater emphasis at the present time. We have all suffered deprivation of some kind. Whether we continue to dwell on it and use it as an excuse for not living reasonably satisfying lives depends to some degree not only on our history, but on our choices as well. Frequently I have been struck by the similarity in life history between people who chose to become prostitutes and those who did not. Often, it is true, there was some saving grace: a kind neighbor, a sympathetic teacher; sometimes even the unquestioning love of a pet. But there are other considerations as well.

One of the most important of these considerations, as I mention elsewhere, is what the sociologists call differential association. That is, girls who become prostitutes usually have been associated with other prostitutes, or pimps, or both. Once they have become prostitutes themselves, the unhappiness of their current life pattern tends to make them see their past lives in equally black terms.

In using hypnosis in the treatment of one girl, I asked her to visualize a happy scene from her childhood in order to deepen the trance. She replied, "I never had a happy moment in my life." When I discussed this reply with her after she had left the profession, she explained that of course it was not true, but that at that moment she was so depressed that it seemed to her she had never known anything but unhappiness.

Another factor to which I would be inclined to give even greater weight than I did previously is the enormous hostility these girls harbor within themselves. Unfortunately for them, they tend to express this hostility by hurting themselves more than others. They are attempting to revenge themselves on the world by their suffering, by proclaiming to a usually indifferent world, "Look what you have done to me." In my later work with prostitutes I have attempted to help them turn anger outward rather than in on themselves. As I have grown more experienced and more secure in my profession, I have been better able to bear the brunt of this hostility even when it was directed at me. For a patient to be able to express anger, she needs a therapist who can take it with neither fear nor the need to retaliate.

Another change has taken place in my own feelings. While I still do not believe that prostitution is a rational or fulfilling choice, I no longer see it as completely destructive. Reluctantly I have come to the realization that there are other self-destructive patterns which may be even worse, and that there could be situations where prostitution might be an understandable attempt to solve certain problems of living. If, for example, society were more accepting of the profession so that it became a branch of, say, social work, it could become a more rewarding occupation. With our newer and more permissive attitudes to sex, it is conceivable that the prostitute could be seen as a sexual-therapist who could help the lonely and the rejected experience sexual pleasure. Also, a trained therapeutic-prostitute might be of great assistance in helping men who are afraid of not performing satisfactorily, such as those who are impotent, or unwillingly homosexual, thus helping them make the transition to a more gratifying sexual life. However, this would require not a glorification but a realistic understanding of how such women can make an important contribution to the well-being of their clients. I would hope that these clients would then go on to more personally involving relationships because most people seem to find sex with involvement more deeply satisfying than uninvolved sex.

Much has changed in public attitudes since I first engaged in research in this area. When I was working on my doctoral dissertation (which was later to become a portion of this book), one of my advisers called me in and said, "Harold, while it is in the tradition of psycho-analytic research to use explicit terminology, it is not in the tradition of the social sciences. So in your verbatim portion where the girl says, 'Why should I suck his cock?' couldn't you have her say, 'Why should I perform fellatio on him?' "

I explained to my advisor that fellatio was not the way this girl or most call girls described oral sex. We struck a compromise. Thereafter I carefully left blanks for offensive terms but always made certain that my blanks matched the letters of the omitted words. I later learned that when my dissertation was deposited at the University Library under the innocuous title of "A Study of Deviant Sexual Occupational Choice in a Group of Twenty Women," it became quite a sport for students to take it out and fill in the blanks.

My adviser was far from puritanical and was, in fact, unusually urbane for an academic type, but he was correct within the context of his time. Now that such language is a commonplace in the theater, and books formerly smuggled in from abroad are openly displayed on the bookshelves, I am interested in what reception my book will receive in its new format. While innocently believing I was presenting a scientific document when it was first published, I soon realized (when a young actress friend told me, "You have written one of the great stroke masturbatory books") that others were reading it for personal titillation which perhaps helped to explain the phenomenal sale of a revised doctoral dissertation.

Another even more unprepared-for surprise came when I began to meet new call girls who had purchased it as a "How to" book. A number of novitiate call girls informed me that they had studied it to "learn the ropes." I thought that my book amply demonstrated what I then considered the extreme degradation of their lives, but I did not fully appreciate the large percentage of girls for whom this very degradation was one of the most attractive features of the profession. It was only when I became fully emotionally convinced that prostitution was not necessarily more degrading than working at a job one hated or being married to a man one found physically repulsive, that I became more effective in dealing with both practicing prostitutes and those who were preparing to enter the profession. Then I could free myself somewhat from my moral preconceptions and could discuss their choice of occupation as objectively as I would any other job, I was better able to understand and deal with their problems. This was brought home to me when a young man brought his wife to see me because she had a "work problem." She had difficulties about fulfilling her role of a call girl. Without making a commitment either way, I accepted the case and the more we explored her work problem, the more convinced she became that she did not want to be a call girl any more. She was a member of a therapy group and eventually her husband came into the group to work together with her on their marital problems. The members of the group were immediately hostile to him which would have resulted, if it had been permitted to continue, in hardening his determination to continue his role of pimp. When I intervened and pointed out that the other group members were stereotyping and reacting to his role rather than to him as an individual, they were able to join me in trying to understand the serious problem that led to his behavior.

What I am trying to indicate is that the entire area of prostitution is so laden with emotion, that it is difficult for most of us to divorce ourselves from our preformed conclusions and look objectively at the facts. I would like to ask the reader to make this effort.

Harold Greenwald
August 1969

"I GUESS IT SOUNDS pretty neurotic, but I'm so lonely. I've been alone so long, and yet I try to keep away from all entanglements and involvements until I can get myself straightened out. How can I be of any value to anyone else when I'm of no value to myself? The constant thought in my mind is will anyone ever want me if they know about my background or past? Am I never to be able to live a normal life, or will my past always be crippling?

"Harold, I get so discouraged and so unhappy. I'm trying to find a life for myself. A husband and a home and the security of the self. Am I never to be able to rank myself with the normal things of life because I was mixed up? I'm wondering if even when everything is straightened out in my mind if it will do any good. Have I goofed so irrevocably that I'm just whistling in the dark even with analysis? Would you, even if you loved me, understand my having been to bed with ninety-two thousand men? Is it so fouled up that it just isn't any use? I don't know. And I guess you can't tell me. You'll try to encourage me, because what else can you do? But is it really any use? I'm such a misfit at this point. Where do I go from here?"

—Excerpt from a letter to the author from Beverly, who had been a call girl for sixteen of her thirty-six years.

PART ONE

*The Social and Professional Life
of the Call Girl*

1. INTRODUCTION

THIS IS A BOOK about the elegant prostitute (the call girl):
her psychology, her life and the men in her life.

While the dictionary defines the call girl as an independently operating prostitute, I am using the term in the special way in which I know it. The call girls in this book are the aristocrats of prostitution. They live in the most expensive residential sections of our large cities; they dress in rich, good taste. They usually charge a minimum of fifty dollars per sexual contact.

Since I believe it is impossible to understand any complicated human phenomenon in a vacuum, this book will also deal with the special area of society in which the call girl functions and with some of the forces in society in general which bring about this special type of prostitution. Moreover I believe that the call girl cannot be understood except in relation to the men to whom she caters; therefore attention will be paid to her clients—the men on whom she lives; and to her pimps—the men who live on her.

In writing this book I have had a number of aims in mind. Authorities, such as the president of the British Social Biology Council and the chief magistrate of the city of New York, agree that there is a lack of information about prostitution in general. For example, in his intro-

3

duction to the book *Women of the Streets*,[1] The Earl of Cranbrook, president of the British Social Biology Council, stated:

> By and large, save in those countries where what we would now call prostitution was a part of the organized religion of the state, neither legislators nor sociologists seemed to have had any real knowledge of the problem involved—indeed the same is true today. So far as what may be called the individual problems are concerned, neither did they, nor have we, any real knowledge of the early history of prostitutes, nor how or why they took up this method of earning their living.

That statement was made about prostitution in England.

In New York City, a former chief city magistrate, John N. Murtagh, reported to former Mayor Robert F. Wagner on the problem of prostitution, and stated:

> The prostitute has never been understood by our courts. Indeed she is still an enigma to science itself. The nature of her emotional instability, its causes, its cure, are all matters beyond the knowledge of science, let alone the law.

This book then is first of all an attempt at a scientific exploration of a specific facet of prostitution.

Why is such an exploration needed at this time? Contrary to the opinion of some, prostitution is not yet the dead issue which some social theorists had expected it would become when sexual morals were relaxed. Kinsey and his collaborators in their study of female sexual behavior,[2] note that the number of prostitutes does not seem to have been materially reduced despite strenuous measures of suppression and despite the betterment of

---

[1] British Social Biology Council, *Women of the Streets* (ed. Rolph, C.H.). London: Secker & Warburg, Ltd., 1955.

[2] Kinsey, A. C., *et al., Sexual Behavior in the Human Female.* Philadelphia: W. B. Saunders Company, 1953.

economic conditions. In their study of sexual behavior in the human male,[1] they stated:

> The percentage of males in each social level who are frequenting prostitutes today is almost precisely the same as the percentage which had such experience twenty or more years ago.

Thus, prostitution is still very much alive, still an unsolved problem.

In addition to these reasons for studying prostitution in general, the call girl in particular has, to the best of my knowledge, never received any serious study. Yet the call girl lends herself peculiarly to an illumination of the mystery of prostitution because, unlike her less successful sisters of the street, she is usually better educated, more articulate, and therefore frequently better able to explain some of her motivation.

However, as I became more acquainted with the problems of the call girl I began to see that there were additional reasons for presenting this material. One of these was the prevalence of prostitution fantasies that I found among non-prostitute, even prudishs women. Frequently they imagine themselves as latter-day Madame Pompadours living gay lives of silken luxury and going to bed with a series of handsome and exciting men, all of whom desire them passionately. The occurrence of prostitution fantasies has been mentioned by a number of other psychoanalysts, such as Karl Abraham[2] and Helene Deutsch.[3] The study of the call girl may also help us to understand not only more about women in general, but perhaps about the motivations of men, particularly men who find themselves able to function sexually only with prostitutes: men who are impotent with all other women

---

[1] Kinsey, A. C., et al., *Sexual Behavior in the Human Male*. Philadelphia & London: W. B. Saunders Company, 1948.

[2] Abraham, K., *Selected Papers on Psychoanalysis*. New York: Basic Books, Inc., 1953.

[3] Deutsch, H., *The Psychology of Women*. New York: Grune & Stratton, Inc., 1945.

but the prostitute, or men who find the marital bed dull and insipid and find excitement only in the paid embrace of the call girl.

I believe that a knowledge of the problems of the call girl has even wider implications than providing a greater understanding of sexual problems. First, it has long been understood that the study of the abnormal helps to clarify the normal. Psychologists and psychiatrists usually agree that the difference between the abnormal and the normal is merely a matter of degree. Because of the greater extent to which certain behavioral patterns are evident in the abnormal, it is easier to see and to understand these patterns, and thus to broaden our understanding of the normal. This was brought home to me particularly because certain problems were shown in marked relief among the call girls which are also problems among large numbers of individuals. There is, for example, the problem of masochism, the kind of behavior designed to cause pain rather than pleasure. The novelists[1]—who in the past have done a much better job of describing the prostitute than my colleagues either in the psychiatric or psychological fields have done—have graphically described the prostitute's search for pain. The search for pain is not limited to the prostitute. It is one of the most characteristic yet most puzzling aspects of much neurotic behavior.

A problem which is endemic in our society is the problem which Durkheim[2] the French sociologist described many years ago as *anomie*. As I understand the term *anomie,* it means the lack of social norms and therefore frequently a deficit in the connection that so many individuals in our society have with each other, very similar to that described in *The Lonely Crowd*[3]—the walls of isolation that so many of us put around ourselves which make it impossible for us to enjoy enriching social contacts. In the call girl we can see this phenomenon in its most extreme form.

---

[1] For example, Zola in *Nana* and Kuprin in *Yama, the Pit.*

[2] Durkheim, E., *La Suicide,* Paris: Felix Alcan, 1897.

[3] Riesman, D., *et al., The Lonely Crowd.* Garden City, N. Y.: Doubleday & Company, Inc., 1953.

In another area this book may help to illuminate the relationship between the personality of the individual and the kind of occupation he chooses. Since the choice of occupation is of special significance in the case of the call girl, and since I hope to be able to demonstrate some of the important emotional factors in the choice, perhaps this will help to illustrate and explain some of the factors that are involved in all occupational choice.

Also, the call girl's occupation is closely linked with the entire problem of delinquency, a problem which many authorities believe is today reaching epidemic proportions in our society. Delinquency has frequently been connected with child-rearing practices, and here we will have an opportunity to study the special kinds of child-rearing that these girls experienced. By discovering what was done to *create* delinquents, perhaps we can learn what needs to be done to *prevent* the raising of delinquents.

As a psychoanalyst and therapist I, like many of my colleagues, have been faced with the fact that many of the pure neurotic types described by Freud and some of the earlier writers in the field of psychoanalysis. Increasingly we are faced with the problems of dealing with people who have what have been called behavior disorders; where the difficulties arise out of the way in which these people operate in society. Since I have had the opportunity of working with an extreme type of behavior disorder in the case of the call girl, perhaps my experience may be helpful to some of my colleagues working in similar fields. My study of the very limited literature in this field indicates that I have acquired material that is unique. To my knowledge there have been very few examples of information about the early lives and development of these girls such as I have been able to obtain.

Despite all efforts to make this study as scientific as possible, I recognize full well that there are many limitations in it and I wish to warn the reader of these limitations.

First of all, the number of call girls I was able to study, six psychoanalytically and twenty by interview method, is a very small sample, and there is so little reliable information available on the number of call girls in general—their ages, their socio-economic background—that there is no way to be certain how well this sample of twenty-six call girls represents the typical call girl. Then, since all of these girls had to volunteer either for therapy or for interview, there was a problem of selection. All of the girls were, in a sense, self-selected—that is, they were willing to cooperate. (This has been both an advantage as well as a difficulty since most of the previous information amassed about prostitutes has usually been obtained in a prison atmosphere where they were already smarting under the sting of society's punishment and hardly in a mood to speak frankly and cooperatively.) Another problem was that, with the exception of four cases where the interviews were recorded, my own personal biases may have been a factor in both the selection and the organization of the material I chose to write about. It should be clear that while I believe that many of the psycho-dynamic factors that will be described probably apply to other types of prostitution, all of them were examined within the special social context to which this study is limited, that of the call girl operating in a large American city. It may be that, since the institution of prostitution takes different forms in different lands and in different socio-economic groups, the dynamics of the prostitute also vary.

However, despite these limitations, I felt that the study was worth while because of the unusual opportunities offered by this material: most particularly the opportunity to obtain confidential material from a group against which there has existed historically such widespread social disapproval, and the opportunity to make the first study of the aristocrats of that group: the call girls.

Part of the study was done by a unique method: ten of the call girls were interviewed by others whom I had trained to do such interviewing. I feel that it is important to show the use of this method in dealing with members of a socially disapproved group. In addition, I believe the attempt to combine the disciplines of psychoanalysis and of social psychology in an effort to reach a better understanding of a problem may be a valuable method of exploring social pathology.

The book is divided into four parts:

1. The social and professional life of the call girl.
2. A psychoanalytic study of the call girl, devoted chiefly to two case histories of call girls who were seen for psychoanalytic therapy.
3. A social psychological study of twenty call girls.
4. The men in their lives, illustrated by two psychoanalytic case histories; one of a pimp, the other of a compulsive and frequent client of call girls.

Since I believe that in a democracy social problems can best be solved by an informed citizenry rather than by reliance on experts, I have made an effort to present this material in language as clear as I can command.

Since I also believe that in learning more about any human beings we must inevitably learn more about ourselves, this book is addressed to the general reader, not just the specialist.

2. THE SOCIAL AND PROFESSIONAL LIFE OF THE CALL GIRL

LITTLE IS KNOWN GENERALLY of the life of the call girl. How does she earn her living? How much does she earn? Where does she get her clients? What does she have to do in order to be good at her job? Does she have a code of behavior like, let us say, that of the lawyer or doctor? What is her social life like? With whom does she associate and what is the nature of such associations? These are some of the questions I shall try to answer in this chapter.

INCOME

Call girls now earn in the neighborhood of thirty thousand dollars a year. Since they live outside the law, all of this is untaxed. The girls charge from fifty to a hundred dollars for each session and on occasion are able to charge even more. The higher figures are paid either by extremely affluent people or by those who have special tastes for which the girls want extra pay. A man might require an entire night of a girl's time, perhaps taking her out to a night club to pretend that it wasn't purely a commercial transaction but a semi-social occasion. In such cases the girls usually expect to be compensated accordingly.

EXPENSES

The income of thirty thousand dollars is a gross figure from which a large number of expenses must be deducted. First and foremost in the life of the call girl is the telephone; without it she could not practice her special form of prostitution. Call girls make almost all of their appointments by phone. However, in some instances the girls are so apprehensive about the possibility of arrest or of being traced that they do not use personal telephones but receive their calls from an answering service or a telephone exchange. This is a number which the girl gives to her clients; she herself is never at the number but calls it several times a day and then phones the various callers who have left messages. The cost of telephone and answering service is about forty-five dollars a month.

With few exceptions, the girls live at addresses where they can on occasion entertain clients. Although most of them prefer to go to the client's home or, more often, his hotel room or suite, there are some clients, usually local married men, who do not provide a place of their own; therefore the girls have to have their own apartments—the fee is usually the same. Call girls' apartments are generally in expensive neighborhoods. In a city like New York, for example, they tend to be in the most expensive area; on the upper East Side around Park Avenue. In Chicago they are usually on or near Michigan Boulevard. Not only is the rent high, but the girl often has special expenses because the landlord or superintendent is aware of her occupation and therefore boosts the rent even higher, or she has to compensate the landlord or his representative or the superintendent or manager with extra large monthly bonuses. Rents average about three hundred dollars a month.

It would be difficult to estimate clothing expenses. In the circle in which they move the girls have to make a good appearance. They must, for example, be able to walk in and out of the finest hotels without attracting undue attention because of dressing either too poorly or too garishly. It is difficult, however, to say how much of the clothing expenditure is a necessity. Like many women, a call girl, when depressed or annoyed, may go on a shopping spree and spend a great deal of money on clothes. Some of the clothes are bought from conventional sources: department stores, specialty shops and others. However, there are other sources. Because of their contacts with underworld figures, many of the girls are able to buy their clothes at substantial discounts. In New York, the center of the garment industry, there is organized stealing of high-quality clothes, from trucks and from factories. These clothes are sold through a series of small dealers or fences, and the girls often have contact with such sources and so are able to buy expensive clothing at low prices. In many cases, when clients are themselves owners or executives of apparel firms, the girls may receive gifts, or their services are performed on a barter basis with payment being made in clothes rather than in cash.

In addition to outer wear, the girls understandably spend a great deal of money on their undergarments. Here, too, these garments are obtained from both conventional and unconventional sources. A number of former and some still occasionally practicing call girls have gone into the lingerie business, and call girls frequently patronize such places. There are also dealers who specialize in selling lingerie, negligees and perfumes to the call girls and such dealers frequently visit them at their homes. These dealers are recommended by other call girls.

One special item of expense, particularly for a girl who uses her own apartment a great deal, is the laundry bill. Fastidious clients require a change of sheets and pillow cases before each visit. Large numbers of towels are used. The laundry bill thus frequently runs much higher than any conventional householder's.

A great deal of money is also spent on cosmetics, perfumes and beauty shop expenses. All of the girls try to keep their hair in good condition and spend a large amount of time on their personal appearance. There are a number of all-night beauty shops in cities like New York and Chicago which the girls find convenient. Again, like many of their more respectable sisters, call girls frequently, when depressed, will take themselves off to the beauty parlor for a facial, a hair-do, a wash, a rinse, a dye, and other complicated rituals of the beauty parlor.

Their medical expenses also tend to be higher than average. For one thing they usually patronize physicians who have large call-girl clienteles and who often charge them higher fees than their more respectable clients. Many of the girls go for monthly check-ups to ascertain whether they have venereal disease, and some go to the length of getting prophylactic doses of antibiotics to prevent the possibility of contracting a venereal disease. However, venereal disease in this group does not seem to be a serious problem. With the spread of antibiotic drugs it has lessened in all society and particularly at the socio-economic level at which these girls operate.

Abortions—occasionally necessary—are highly expensive for those call girls who want them. Although the professional call girl is well versed in the facts of contraception, many of them forget to use or dislike using female birth control devices or pills and most of their clients refuse to employ any devices to prevent pregnancy. Also many of the girls believe that they are unlikely to become pregnant as long as they are so active sexually. Their theory is that the different strains of semen destroy each other. Several of the girls reported that they had not used any method of contraception for long periods of time and did not become pregnant. However, when they do conceive they usually know doctors who are willing to perform abortions, the fee for which may be as high as three thousand dollars.

One item of expense which cannot be calculated is the amount of money that has to be spent for direct and indirect protection from arrest. Some of the girls secrete sums of money in their apartments which may run as high as two thousand dollars, or leave sums of money in the hands of friends who can be reached at any hour in case of difficulties with the police. When such difficulties arise, the girls frequently attempt to bribe their way out of them, and such bribery is usually not conducted on a credit basis. Therefore it is important to have money readily available for such emergencies.

There are many other extra expenses. For example, if the girl lives in an apartment house with elevator operators, the operators have to be tipped liberally and frequently, and the doorman as well, if there is one. In general most of the girls tend to be quite liberal tippers in any situation.

The largest drain on a call girl's income arises out of her relationship with a pimp. In most such relationships the call girl will turn over practically her entire income to the pimp, who will then dole out whatever money he feels she needs for expenses. However, as the money given to the pimp cannot be considered a normal living expense and as her reasons for giving this money are intimately connected with her psychology, this aspect of her profession will be dealt with more extensively in a later chapter.

Sources of Clients

One of the girls, Stella, wrote especially for my use a description of the relationship of the professional call girl to her clients:

The first prerequisite is a telephone in good working order, with an answering service connected so that business can continue even when the proprietor is out on a call—away from home. Usually as soon as "business has been completed," the girl will call her answering service for messages, thus enabling her to hop from one address to another without wasting expensive time. If there has been a call at her residence while the present job is in progress, and the phoned-in customer has left a message or number with the girl's answering service, it is not unusual for the amenities of the current business to be completed quickly (the passage of fee from "John" [client] to girl) and a hasty departure for the next destination made by the busy young lady. For example:

Jim Jones calls Terry Toon. He says: "I'm a friend of Bill Brown; he gave me your number."

She says: "Oh yes, Bill Brown. Where are you staying?" (Most calls seem to come from out-of-towners—the local chaps are less active, although when in Chicago a New Yorker acts like a Chicagoan in New York.)

He says: "Blank Hotel." (This is rarely more than a forty-or fifty-dollar call—usually a "quickie," about forty-five minutes to one hour.) Some girls pride themselves on giving less or more time according to their tastes and styles, but all do so with the attitude of having a successful, effective approach to conducting their business. It is of considerable pride whether they do a twenty-minute "fifty" or an hour "fifty." But time and money usually determine each other in this income bracket. The seventy-five or hundred-dollar John has a more elastic schedule granted him; also a clever girl will not phone into the "office" for messages too frequently while on duty with a seventy-five or hundred-dollar man. It is bad taste, as it reminds the buyer that his purchase is not exclusive. A man spending this amount of money expects deception and romance, as well as the orgasm. The girls often prefer to do several quick thirties rather than one slow, long-drawn out job for a hundred dollars.

Back to Jim Jones and Terry Toon. He identifies himself and the source of his information regarding her, and if the name he uses as introduction is a valid customer, the girl will accept business thus recommended. If the name of the original customer, however, recalls any problems sexually, a demanding tough John or financial hazards (arguments about amount or rubber checks, et cetera), the girl will frequently refuse the new applicant, considering him not a good risk if his friend has created a bad impression before him.

However, if everything is in order, and there is no doubt in the girl's mind that this is a legitimate John, not a cop playing her for trouble (as some arrests have been planned and effected this way), she will make a note of his hotel and room number and set an appointment. Usually the John says, "Come over in a hurry, I have to leave soon." This also reassures the girl that it will be a "quick one."

This type is one classification; a cut-and-dried affair in which there is no illusion of romance or subterfuge.

The girl arrives and the man often is already disrobed totally or partially, and he answers the door furtively, removing her coat and exchanging amenities on the way to the bedroom (if it's a suite). The preliminaries in this case are dispensed with quickly and the physical action begins. The John expresses his sexual preference or in some cases inquires as to the girl's preference. One type of girl considers this stupid, figuring that he is paying, why ask her her preference; another girl would find this an act of consideration, but the finer functionings of these affairs are full of contradictions. (There I go analyzing!)

This is an example of word-of-mouth advertising which is the basis for increasing a clientele. A call girl's business should constantly increase as Johns distribute her number to their friends. One John can recommend as many as four others and sometimes more, depending on his number of contacts.

Another source of enlarging clientele is fellow call girls who exchange "numbers" and "dates." A "number" is a man who is on the John list. In this maneuver the positions are reversed. The girl calls the man and says that her girl friend told her to call him. A date is arranged and these cases usually are local businessmen who come to the girl's place.

Location and style are important here. The fee of the girl often depends on the address and furnishings of her place of business, as much as her attractiveness of physique and manner.

It will be seen from Stella's description, which seems quite accurate on the basis of the information I was given by other girls, that most of the clients are not obtained by direct solicitation. Usually they acquire clients from each other or by recommendation from previously satisfied clients. Occasionally, however, when business is slack, the call girl will initiate calls. She doesn't solicit in the usual sense of streetwalking, but she will call a number of men in an effort to drum up trade.

There are other sources of clientele, too. In breaking into the profession, girls usually work first through some type of procurer or madam. Some of these procurers are themselves practicing call girls who, for a percentage, will pass on excess business to other girls. This percentage varies from as high as two-thirds of the total fee in cases of the raw beginners who are breaking into the field, to as low as twenty per cent. In the twenty-per-cent bracket there is a special twist. The standard minimum fee for a call girl in most of the large cities is twenty dollars for a beginner. Sometimes madams add an extra five dollars, making the fee twenty-five dollars, and this five dollars is deducted by the madam, although such a small percentage is rare. It usually runs to at least fifty per cent.

In addition to madams who are practicing or former call girls, another source of outside business is a male procurer. There is a distinction between the procurer and the pimp. The pimp as such, as will be explained later, performs no economic function. The procurer performs the function of getting clients for the girl. Call-girl pimps are rarely procurers.

Another source of clients is the voluntary procurer, the businessman who entertains male acquaintances by providing them with call girls. The girls are used in the entertainment of out-of-town buyers, lucrative customers, and sometimes even important personnel who may be taken out on the town by their employer, included in which evening will be the treat of visiting a call girl.[1]

There are a number of cocktail lounges and restaurants which are known haunts of call girls, but the solicitation here is usually not direct. In these places the management encourages the trade of call girls. They usually sit at the bars, drinking by themselves; occasionally introduction is made by the bartender or manager where the potential client is not very adventurous and asks aid. The more adventurous clients will approach the girl themselves, in

---

[1] The high-priced call girl is thus a phenomenon of a lush economy and of the income-tax structure. "Entertainment" of clients and customers is a deductible expense under the income-tax laws and a call girl's fee can be treated as a "business expense" for tax purposes. In effect, then, the United States Treasury frequently pays more than half the cost of the "entertainment."

which case the encounter frequently takes on the appearance of an ordinary barroom conversation. It is then important for the call girl to display her skill in negotiation so that she can obtain the promise of a fee without being too crudely commercial in her negotiations, as many men find such an attitude dampening to their ardor.

In addition to the exchange of telephone numbers, customer lists are also sold. One way in which this is done is through the sale of the "black book." A girl planning to leave the city or planning to retire from the profession will sell her black book of addresses to another girl. Black books of good clients have been known to sell for as much as five thousand dollars. Sometimes a pimp will advance this money, secure in the knowledge that the girl for whom he buys the book will soon earn it back.

SPECIAL SERVICES

One of the special services that call girls are often called upon to fulfill is to cater to those with deviant sexual appetites. An experienced call girl is usually adept at giving oral satisfaction and some can perform it with an amazing amount of sensuality and tenderness. Not only are there men who wish to have these girls satisfy them sexually but many Johns like to perform oral sex on the girls and many of the girls reported having clients who only required the girl to lie back relaxed and permit themselves to be stimulated orally.

However, there are other men who have more eccentric tastes. One man would come to his appointments armed with a twig and request the girl to tie a noose around his testicles, pull them up between his legs and beat him with the twig. On the other hand, the young scion of a socially distinguished family would pay handsomely for the privilege of taking a girl to the park, have her climb up on the limb of a tree and urinate on him while he stood below, savoring this golden shower. Other more conventional masochists require only to be tied and beaten, to be humiliated, or to crawl on the floor begging to kiss the shoes of the girl, which is enough to cause them an ejaculation.

In Paris one can see streetwalkers (called *les Perles* or *Specialiste*) dressed in old-fashioned riding habits and swinging their whips for the benefit of clients in search of such gratification. I met one aged former actress who had a clientele that was composed exclusively of masochists whom she never gratified in any other way than by insulting them, beating them, or if the price was right, urinating or defecating on them.

Of course, the other side of the coin is equally prominent and although the call girls I interviewed were more reluctant to discuss this matter, many of them did gratify their clients' sadistic desires. Most often this gratification was on a symbolic level. For example, many men require the girl to permit herself to be tied down while they beat them (usually light) with a belt. Sometimes in the heat of passion such men are carried away by their enthusiasm and may seriously hurt the recipient of their favors. So prevalent are sadistic degrading fantasies that some girls invite favored clients to urinate on them because they know it is a good way to earn an extra fee and develop a steady client.

There are a wide variety of fantasies that some men ask to be gratified that are even more bizarre. One regular client would require the girl to take an enema and retain the water while he had intercourse with her. During this time, he would make it clear that he imagined that she was giving birth while he was inside her. Of course, there are many givers and takers of enemas who would simply limit their relationship to either donating or receiving the kind ministrations of this bygone aid to regularity, which was enough in itself to gratify them sexually.

Many men in the past sought out prostitutes because they could indulge freely in obscene conversation before and during the act. Frequently, such men request that the call girl describe in most explicit terms her experiences with other men or women. Paralleling the sexual research of Kinsey, along with Masters and Johnson, such men inquire as to the girls' reactions to penises of different size, shape, or ejaculatory production.

One of the most complete and involved fantasy productions was carried through by a highly successful, middle-aged physician. He had a variety of scenes that he would act out with call girls that needed considerable histrionic ability on their part. First he would rent a hotel room, dress himself in female clothing and require that the girl exclaim over his feminine allure and how much she would enjoy a lesbian relationship with him. Then he would change back to his male attire, sit himself in a wheel chair and have the girl wheel him first to an expensive restaurant for dinner and then to a round of night clubs. In addition, the girl had to wear very short dresses with no undergarments and sit in such a posture that men could easily see her pubic hair. When a man looked, she was supposed to react with intense embarrassment and shame. After all this, he would not have intercourse with his companion of the evening, but would pick up a streetwalker (preferably disheveled and ugly) and engage her sexually while the call girl was supposed to look on in horror and disgust.

As a result of several years of intensive analysis, he could explain the meaning of this fetishistic behavior to the girls but seemed powerless to stop it, despite his great fear of being found out and the resultant effect on his professional career. He remembered peeking up his mother's dress and seeing her pubic hair when he was a young adolescent. He found it so sexually stimulating that he had an orgasm then and there. He explained his dependency needs which required the wheel chair and his identification with the girls in their exposure of themselves to other men. However, he never recognized or would accept the hostility and need to control women which would seem to be the most important determinant for his behavior, plus his erroneous conviction that this was the only way he could experience gratification. When he came to see me at the insistence of one of the call girls, I stressed only the danger to which he was exposing himself and insisted that he control the impulse to *act out* his fantasies and use

them instead in *imagining* such situations when he engaged in intercourse with his girl friend. In a short time he
gave up the acting out and, after his behavior had
changed, was able to recognize his hostility and need to
control. Now, eight years later, when I run into him
socially, he is able to laugh at his earlier obsessions.

Voyeurism plays an important role in many of the
special requirements that some men make. Prostitutes at
the higher levels have always catered to this tendency in
their clients. The elaborate houses of pleasure in Paris,
pre-Castro Havana, and New Orleans were frequently
provided with peepholes so that favored clients could
observe other clients who were unaware of this attention
while engaged in intercourse. At "stags" which used to be
part of the prenuptial rites of young men about town,
prostitutes were hired to perform with each other and with
various guests for the pleasure of those who observed. The
recent growth of group sex and of a more permissive
attitude in the theater and motion pictures to the depiction
of explicit sexual intercourse has tended to make the illicit
stag show obsolete in the United States. However, clients
who can afford the extra charge frequently request two
girls and enjoy watching them in homosexual lovemaking.
Others reverse the procedure and prefer to watch
heterosexual activity and will ask a girl to perform with
another man while they watch.

The prominent Protestant minister of a fashionable
suburban church always shows up with a young male
whose activity he likes to observe while he solemnly mas-
turbates.

Some girls have the walls and ceilings of their places of
work completely covered with mirrors so that the client
can observe himself from every possible angle while he is
with her. Sometimes the client provides the mirrored bedroom and now some have home TV setups so that they
can record their activities on magnetic tape. Polaroid
cameras have also been a boon for those who wish to
record the high point of their activity for later perusal.

Pseudo-necrophiliacs, too, require gratification and a
wealthy undertaker is notorious in call-girl circles for his

penchant for having the girl lie immobile in an ornate silk-lined casket while he has intercourse with her. Sometimes he reverses roles and has the girl ushered into the room where she discovers him lying in the casket, before he "comes to life." He then arises Lazarus-like to engage in sexual play.

As has been noted above, there are men who do not wish to have actual intercourse. Some ask the girl to disrobe with excruciating slowness while they masturbate. Others prefer to have the girl masturbate as they watch and either ejaculate spontaneously or join in the masturbation. A number of men are still arrested at the "playing doctor" stage and conduct careful examinations of the breasts, anus and vulva while bringing themselves to a climax.

There are a sizable number of men who prefer to dress in women's clothes while engaged in intercourse. They are usually not homosexual but find the experience of dressing in "drag" (feminine attire) sexually stimulating. Others, on the other hand, prefer the girl to dress in man's clothing and to take all inititative for the sexual act, sometimes even requesting that they be "raped."

With the exception of the uncontrolled sadists, most of these men who require special services are harmless and are too inhibited or unaware that they can find similar stimulation with wives or girl friends. For them, the existence of call girls is the only thing that makes gratification of their sexual idiosyncracies possible.

WORKING HOURS

Because of the nature of their work the girls usually are late sleepers, rising at one or two o'clock in the afternoon, which is the time that the telephone first starts to ring. Quite a few men seem to be interested in the services of a call girl in the afternoon. For the next few hours the girl is usually busy tidying up her apartment, making herself up and in general preparing for the evening's activities, at the same time receiving telephone calls. Her active work usually starts at about four o'clock, with businessmen who stop in on their way home from the office, and usually continues until two or three in the morning. At that time, girls will often gather in restaurants, go to late movies, one of the all-night beauty parlors, or to an after-hours spot. The after-hours spots are restaurants, often in the guise of private clubs, which operate after the legal curfew. Many of these are frequented by call girls and pimps.

LANGUAGE

As Sutherland described it, in the case of the professional thief,[1] so call girls too have ways of recognizing each other by the use of special slang. Not all of this slang is peculiar only to the call girl; many of the words are also part of the vernacular of various groups in and around the marijuana world, and many are taken from the slang of jazz musicians. Words like "bread" for money, "stoned" for drunk, "dig" for understand, "pad" for a place to sleep are just as common with the call girl as they are with jazz musicians and their fans.[2] Of special interest is the way the girls describe fellow-professionals. They speak of them as being "in the racket," as being "in the life," as "a regular girl," or "one of the girls," with particular emphasis given to the word "girl." This emphasis is extremely important in their discussions. Frequently when they use ordinary words, the inflection or the emphasis or the accompanying winks give them special meaning. Numbers, for example, are never given in their original form. If a client wants to discuss a fee, the call girl will never say, "Fifty dollars"; she may say, "It will be fifty blocks away." If a girl is giving the telephone number of another girl, usually she will not give it as a telephone number, but perhaps as a price. Thus Spring 7-3100 might be given as: "The spring price is seven for thirty-one hundred

---

[1] Sutherland, E. H. (Ed.), *The Professional Thief, By a Professional Thief*. Chicago: University of Chicago Press, 1937.

[2] Of course this language is now part of the general hip vocabulary, particularly of young people.

dollars." In special circumstances when call girls need to communicate with each other while working together on a job, they may use "carny" talk, a complicated form of pig latin which supposedly originated among carnival employees, but which is very popular among people having connections in and around the underworld. For example, call girl would be ceeazall breeazbad.

CODE

The professional call girl has a code regulating her relations with the client. For example, it is customary for a call girl never to show any signs of recognizing a customer when she meets him in public, unless he greets her first. If their clients are prominent people the girls will not readily identify them or name them in conversation even with each other. Also a girl with an established clientele will not steal from her customers nor permit them to overpay her if she feels they are doing so because they are drunk. A professional call girl will make every effort to satisfy a client even if he has difficulties. When working with groups of men she will not reveal the inadequacies of one of the men to the others in the group, but will praise him.

Their code also regulates their relations with each other. If one girl sends a client to another she expects reciprocity. Similarly, if one girl takes another girl along on a job with her, she expects the other to return the favor at the earliest opportunity. This code is learned during the period of indoctrination usually from a madam who also acts as teacher for her percentage.

STATUS

The call girl gives a great deal of attention to her status. She is particularly anxious to distinguish herself from the ordinary streetwalker or house girl—Karen, in discussing an example of mistreatment, said of a man: "He acted as if I was a street girl."

Her status is based on her attractiveness, financial standing, political connections, dress, apartment, manners and the state in which she keeps her "old man" or pimp. Call girls have more scorn for the streetwalker than does the most puritanical reformer. They will avoid bars and restaurants that are patronized by girls who, they feel, have inferior status as professionals or whom they consider amateurs just "chippying around," girls who occasionally "turn a trick" (accept men for a fee) even though they have other means of earning a living. They want nothing to do with girls who in their opinion are not truly professional in their approach. Many girls also avoid associating with addicted call girls who are considered unreliable and therefore dangerous.

While there is no common agreement as to the gradations within the general profession of prostitute, Stella divided them into three broad categories:

The "party girl" (who is often also a model, actress, or a chorus "broad").

The "hustler," or "hooker."

The prostitute, or whore.

By the "party girl," Stella meant the girl who goes out on no more than one date per evening and where the question of fee is not made explicit. That is, the girl never discusses fee with clients, but it is understood, usually by arrangement with the person making the introduction, that at the end of the evening the man will unobtrusively slip her an envelope containing anywhere from a hundred dollars up for "taxi fare." Also, most girls in the "party girl" category will occasionally refuse their favors to a man who does not appeal to them. "Party girls" are very careful to keep this prerogative of refusal as a means of denying that they are engaged in prostitution.

The "hustler," or "hooker," is the call girl who operates on an appointment basis, maintaining her own residence, which may or may not serve as a place for entertaining clients. It is interesting to note that Stella applied the term "prostitute" only to the streetwalker in order to avoid using the term for her own group, which included the call girl and the party girl, because she had been both.

In addition to the categories that Stella mentioned, there are others. The "house girl" operates within a house of prostitution. Except for special sections of New York where there is much poverty, like Harlem or some of the Puerto Rican neighborhoods, there seem to be very few houses of prostitution in operation at the present time. Occasionally two girls will share an apartment, but not in the organized way that houses of prostitution flourished in New York in pre-World War II days, as described by Polly Adler.[1] The "kept woman" is another category that Stella omitted. The kept woman usually gives her favors to only one man at a time in return for financial security during the time that the arrangement is in effect. Kept women differ from a girl who is living with a man without benefit of marriage in that they frequently move on from one lover to another, and when not being kept they are usually looking for someone to attach themselves to in order to secure a livelihood. What distinguishes the kept woman further is that her relationship with the man is solely and frankly an economic one, in which she may pretend affection, but where her own subjective feelings are that he is a John or "sucker." Occasionally one of the girls in the other categories will move into the kept woman class for a short period of time. However, the typical call girl is not interested in this arrangement and usually finds such a life much too boring and dull to be able to tolerate it for long.

The clothes the call girl wears are very important to her status, both in her own eyes and in the eyes of her clients. Etta, for example, usually bought a new mink coat every season, trading in last season's coat, in very much the same way many people trade in their cars. She told how a regular customer of hers in describing her to a friend of his said: "Wait till you see what a gorgeous mink coat this kid has."

The amount of money a girl charges as her customary fee is obviously important to her status. For example, as previously mentioned, none of the girls included in this

---

[1] Adler, P., *A House Is Not a Home*. New York: Rinehart & Company, Inc., 1953.

study would dream of charging less than fifty dollars. To do so would make them feel like "common prostitutes." Girls who charge above this minimum consider themselves on a higher status and one assured me during our interview that she was "strictly a seventy-five dollar girl."

The dress and standard of living of the pimp (paid lover) supported by the girl—if she has one—are important to her status. One of the reasons why many of the girls are willing to part with large sums of money to keep their pimps well dressed and riding around in Cadillac convertibles is that this enhances their status in the profession.

The type of clientele to which a girl caters is another factor in establishing her status. Girls will often boast that they see only "the nicest type of men," businessmen, professionals and people from the theatrical world. Many of the girls during their interviews managed to mention casually that they had had business relations with leading television or movie stars at one time or another but usually remained true to their code by not mentioning names.

It is important for the girl to have her status as a professional recognized by others in the group. Trading of telephone numbers will be done only with other professionals who are considered of equal status. Thus a girl who is on the seventy-five dollar level will not be likely to trade names with a fifty-dollar girl. Also, a girl will not trade names with another one who she thinks will injure her reputation with a client because of not knowing how to handle herself properly in the situation. When several girls work together at an occasion where a number of men are present, such as during conventions or arrangement of big business or political deals, a girl will be very careful as to which girls she works with. On such occasions a girl who is liable to lose self-control or mistreat clients may become dangerous. Since such parties are usually accompanied by heavy drinking, one girl who behaves in such a way as to arouse the anger of some of the inebriated clients may cause all of the girls to lose their fees, receive beatings, or even in some cases to risk arrest.

ASSOCIATIONS

Call girls prefer to associate with people like themselves who are in the racket, or who know what they are
doing.

Chief among their associates are the members of that
special sub-culture which is described later as the "gray
world"—bookmakers, promoters of worthless stock and
others who live in the gray area between respectability and
outright criminality.

Since the girls recognize that society at large considers
them outcasts, they are very apprehensive when with
strangers that somebody will discover their profession.
This worry about what other people would think of them
if their profession became known is a chief reason for
restricting their contacts with respectable society. Their
awareness of society's attitude toward them is a great
obstacle in the path of many of the girls who would like to
choose a more respectable way of life. Stella, for example,
was worried, when she became interested in a theatrical
career, that she might be recognized on television by
former clients. Frequently their associates who are not in
and around the racket are creative people—artists, musicians, writers—who tend to be more tolerant of them.

All of the girls I interviewed were working at the time
in New York City. However, several of them had worked
at various times as call girls in Chicago, Los Angeles,
Miami Beach and Las Vegas. While call girls may be
numerous in other cities, these were the cities and loca-
tions that were mentioned most frequently. The conditions
of work in these places are almost identical to those in
New York. The only ascertainable difference seems to be
that the police in the other cities were accused by the girls
of being more graft-hungry than the New York police. In
Miami Beach, they stated that the cupidity of the personnel of the large hotels was so great that they found that
they were working for the elevator operators, bellhops,
room clerks and chambermaids—in the words of one of
them: "I found that I was working to support all these
parasites and making hardly anything for myself." In

Chicago, the girls reported that there were organized mobs who had to be paid off with regular contributions.

AMUSEMENTS

The amusements of the call girl are not much different from those of other girls of the same educational level. They like the movies and television. They tend to read a great deal and their tastes in reading material vary with their education and background. I have frequently been in respectable homes where no books were in evidence. I have never been in a call girl's home where there were not at least some books to be seen and, in many cases, large numbers of books. Marie, for example, had one wall completely covered with filled bookshelves. Large numbers of these books were paperback romantic novels, but there was a good selection of serious plays and of novels, chiefly of the best-seller variety. Their preference in reading matter would seem to be, first, periodical literature, tabloid newspapers, the exposé type of magazines, and other mass circulation magazines, including a variety of women's magazines. After that come romantic novels. Books about prostitutes are quite popular if the prostitute is a romantic figure. Even though they are derisively aware of the inaccuracy and distortion of some of the fictional portraits, many of the girls stated they enjoyed such books. Most of them were avid television fans, especially of programs on which their clients appeared.

There was very little evidence that the girls had any great interest in gambling. While many of them would go to race tracks in the company of male friends or habitual customers—who would sometimes even pay them for their time either because they felt they brought them good luck or because they liked their company—the girls rarely bet with their own money. Sometimes they would bet with their companions' money. Gambling did not seem to be an important activity with them.

The movies, particularly those movie houses that are open in the early hours of the morning, were a great attraction for the girls. A number of the girls were theater enthusiasts and went to the hit plays, frequently in the company of good customers. Since many of them knew men who were interested in sports, they frequently went to important prize-fighting events, in addition to the horse races mentioned previously. Their work took many of them into night clubs, but they usually found the night-club shows boring, except that they often enjoyed sentimental, sad singers.

PART TWO

Psychoanalytic Study

PSYCHOANALYSIS IS ESSENTIALLY a therapeutic method. Its effectiveness lies in uncovering psychic conflict. In order to do this, the psychonalyst devotes a large portion of his effort to removal of the roadblocks to communication. His aim at all times is to obtain a meaningful emotional history of the person who comes to him for assistance.

In this part I shall present material obtained from the psychoanalytic investigation of two girls who came for help. They were deeply troubled and were strongly motivated to tell as much as they could about themselves. During our work together both girls put some of their thoughts into writing. Because they were writing to their analyst, this material belongs with the analytic study, and excerpts are therefore included.

The unique opportunities that psychoanalysts have for intensive investigation of the human psyche also give them a body of knowledge about the causes of individual human behavior. I shall therefore attempt subsequently to apply some of these principles to the individuals studied in this part.

3. SANDRA

SEVERAL YEARS AGO I received a call from a friend asking me whether I would accept a call girl for analysis. I explained that what mattered to me was the kind of problem she had and whether I could be helpful to her, not her occupation. Shortly thereafter, Sandra telephoned and made an appointment.

When she came in, my first impression was that my friend had played a cruel joke. While at that time I had only the foggiest notions as to what was meant by the term "call girl," it was hard to believe that the girl who sat so uncertainly facing me was involved in any unusual behavior.

She was slim and petite, with honey-blond hair and the quiet kind of beauty that comes to each one who sees it as a personal discovery. She was dressed with unostentatious good taste in a suit that blended pleasantly with the color of her hair; her make-up was subdued, and she wore small copper earrings as her only jewelry. She looked like a modern dancer or art student with a wealthy family supporting her. When she spoke there was nothing about her speech that clashed with her appearance. In fact it was a year before she ever used any of the simple four-letter words that some Westchester matrons employ with abandon in an analyst's office.

Sandra explained that she had come for treatment because of frequent, intense depression. On two occasions she had made efforts to commit suicide by taking overdoses of sleeping pills, but both times friends had found her before the pills could take effect. She was then twenty-three years old and said that she had been working as a call girl for the past five years.

At this point, partly because I wasn't quite sure of the term "call girl" and partly because I had not yet recovered from the surprise caused by her appearance, I asked her precisely what she meant by "call girl." She explained with great reticence and embarrassment that men would call her, she would go to their apartments or hotel suites, and: "Then we have sexual intercourse, I get paid, and that's all."

Too late I realized that this was a poor question for an analyst to ask because it implied a judgment about her work, that it could be and probably was interpreted as: "How could a nice girl like you do that kind of thing?" Apparently I, too, was not quite free of the usual social attitude toward prostitutes at that time.[1]

Nevertheless with very little prompting Sandra began the story of her life. She was born in a small New Jersey town near New York. She was four years old when the depression struck her family, and her father found himself out of work. Sandra was the youngest of three daughters. When her parents decided they could not support all three of the children, the oldest sister—five years older than Sandra—was kept at home to help with the housework while the mother went to work as a domestic. The middle sister was sent to live with an aunt and Sandra was placed in an orphan asylum. After spending a few months in the asylum she was sent to a foster home.

The social worker who made the placement must have felt that it was an ideal one. There was another girl of Sandra's age in the home; this girl, Helena, was the child of Sandra's foster parents. Helena had many toys, clothes,

---

[1] When I read this portion to Sandra later, she explained that she had thought I was "kidding" her.

a bicycle. Sandra had only the dress she wore and two others. Sandra remembers trying to play with Helena's toys and having them snatched away from her. Every time she chose a toy to play with, Helena decided that she wanted it. Every time she tried to ride the bicycle, Helena decided that she wanted to ride it. The stage was set for the next act—an act that Sandra blamed for many of her difficulties.

One day she was left alone in the house with her foster father while his wife took Helena shopping. The foster father called Sandra over and put her on his lap. She was pleased by this unaccustomed attention but soon began to feel that something was going on she couldn't understand and that was disturbing. The foster father began to breathe heavily and to get red in the face. Suddenly he thrust her off his lap and Sandra felt she had done something to displease him. She was reassured, therefore, when he asked her to come into the bedroom with him and she went willingly. In the bedroom he exposed himself to her and tried to force her to perform fellatio. Frightened, she refused. The foster father became enraged and thrust her leg against a hot radiator, causing a scar which Sandra still bears. She gave in then. After the act was over, he said to her, "Don't forget, if you tell anybody, I'll kill you."

Sandra replied, "Oh, I wouldn't tell anybody."

The foster father laughed and said: "You're a funny kid."

That afternoon she received her first fee, a ball and jacks. A pitiful little present, but it was the first gift she had ever received for herself alone. Both in the foster home and in her own home the only toys she had known up to that moment were the ones that belonged to others.

The next evening Sandra was out in front of her foster home playing with Helena when the foster father came down the street toward them from work. Sandra rushed toward him, ahead of his own daughter, yelling: "Daddy, hello Daddy." The foster father passed right by her and picked Helena up in his arms, nodding curtly at Sandra.

During the week Sandra developed badly chapped lips

and the foster father put a strip of adhesive tape over the lips, supposedly to protect them. Sandra felt, however, that the tape had been put on her mouth to prevent her from talking about what had happened. That weekend Sandra's own parents came to visit her and she started to run to greet them. The foster father stopped her, ripped the adhesive plaster off her mouth, and she then ran to greet her parents.

Sandra remained in this home for about two years, until she was six years old. At that time her family's finances improved and Sandra came back to her own home and started school. At school she didn't find the work difficult—her intelligence is above average—but she did find herself constantly bored and had difficulty paying attention to the tedious drill that was then part of the curriculum. When Sandra was eleven the family again felt the pinch of economic pressure, and once more she was farmed out to a foster home. In this home there were five other girls and in some ways Sandra liked this home better than either her own home or the previous foster home she had been in. Her reason for preferring this home was interesting:

> The woman in this home was very strict with me— she made me wash very thoroughly; she made me dress neatly and she would make me sit on the toilet seat every day, no matter how long it took, until I moved my bowels. She was the only one I felt was interested or ever gave a damn about what happened to me.

On one occasion a ring disappeared. That afternoon all of the six foster children were supposed to go to the movies. The foster mother lined them up and said there would be no movies unless the one who had taken the ring confessed. Sandra had not taken the ring but she didn't want the others to be penalized, so she confessed to stealing the ring, saying that she had thrown it into the garbage. Sandra explained that she preferred being punished for something definite, even something she didn't do, to the constant feeling of being punished for "just living."

The other five children went to the movies and Sandra remained at home with her foster father. She didn't feel this was much of a deprivation because she enjoyed washing the dishes and she felt that if she stayed at home she would get a chance to wash the family dishes. She was bitterly disappointed, though, when the foster father refused to permit her to wash the dishes, only allowing her to dry them.

One night she woke up to find the foster father in bed with her. He persuaded her to submit to fondling and caressing. This happened on a number of occasions and while she felt some distaste for this activity, she liked the foster father, wanted him to like her and did not wish to offend him by refusing. On other nights she heard the foster father going into the bedroom of one of the other wards. While she was pleased not to have to submit to his advances, she nevertheless felt jealous at the thought that he preferred somebody else to her.

At fourteen she returned to her own home. At this time there was a pleasant interlude at school. She was made a monitor and it was her job to enforce discipline in the yard and in the hallways:

> I felt like a policeman. I had a book of tickets, and if a kid talked or fought, I would go up to them and say, "What's your name?" and hand them a ticket. If they tried to give me an excuse or anything like that, I'd just say, "What's your name?" and write in my ticket book just like a cop. It was great, but for some reason they took the job away from me.

Most of this time Sandra was quite lonely. She had few friends and her family was very strict with her, insisting that she be home early, and sending one of her older sisters for her if she stayed out later than eight o'clock. She remembers once sitting in front of the local public library talking with four boys she had met inside. Her older sister arrived and said: "Get home or Mother will come after you." She felt humiliated and went home with her sister. The next time she saw the same boys in the street she was too embarrassed to talk to them. When she was about fourteen and a half years, she met a group of girls who took her in as part of their gang. They would go on walks together, play handball and roast potatoes in bonfires on open lots. The girls decided to form a club and buy identical sweaters. In order to finance the purchase of the sweaters, each girl was to pay fifty cents a week dues. Sandra loved the idea of belonging to something and wearing the sweater to show that she belonged. She ran home in great excitement and told her father about the club. He refused to give her the fifty cents, and when she started to plead with him for the money he slapped her face and locked her in the bedroom. Sandra never joined the club.

It was about this time that boys began to be interested in Sandra. They would follow her home from school, ask her to go for walks with them, and in other ways show her attention. Sandra was pleased by these attentions and was especially pleased when one particular boy, Tom, took her for rides on the handlebars of his bicycle. Tom belonged to a club that had a little shanty clubhouse behind some billboards on one of the vacant lots. Frequently he asked her to come to the clubroom with him; she would go with him and they would neck. Once she was in the clubhouse with Tom and his friend Jerry. Jerry asked her: "Who do you like better, Tom or me?" She liked Tom much better but felt she couldn't hurt Jerry so she told Jerry that she liked him better.

Gradually she drifted from necking sessions in the clubhouse to more intimate relations, until she was having sexual relations with many of the boys in the neighborhood.

Once when one of the boys asked to have relations with her she said: "I will, if you give me something." Frequently she would accommodate five or six boys at a time, not because of any sexual desire on her part, but because as she said:

It didn't mean anything to me so why shouldn't I do it if they made such a big deal out of it? It seemed so important to them and all I wanted to do was to give something to them that I never got myself—attention.

She went to high school without much interest, except for the class of one English teacher who encouraged her to write after reading one of her compositions. He felt that she had promise as a writer and for a short period she found school exciting and challenging, warmed by the interest of this teacher.

At sixteen she left high school and started to work. Up to this time her family had tried to maintain strict curbs on her conduct. She was still required to come home early and she still had to account for her time. After she started to work, her father would take her unopened pay envelope from her and give her an allowance that was just enough to cover her carfare and the daily bottle of Coke that she drank with the lunch she took from home. Her mother would buy her clothes when her father decided that she was permitted to have some new ones.

Her first job was with the telephone company as an operator. She appreciated the training in speech that she received. However, she found the work very boring and she started to make dates and stay away from the job. It was during this time that she met Phil, who was to remain her boy friend on and off for the next twelve years. On a date with Phil one evening she was introduced to marijuana. She didn't like the sensation. After they had each smoked a stick they went into an ice cream parlor and as she caught sight of herself in the mirror, she felt that all the people in the ice-cream parlor were looking at her, shaking their heads and saying to themselves: "Boy, is this kid mixed up." This feeling continued to plague her and was one of the factors in her decision to come for analysis. Wherever she went she constantly felt that people were looking at her, thinking she was crazy. On several occasions she felt that I, too, had smiled in the same way with the same attitude.

At eighteen she started work in a retail store as a

salesgirl. Her employer was unlike anyone she had ever met, with the possible exception of the high school English teacher. He didn't make any passes at her. He was kind to her, took great pains to teach her how to dress well and to make up with good taste, and introduced her to the art museums which she found exciting. As a result of visiting the museums she started to sketch and draw for her own amusement. After several months this kind employer called her into his back room and indicated that he wanted to have relations with her. She was shocked by his proposal because she had felt that he was "different." Mistaking her shock for refusal he threatened her with the loss of her job if she did not accede. She gave in. Shortly thereafter, she started to make dates with the customers in the store indicating, at the suggestion of her boy friend Phil, that if they paid her she would be willing to have relations with them. Phil explained that they needed the money that she could earn in this way in order to get married. For ten years, during the times that they were on good terms, Sandra was earning money this way and turning it over to Phil so that they could get married.

Once she quarreled with Phil and took a job in Boston. She was lonely away from home and came back without notifying her family. When she returned she frequented various bars for several days picking up men, who occasionally bought her meals or took her home to sleep with them. In one of these bars she met a man she liked who said to her, "What's the sense of giving it away when a kid with your looks could make herself sixty or seventy dollars a night?" He introduced her to a woman called Madame Bertha.

Madame Bertha was one of the new crop of madams, who do not operate through a house but act as central dispatchers for a number of girls. She had the contacts and would send the girls out on calls, receiving half the fee for her help in arrangements. Sandra gave the man who had introduced her to Madame Bertha one hundred and fifty dollars:

I didn't know what to do with the money anyway. I had moved back with my family and how could I show up with that kind of money?

The man wanted to become her regular boy friend and take care of her and her earnings. However, she met Phil again and when she proudly told him how much money she was earning he was pleased that they would be able to get married so much sooner, and they were reconciled.

Sandra began to find it increasingly difficult to come home before the early hours of the morning. Her parents raged at her and on occasion her father would take her clothes away and lock her in her room in an effort to get her to reform. The final blow came as a result of an ingenious arrangement that Madame Bertha had worked out. Every week she gave Sandra a sum of money, equivalent to what she could have earned at a regular job, in a pay envelope with the name of a legitimate business firm on it. One night when Sandra was home her father appeared with a strange man in tow. He started to question her: "Where do you work? What is the address of the place? Do you know any of the other people who work there?" Sandra answered the questions as best she could, and then her father turned triumphantly to the strange man and said: "Do you know her?" The man said he had never seen her before. Her father slapped her across the face and sent her into her room again. Somehow he had made the acquaintance of the stranger and found out that he was working for the business firm whose name appeared on the pay envelope which Madame Bertha had so carefully prepared for Sandra.

Her family apparently held a council and decided on a radical measure: the thing to do was to get Sandra safely married. Sandra's parents were Greek and her father was a frequenter of Greek coffee houses. In one of these coffee houses he met a young man who had recently come over from the mother country to manage the American end of his family's importing business. He confided to Sandra's father that he was interested in getting married to a nice American girl, and when he met Sandra the interest was strengthened. She consented to the marriage chiefly because of the insistence of her family and also because:

> Once I got married they wouldn't be able to tell me what to do and I'd be a person. I'd have freedom and I couldn't be pushed around by them any more. Also, this fellow had lots of loot [money] and it seemed like a pretty good thing.

The marriage lasted seven days. In the first place Sandra knew very little Greek and her husband very little English. On the wedding night Sandra had been much concerned because she would not be able to produce the traditional proof of virginity. She had therefore taken the precaution of bringing a small bottle of iodine to bed with her and had emptied it on the sheets. Unfortunately the iodine apparently reacted with the starch in the sheets to produce an orange rather than a brown stain. The next night he said he knew she had been in love with somebody else before but that he forgave her. However, she found herself very bored with his romantic lovemaking. "I never did go for that mushy stuff—kissing my hands, my eyes, and all that kinda bullshit." However, what she found most disturbing were his incessant sexual demands. "Can you imagine—five, six times a night were like nothing to him! I didn't get married for that. To me marriage was supposed to be one beautiful thing." After a week they parted.

With the marriage behind her, Sandra greatly loosened the ties to her family and went out on her own. She was reconciled with Phil, who came to her and said, "Look, baby, you know you'll never love anybody else and I know I couldn't make it with anybody else. Let's cut out the goofing around and really work hard for a year, save our money, and take off for the Coast where I can go into business and we can really have a nice life together."

Sandra suggested that they get married immediately. Phil declared, "What kind of a jerk do you think I am? I wouldn't want my wife to live the way we'd have to live now without any real dough, worrying about the rent and the groceries." Sandra suggested that they get married and that she continue to work as a call girl until they had enough money. Phil's answer was, "Look, when I get married I don't want my wife to go around peddling herself to every Tom, Dick and Harry. When we get married, we're going to do it right."

This argument was repeated many times during their relationship. However, Sandra accepted Phil's point of view and in her world it didn't seem particularly strange that her man should expect her to continue to earn money as a call girl in order to avoid a life of economic insecurity.

Sandra became a full-time professional call girl with a smart apartment in the east Eighties and a well-filled little black book containing the phone numbers of several hundred Johns. Throughout all this time she attributed many of her periods of depression not to her work, but to her relations with Phil.

One early morning when she met Phil after her night's work was done, as was their usual custom, he greeted her cheerfully. "I got good news for you. We're going to be able to make it and get married sooner than I thought. I got another kid, Elaine, who's going to give me her pay."

Sandra was furious at the suggestion and said, "I'd rather take longer than have you take up with another girl." Phil was angry because she didn't understand how much he loved her and the extent of the sacrifice he was willing to make for her.

"Look, baby, can't you see I'm only doing it so we can get married sooner? How do you think I feel having my girl in the racket! I wanna get rid of this crap and the sooner we can make it, the better off we'll both be."

Finally Sandra agreed and she began to see Phil alternate nights so that he could spend time with Elaine in payment for the money he was receiving from her. In addition, Sandra began to supply Elaine with clients because Elaine was comparatively new at the racket and didn't have Sandra's contacts.

During this period the fights between Sandra and Phil became more numerous and violent. Occasionally Phil would be late when it was Sandra's night to see him. She would then call Elaine's house to find out whether Phil was there. On one occasion when there was no answer to the phone call, Sandra went over to Elaine's apartment and rang the bell until Elaine opened the door. She pushed the door open and forced herself into the apartment. Phil was there. He became so enraged at the instrusion that he beat her up. Sandra had to cover her black eye with make-up in order to be able to work the next day.

After that they stayed apart for about six weeks. At the end of the six weeks Sandra called Phil saying that she wanted to see him again. They met and Phil laid down a set of conditions under which he would be willing to be with her on alternate nights. First, he requested that she give him at least three hundred dollars every week to put away into the account for their "marriage"; second, she would have to stop calling Elaine, and third, she must ask him for permission before she spent any money.

Because she had been so intensely lonely during their separation, Sandra accepted these conditions. She was so pleased that they were together again that she gave Phil the convertible automobile she had purchased for herself. For a short time Sandra tried to live up to the agreement. However, she found it impossible not to call Elaine when Phil didn't appear on time or when she felt that she had to talk to him. Afterward she would feel guilty and responsible for the arguments that developed as a result of her violation of their agreement.

On one occasion, after a particularly violent argument, she decided to revenge herself on Phil. She felt that the nature of the revenge was so horrible that she had great difficulty in telling me about it. She obtained the name of a Negro musician from a friend of hers and called him up. He came to her apartment and they had relations.[1] The

---

[1] Sandra shared the attitudes described on pages 193-194 toward sexual relations between white women and Negro men. She felt that she had degraded herself and by doing so had also degraded Phil.

next morning she slipped a fifty-dollar bill into his pants pocket. She felt that there were other motives in her having had the affair with the Negro in addition to revenge.

> Colored men are different. They put you up on a pedestal while Phil is always putting me down. Also by calling him and paying him I felt that made him lower than me and so I wasn't so low.

Sandra frequently tried to explain to me her relationship with Phil and why she returned to him so often. At first she put it on the basis that their relationship was "different" from those which existed between most girls in the racket and their "old men." She and Phil really loved each other and were going to get married. Later she offered another explanation:

> Men are like babies and after all I would like to have a baby of my own. I want somebody to give things to so I give it to Phil.

She also described the many periods of loneliness she experienced: being alone on a Sunday and crying from sheer loneliness. At least when she was with Phil she had someone to talk to, someone who was around. "Every other night is better than no night." Later on she explained it on a different basis:

> I hate the money I get from the racket—it's like shit. I want to get rid of it as soon as possible. If I didn't have Phil I would just waste it. This way at least I give it to him and it might do him some good. Also it doesn't make me feel so low. At least somebody else gets the money and in some ways that makes him lower than me and I'm on a pedestal again, just like with a colored fellow. Many times I've had offers by guys with a lot of dough who wanted to keep me. But I couldn't do it because what would Phil do then? He needs the money.

Phil began to drink more heavily and became a chronic alcoholic. He often blamed Sandra for his condition, saying that it was the irritation she caused him that made him drink. Sometimes she felt that this was true and that it *was* her fault. At other times she was contemptuous of him for letting himself go in this way. She thought of many ways of trying to get him over his alcoholism. Once she even suggested that he go into psychoanalysis. He gave her the customary response that he wasn't crazy and he didn't need any head-shrinker. She told him then, for the first time, that she was in analysis. She expected him to be angry but to her amazement Phil was very impressed with her courage in being able to face an analyst; he told her that once he had got as far as making an appointment with a psychiatrist but had been so frightened that he ran out of the waiting room when it was his turn to go into the private office.

At another time she herself contemplated becoming a heavy drinker. She didn't care for alcohol, had been drunk only once in her life and had decided then that this was not for her. However, she thought that if she became an alcoholic too, Phil might reform when he saw what he had done to her by getting her into the same state. She felt that Phil wasn't a man any longer since he had become an alcoholic.

He can't even make love. When he tries it's pathetic. And if a man can't make love, he's no man. Sometimes I wonder if I didn't do this to him by giving him the money. By being the man of the house, I've made him into a woman.

Sandra recognized that she had strong feelings against being a woman. She said that she had always wanted to be a boy. When she was young she wouldn't ride on a girl's bicycle and insisted on using a boy's bike. Yet she felt that girls are wanted because men usually pay for sex and how often do you hear of a woman paying a man? Also, during the course of analysis, she began to verbalize feelings about wanting a child. In this connection it may be interesting to recount one of her dreams.

She dreamed that she had a baby that was normal in every detail except that it was no larger than her thumb. One day she dressed the baby and wrapped it up in a blanket but was afraid that she wouldn't find it when she came home. She went to a movie with another woman. But when she got home she was worried. She looked all over the apartment and finally found the baby. She was very happy; this was her baby and this was the way she wanted things. Her associations to the dream were that she wanted to stop working and get out of the racket and that what she really wanted very badly was a baby—something to hold onto, some goal.

In the course of her therapy Sandra rarely spoke about her father but frequently discussed her mother. Her mother figured very often, particularly in dreams. One dream that seemed to express some of her feelings about her mother was the following: She dreamed that her mother was going to have a baby and die of syphilis. Her sister telephoned this information to her. In the next scene of the same dream two men were in the room, one of whom was necking with her mother. Then he picked her mother up and carried her into another room, a bedroom. The remaining man slipped his finger under Sandra's dress and tickled her. Sandra was furious with him and said: "Just because my mother acts this way is no reason for you to think that you can get away with acting like that toward me."

In her associations for this dream she remembered that at about age eleven she used to hear her parents having intercourse in the next room. She knew about intercourse and felt that her father would never do such a thing but that her mother, who knew her way around, probably forced him to act this way. She often thought that her mother was very "sexy" and that she had inherited her own proclivities from her mother.

In another dream her mother was married to one of Sandra's Johns. The John had a girl friend (Sandra), and her mother took sleeping pills when she found out about this girl friend. Sandra refused to give any association for this dream and acted as though there was a good possibility that she understood it but did not want to discuss it. In general Sandra had an unusual ability to understand and interpret both her own dreams and those of others.

At the beginning of the analysis, Sandra found it difficult to come regularly for her sessions. On many occasions she would make appointments and then not appear. On other occasions she would leave the analysis for weeks or months. At one time during the course of the analysis she came in very frightened and said, "I think I really flipped. You know what I did last night? I had an orgasm with a John." In response to my inquiries she explained that she had been taught: "You never give a sucker an even break;" and said if she were going to have orgasms with Johns, how could she charge them? Apparently one of the difficulties she faced was her need to repress feeling and emotion in order to be able to endure her work. The analysis, by restoring her capacity to feel, threatened the shaky adjustment she had made to a very trying situation.

Phil eventually married another girl. At this point, after an absence of several months, Sandra came back to analysis in an attempt to discover what had caused her to remain with Phil for so many years. She recapitulated some of the things mentioned previously and then went on with an interesting association:

> You know, in many ways he reminded me of that first foster father. He, too, didn't want regular sex. He looked something like my first foster father and sometimes he would even give me presents. I think I'm better off without him.

A few weeks later Sandra left for Detroit to live with her mother and work at a legitimate job. At that time I wrote the following brief analysis of some of the factors in Sandra's case. This was before my study of the twenty call girls had given me additional insights into the motivation of call girls:

Much of Sandra's story is a story of rejection—rejection of the most traumatic kind. At the age of four, when children are still very dependent upon their parents, Sandra was thrust out of her home and into an orphan asylum, while one sister remained at home and another was placed with an aunt.

Here was the beginning of Sandra's feeling of not being wanted and of not belonging. Later events were to reinforce these feelings. When she returned home and went to school she felt different from other children who had been raised in their own homes. When she wanted to join a club and wear the same sweater as the rest of the members, she was expressing her wish to belong, and when her father refused the dues, this made her goal seem impossible.

Sandra's beauty added to her feeling of being different. Her feeling of being looked at was not completely unreal. Her extreme attractiveness did cause people to look at her wherever she went. She felt that her mother's envy of her beauty was one of the factors that had made the family decide to put Sandra into an orphanage. This may help to explain why to Sandra her attractiveness was a curse rather than an asset: "People always looking at you— people always expecting things of you. Many times I wished I was ugly."

Of crucial importance in her development was, of course, the fellatic experience with the first foster father. One possibility that must be raised is that this was a fantasy rather than a real experience. It is my belief that this was not a fantasy but even if it was, its importance would still be the same. If it was a fantasy, it still would be a reflection of her feelings to the foster father and possibly of his feelings toward her. In this story, as she remembers it, there seems to be a great deal that helps explain Sandra's later behavior.

First, she remembers sitting on her foster father's lap and his pushing her off. Here was the same inexplicable situation as that which had happened to her in her home: being thrust out; being pushed away from warmth and affection. This very action made her all the more ready to accede to the foster father's next demand. After she acceded, she received a fee; the training in prostitution had begun. If she acceded to men's wishes, she received gifts that were otherwise denied her. But even then she did not belong because after getting the gift, the very next day he passed her on the street to greet his own daughter. Not belonging became a punishment for the guilt feelings aroused by the relationship.

Another painful tendency of Sandra's found its beginning in this same incident—the feeling that people were laughing at her. It was at the moment of heightened sensitivity that her foster father laughed at her and said: "You're a funny kid." For years thereafter it seemed to her that others were echoing the same words in other situations of heightened sensitivity.

An important implication (for parents and others interested in child-rearing) can be drawn from Sandra's desire for imposed limitations upon her. She pointed out that she enjoyed best the foster home in which the woman was very strict with her and made her wash and dress and watch her toilet habits. Apparently Sandra recognized that she needed to have limits imposed upon her and accepted such limitations as a sign that somebody was interested in her and that somewhere she belonged. One of the reasons she returned to Phil time after time and accepted his rigorous conditions was that in this relationship someone was interested enough to tell her what she could and could not do. Once again she had found limits.

Because she had had so few experiences with discipline she had never learned sufficient self-control, how to defer the immediate gratification of impulses. At some level she appeared to recognize this and tried to establish self-control by her efforts to control her friends and on many occasions her clients. This was particularly evident in the analytic situation itself, where she tried to control the analysis by a whole series of maneuvers that included breaking appointments, trying to change the hours, attempts to seduce the analyst, and when all these maneuvers failed, breaking off the analytic relationship for varying lengths of time.

The wish to belong seems to have been the drive in many of Sandra's actions. In the first foster home and in the later foster home she had learned that the one path that seemed open to her was the path of sex, that this could be used to obtain some temporary feeling of belonging. As she entered adolescence, again she found that sex could be used this way and that for a short time she could get a feeling of belonging with the boys with whom she engaged in sexual activity. The group nature of some of the sexual activities even added to the feeling of belonging.

For a woman who had had so many dealings with men, she had a remarkable lack of understanding of the men in her life. For example, her feeling that her father was not interested in sex and would never have been involved in such activities with her mother if her mother had not seduced him into them; her inability to understand what her employer wanted from her and her complete amazement when he made his intentions clear; her belief that Phil would marry her even though she came to recognize that in many ways their relationship was a classic example of that between pimp and girl friend.

Perhaps this lack of understanding was due to the fact that she had so often felt fooled and betrayed by men: first, by her father, who had permitted her to be put into the orphan home and had later tricked her into betraying the source of her earnings; later, by her employer, who tricked her into believing that his interest in her was entirely platonic; still later by Phil, who constantly tricked her by holding the mirage of marriage before her as the bait for continuing their relationship. Frequently a client attempted to trick her out of her fee and despite all her precautions, some succeeded. It was probably all these betrayals that helped Sandra develop great hostility toward men and the need to fool and betray them. Her stratagem with her husband, pouring iodine on the sheets in lieu of the blood of maidenhead, is an example of such a trick. In a way her profession helped to gratify this need to betray. She was quite proficient at pretending that she was carried away with passion but, actually, with the one exception mentioned, she was always cold and indifferent to the men with whom she had intercourse. In mocking this passion she was in a sense tricking all of her customers, and in having so many men she was acting out her betrayal of them.

Because of the fact that Sandra never established a close relationship with either father or mother or with any other significant adult, she apparently never clearly defined for herself her sexual role. While she reported only one homosexual experience, there were a number of indications that Sandra was not clearly differentiated sexually. In her relations with Phil there was a reversal of the traditional role of male and female in our society. Sandra was the breadwinner; Sandra worked and supported Phil. She bought him expensive gifts; she was the one who felt that his dressing well reflected on her status in her profession, very much like a businessman clothing his wife in furs and jewels as a display of his success. An interesting example of this reversal, an example played out in the terms she knew best, was the incident when she invited the Negro to her bed and paid him for his services; he was the call girl, she the John.

One of the puzzles to all those who have studied the behavior of prostitutes is why they are willing to use the money they earn to support men who seem to give them so little in return. The law is generally harsh with these men, and society frequently takes the attitude that it is they who force the women into the life they lead. It seems to me that a study of Sandra's case will indicate that Phil fulfilled many needs in her attempt to adapt to the pattern of her life.

Sandra was frequently plagued by feelings of loneliness and separation. Phil helped to assuage these feelings and served as company in the early hours of the morning after her night's work was done. Owing to her lack of self-control, she attempted to solve this problem by manipulating others. Phil lent himself to such manipulation because of his own need of the money that Sandra could supply. Also, Phil took his appointed part in Sandra's attempted reversal of roles. In addition to being the breadwinner, she also felt in this relationship that she was the superior one—for society's attitude is that the one creature lower than the prostitute is the pimp. Sandra often expressed hatred for the money that she earned as a call girl; giving Phil the money was a way of turning this contempt away from herself and onto a man, saying in effect: "This money which I earn in this low way I give to you and make you even lower than I am."

On a deeper level Phil fulfilled another and greater need. Her original rejection by her father had been caused by the father's financial inadequacy. By giving Phil money she was symbolically saying, "If I give this father money, he will love me and keep me and won't throw me out as my first father did."

Interpreting Sandra's dreams was usually easier than with most patients because of the richness of associations that she volunteered and because of her ease in handling symbolic material. In addition to the associations given by her for the dream in which she had the thumb-sized baby, there is also what she did not at first see—the wish to be masculine, to have a penis, which the thumb-sized baby seemed to represent, so that she would not suffer from the helplessness of being female and having to continue in the racket.

In the second and third dreams we find indications of the role that unresolved Oedipal feelings[1] appear to play in Sandra's choice of a profession. In the second dream massive repressions were in operation to disguise and reverse the actual nature of her feelings. Her first account of the dream indicated that she was furious when one of the men who made advances to her had taken her mother off into another room. Her associations for this were the memory of hearing parental intercourse and the feeling that her mother had forced her father. How does this association fit the first part of the dream? Careful questioning revealed that the actual fury was directed at losing the man, i.e., her father, to her mother. The early childhood feeling had been that if the mother had not forced the father to go to bed with her, he would have chosen Sandra. The other man in the dream, the one who was left with Sandra, played a part in the dream similar to the part that the hundreds of Johns played in her life. By remain-

---

[1] The wish for the love of the parent of the opposite sex, and the fear of the vengeance of the parent of the same sex.

ing with him she was protected from her incestuous wishes for her mother's man and from the revenge her mother would exact if she took her man away; by going to bed with all the Johns she felt protected in real life.

In the third dream, Sandra is much more ready, even in her dream life, to face the Oedipal situation. In this dream her mother is married to one of her Johns and when she finds out that this John has a girl friend (Sandra), the mother takes sleeping pills to kill herself. Here is a much clearer statement of the wish to get rid of the hated rival, the mother, so that she can have her man.

Several months after I wrote the preceding analysis, I started to receive letters from Sandra. Below I quote excerpts from some of these letters and my answers to them, to indicate the struggle Sandra faced in trying to build a new life for herself.

Sandra's declarations of gratitude to me were included in order to indicate the nature of her transference to me as an analyst, not as an individual. Most analysts believe that without a transference or displacement of feeling from a significant person or persons in the analysand's childhood onto the analyst, successful psychoanalysis is impossible. Actually Sandra was expressing chiefly her dependency needs in what seem like grateful statements; she was asking that I help her rather than saying that I had helped her.

May 7

Dear Harold:

This letter has been started at least six times of which this is the seventh. Every word brings a new fear plus an over-abundance of anxiety and lack of confidence.

These past weeks have been nothing short of mild murder.

I prefer to tell you good news. Unfortunately there is none. The new adjustment has left me limp and mentally haggard.

Until recently I have been employed by the Michigan Athletic Club. I was hired as PBY typist and doubled as cashier-hostess. Its long life expectancy was short-lived, for five days later found me on the streets looking for another position. By realizing this would not help me in the morale dept. I began slowly but definitely to think affirmatively.

At this moment I am not quite sure of my predicament nor am I completely assured this whole new way of living is cut out for me. There is very little to look forward to, coming home after a tedious day. In a sense, there is much less to look forward to going from one job to another.

At any rate, I shall make one more attempt. If that does not work out, I have no choice but to try again.

Perhaps someday I will find pleasure in complete exhaustion. There is little else to look for—

There are many things you've brought to light and many more which have yet to be seen, but with your understanding behind me, I cannot go wrong.

Best regards,
Sandra

May 11

Dear Sandra:

Thank you very much for your wonderfully honest letter. I can't agree with you that you have no good news to report. The courage you have shown in going out and trying to get a job seems to me like very good news indeed. Whether or not you will be able at this time to adjust to the new way of life is not the important thing; the important thing is that you were brave enough to try it.

It seems to me that you have a right to look forward to more than exhaustion. There is no reason to believe that you could not eventually get married and have the kind of life that I believe you really want but don't seem to consider you deserve.

I know another girl who went through a similar transition. If you think it might be helpful to you to meet her, I will be glad to send you her name and to write her, telling her a little bit about you.

You need not thank me for anything. Your courage is thanks enough.

Sincerely,
Harold

May 15

Dear Harold:

Without the encouragement you alone can give, I could not go on. Your letter had been read with trembling fingers for I knew then its contents were written by a dear friend.

Every pent-up emotion released itself in a flood of gratitude and well-being until the very last word. By then I had gained complete reassurance.

The "outside world" is vast, Harold. It has been painfully introduced with a grim smirk. The challenge is almost death-defying, its enormity frightening to say the least.

The next voice pleads for me not to be frightened; that there's a job to be fulfilled and I alone must fulfill it.

Perhaps someday soon these efforts will not have been in vain, perhaps too your faith in me will be proven and will not have gone unjustified.

The thought of meeting the girl you mentioned is a consoling one. I should very much like her name.

With all good wishes and best regards, I am

Fondly,
Sandra

May 19

Dear Sandra:

Thank you for your letter. I too, need encouragement sometimes and letters like yours are very helpful during the dark periods when nothing seems to happen, periods that I think you remember only too well. If you have found my letter at all helpful, good. I have a new ribbon in my typewriter and there are plenty more letters in it, so write as often as you wish.

The girl I told you about is Beverly ——————, her address is ———————————————. I am also writing to tell her that you may be in touch with her. From all I have heard Beverly is quite cheerful and happy these days and I hope that she will be able to give you additional encouragement.

I am glad you recognize that I have faith in you and I hope you know there is almost nothing you can do that will destroy this faith.

Sincerely,
Harold

June 27

Dear Harold:

At present I am working for Consolidated Motors. Things seem to be going great guns as far as solving those immediate problems of mine. Getting along with the girls I work with is not the easiest task in the world, but I *am* trying. Occasionally, I have found, their acceptance of me is easy to digest. Other times I am completely bewildered as to why they are so damn envious of not only me but others around them. I have come to the conclusion this switchboard cubicle is like another small town, and people are people no matter where one lives. But why can't they all *live together!*

Still waiting for some word from Beverly. Haven't gotten in touch with her until rather recently, having been so busy with so little time to do things in. Somehow I'm almost AFRAID to meet her, don't know why . . . if she don't hurry, however, I may never find out.

Hope to hear from you soon. If for some reason you may not have the time to write, I shall inform you of anything that transpires between Beverly and I. Thanks again.

Best regards,
Sandra

At this time Sandra's father died and she moved in with her mother. She had high hopes of this move back to the home. Her hope was that now at last she and her mother would be friends, that with her father dead her mother would lean on her and accept her.

These hopes were soon destroyed. Sandra found her mother cold, demanding and critical. It was impossible for her to stay in the house and she moved out.

July 7

Dear Sandra:

Thank you for writing, even though I didn't have an opportunity to answer your letter earlier.

I am certain that you made a very great effort to get along with your mother and I believe that your move out of the house was a wise one. Not only for you and your mother, but in my total experience I know of no house that is large enough for two grown women; there must be conflict between them. I think you touch on part of the reason for this kind of conflict when you mention the envy that you find in the girls you work with. It is encouraging, though, that you recognize that side by side with this envy there is also acceptance.

The question you ask, "Why can't they all live together?" is a question that has preoccupied all the great philosophers since the beginning of time. Perhaps they have been so interested in this question because they have suffered, like you, from great sensitivity to rejection.

About the incident with the man out of your past, I am happy to hear that it seems to be working out well. Among the several girls that I know who make the break, such incidents have happened occasionally and, so far as I know, the men never said anything or used the information. One of the girls who quit to become a TV actress was horrified when the director of a show she was in turned out to be one of the freakiest Johns she had ever known. However, throughout the rehearsals he never indicated in any way that he had seen her before.

When you write again it would be interesting to know more about your job and how you spend your spare time.

Sincerely,
Harold

July 15

Dear Harold:

Your letter was most encouraging to say the least. It is always a great pleasure hearing from you, really.

Have never heard another word on the friend out of the past. [A former client of Sandra's whom she saw in the office in which she worked and who she feared would disclose her past to her boss.] People are kind, after all, despite others who may not be.

Lately, I've been wondering how you are getting on with your study of the call girl. Perhaps you could call it On the Inside Looking Out . . . (oooh, I'm sick!) Truly, I am interested in knowing for my own satisfaction. Would appreciate your letting me know.

Not too long ago, I glanced over a book known as *Sexual Deviations*.[1] It was quite interesting inasmuch as certain parts of it were thought of in retrospect. At the moment the author's name escapes me; perhaps you are familiar with the one I am referring to.

As for your friend Beverly, perhaps she means to have nothing to do with anything resembling her former self. If that is so, can't say I blame her. Perhaps the letter never arrived. What sort of a person is she, Harold? Can you tell me her age?

Everything else going favorably, Harold. Occasionally, I become distressed in some of the things I do, things that can so easily be avoided. I fear my end will not be a happy one.

Bless you. . . .

As always,
Sandra

Aug. 12, 11 P.M.

Harold dear,

Tonite is the first time since my last vision of New York, I have felt this extreme tension. So much so, I can barely write, let alone count a minimum of I's.

Let's see. They say when one puts things in writing it can generally ease their pained and troubled mind.

---

[1] Probably: London, L. S., & Caprio, F. S., *Sexual Deviations*. Washington, D.C.: The Linacre Press, 1950.

Of course my need for you recalls again (in my opinion) several events which have led up to this need for your understanding, your sympathy, and most of all your unmatched encouragement.

Harold, I don't know— Gosh, I very often wonder if I've done the right thing leaving the way I have. Pessimistic as I may seem, I am 99-99/100 convinced it cannot be done.

Ever since I was fired things just have not been right. The big boss let me go only because I told him his "ole lady called." It would be wrong for me to say I was not wrong or did not respect him as my superior, but if he addresses me as "Buttercup" and "Honey" . . . well, I do have lots to learn.

Tomorrow, I may move to my sister's. Perhaps my anxiety lies here also. How can I tell you how very hard I've prayed to have my mom *ask* me to come live with her again. Honestly—I'm so distraught and bewildered I hardly know where to turn. Could this be the reason my breasts have been aching sensually and literally "demanding" attention?

I can only wish my nieces will complete the pretty picture I myself find inadequate to complete. My sister understands my situation fully, all except the real association I had with Phil. She knows I cannot find the dollars in which to keep an apartment, continue car payments, etc., and so the monetary problem slightly diminishes.

Only once about four weeks ago I "saw" a friend of mine whom I've known quite well in N.Y. He's pretty well known, but also I consider him one of the tops as a friend, and a real person. I felt none of the usual pangs of guilt that would ordinarily follow, so I cannot feel remorse there.

Your weather is not the most beautiful, I understand. Rather sloppy, eh? If it had not been for the fact so many planes had been grounded I would no doubt find this another session in person.

As for Beverly—we have spoken several times in the past. I must admit she's quite a gal.

Harold, I just don't know what to say—corny but I

wish you were here. If I can only find the will to summon reserve stamina to stand up for one more try, I shall have it made. Just once more! Three homes in four months, three jobs in the same amount of time is difficult to perceive, yet I can recall someone having told me, HE gives us no more weight than we can carry— We shall soon see.

Harold, you are a dear for spending this time with me and for me.

I am always quite touched by your presence even as you are there and I am not. It's almost as though I cannot see you because of an appointment book that is booked solid.

Bless you.

Always,
Sandra

P.S. After re-reading this, good God, it seems all mixed. But then who can see, for the tears. Who can think with this bitch of a headache, and somehow I believe you wouldn't want it any way but just how it reads.

Aug. 23

Dear Sandra:

You are right in what you say at the end of your letter. I do prefer it as it is, a free and honest expression of your feelings rather than a carefully thought out, planned letter. This kind of letter is more helpful to me in understanding you and of more benefit to you in expressing the pains and aches that your very difficult transition is causing you.

One thing that is particularly impressive is that you are tackling, in your letter, a problem which was formerly too painful for you to discuss in our personal sessions. I am referring to the great desire you now have and I believe always had for your mother's love and acceptance. If she had been the kind of person who had been able to give it to you freely, in the past, I doubt that you would have had anywhere near the problems and the kind of life that you did lead. Even your aching breasts is a way of saying that you are aching to give mother love in a way that you would have liked to receive it. It must be very hard for you to accept it, but it seems improbable that your mother will change at this late date. In trying to win her support, I am afraid you may be beating your head against a stone wall. If you can, it would be better for you to think in terms of yourself becoming the kind of mother you never had.

About the jobs, I cannot see it in as discouraging a light as you do. Considering your lack of recent experience with the discipline of everyday work, I think you have made a remarkably brave and gallant effort. It is hard for me to believe that such bravery and gallantry will be completely unrewarded. In fact the effort itself and your ability to make it should in itself be a kind of reward, but I still believe that you will earn more substantial ones.

Please write me as often as you feel the urge; my appointment book will never be so full that I cannot see you by letter or in person if you should come back.

Sincerely,
Harold

Friday

Dear Harold:

This is my new address. Despite all my efforts to get along with Mom, she just would not accept me.

I have concluded this is not *me* at fault, and all indications have shown she prefers her *entire* family away from her. She adores us from afar, so to speak, which is all right with me.

Truly, I may add, I *have tried!* Nothing can change that, Harold.

Miss you very, very much. Wish you were here.

Best regards,
Sandra

Several weeks after this last letter, I received a telephone call from Sandra. She was back in New York and back in the racket.

Sandra had gone to Detroit with two wishes: the wish to leave the racket and the wish to be accepted by her mother. Leaving the racket and taking an ordinary job were difficult and painful sacrifices which Sandra was willing to make in the hope of winning her mother. When the mother showed herself incapable of being won there didn't seem to be any reason for Sandra to continue the struggle; therefore she returned to New York and the racket.

Frequently an interruption in the analysis seems to give patients an opportunity to integrate into their personalities many of the insights they have gathered from therapy. Sandra had apparently been able to do that. In addition, the experience of having worked successfully for some time at a respectable job had apparently given Sandra new confidence and a new feeling of maturity. There was a subtle change even in the way she dressed. Her clothes were a little more mature; she seemed more certain of herself. She had lost something of the frightened-child look that had previously been characteristic of her.

Two incidents she reported shortly after her return were indicative of another change. One day she took a taxi to go shopping and asked the driver to take her to Macy's at 34th Street and Broadway. She sat back in the cab and started to think of other things; when she looked out she suddenly realized that the driver was down at 30th Street. She asked him the reason and he said, "Ah, lady, don't give me a hard time—there's too much traffic on 34th."

She said: "I want you to take me right back."

The driver said, "I'm going down to 23rd Street to cut across and go back."

She said, "I want you to take me right to Macy's."

The driver opened the door of the cab and said, "You can get out right here."

When she got out she said, "Because you've acted that way, I'm not paying you."

The taxi driver said, "You've got to pay me."

She said, "I refuse. There's a cop, go get him and make a complaint."

The driver went for the policeman, she followed him, and both told their stories to the policeman. She was ready to go to the police station rather than pay the fare.

The policeman took her aside and said, "Why start all this trouble? Suppose you pay him and save yourself a lot of difficulty." She refused to pay the driver directly, but gave the money to the policeman.

The next week when she attempted to start her car she found that the battery was dead. She called a neighborhood garage and asked them to send a man to start the car for her. When the man arrived, he started the car and asked her for seven dollars. Sandra felt that this was an unreasonable sum and told him that she didn't have that much money with her. After a bitter argument the mechanic agreed to take two dollars.

At first glance these seem like angry, aggressive actions on Sandra's part. But it must be remembered that previously she had never been able to stand up for her rights. She had never felt she had any rights. Her ability in both these cases to fight for what she thought was right and even to enlist the aid of the police, whom she had formerly regarded as her natural enemies, was an indication of change. She now felt she had the right to be treated the same as anyone else; she now felt that the police and the society they represent were not necessarily her enemies.

An even more impressive example of the change in Sandra was the fact that she enrolled for a course in beauty culture. Although she worked every evening, frequently until three or four in the morning, she made it her business to be at school promptly at 10:00 A.M. She completed the entire course and took several part-time jobs as a beautician in addition to her work at night as a call girl. This was the first time in her adult life that Sandra, who had started courses before, had been able to complete one.

In the analytic sessions there was also a change. In the three years during which I had seen her before she left for Detroit, Sandra had rarely been punctual. Many times she canceled appointments; many times she came ten or fifteen minutes before the end of the hour. When she returned, after a short period of readjustment Sandra started to come on time and to meet every appointment. This, again, was change in someone who had never before had sufficient self-control to arrive anywhere punctually,

particularly at the analyst's office. Her experience of legitimate work, the new strength that she had gained from the
insights that she had assimilated, had helped Sandra build
some of the inner controls that had been lacking.

Because of these changes I decided to alter my therapeutic approach to Sandra. Previously I had done chiefly
supportive therapy. I had worked at demonstrating that
she was not just the "bad, horrible person" that she
thought she was. I had striven to indicate that some of her
behavior was determined by forces beyond her control,
and also to demonstrate that she had a good deal more
ability and strength than she had supposed. During that
early period it seemed impossible and would probably
have proved dangerous to deal too deeply with the fundamental conflicts in her personality.

On the basis of the new strength she showed I decided
it was time to help her deal with her more fundamental
problems, and to attempt to work collaboratively with her
to discover the sources from which her difficulties had
arisen.

The change, of course, was instituted gently, and as
much support as possible was given during the early stages
of the change. The support was slowly withdrawn so that
Sandra could become more mature and "walk on her own
feet" without constantly being reassured. However, I cannot say that she accepted this change without any protest.
Many times she fought against it. Many times she threatened to break off analysis. Many times she protested that I
didn't care for her any more and that she didn't know
what she had done that caused me to treat her so badly.
However, we interpreted this behavior on her part and
indicated what it was: namely, an attempt to remain in a
more childish and dependent state and an attempt to
prevent me from dealing with her fundamental problems.

What were the problems that we uncovered at this
time? First, from her letters, it had become clear that
Sandra's difficulties were not just the difficulties that grew
out of her rivalry with her mother for her father's affection, which are so frequently found in neurotics, but that
behind these there was a more deeply entrenched and

more serious difficulty: specifically the conviction that her mother didn't love her, and preferred her two sisters to her. As Sandra put it once:

> I spend all my time crying for Mama. I can't even quit talking baby talk. The idea of her sweet mother comfort is overwhelming. I am racked with tears, prayers and pain. Having been rejected is not the fear, but perhaps never to be admitted is not a bit comforting. How could I let her know when it is she who is busily seeking consolation?

Sandra here had begun to recognize that her mother was an infantile and inadequate personality who, instead of being able to accept her responsibilities as a mother, was trying to reverse roles with Sandra and to relate as if she, the mother, were the child. When Sandra had been working in Detroit and came home from a hard day's work at the office, her mother would greet her with a series of complaints and difficulties. The mother complained that Sandra wasn't doing enough for her. She never listened to Sandra, never comforted her. Instead she complained constantly, and frequently compared Sandra to her two sisters. This, of course, had helped to reactivate Sandra's earlier feelings of worthlessness, helped make her feel again that the sisters were the preferred ones. After all, they had not been put into foster homes as she had.

The rivalry with her sisters had been intensified by the lack of material comforts in their home. When Sandra was growing up she frequently had to compete with her sisters for clothing and for most of the things that many girls growing up in our country take for granted. It was out of this rivalry that, apparently, some of Sandra's earliest seductive behavior had arisen. What she couldn't get at home she could get from boys and men by her sexual provocation.

An experience that brought some of this into focus and that indicated how it was still operating was the following: Sandra met another call girl with whom she went on several joint dates. On the first one of these dates, Sandra and the other girl whose name was Terry, had both accommodated one man, simultaneously. While this was taking place Sandra experienced feelings of jealousy. She felt that Terry was in control of the situation because Terry was the one who had caused the man to have an orgasm.

Sandra also realized that she felt some attraction to Terry. She thought this was due to a resemblance between Terry and one of her sisters. On the next job, Sandra took Terry along to see one of her clients. This client had intercourse with Sandra while at the same time caressing Terry.

Shortly thereafter Sandra learned that Terry had a boy friend, Allan. She first met Allan through Terry and then some time later met Allan alone in a restaurant. They started talking, and Allan made it clear that he was interested in Sandra. When Allan called her a few days later and invited her to go out with him, Sandra accepted and ended the date by spending the night with him. Allan was Terry's pimp, and he suggested to Sandra that he would be willing to leave Terry for her if she would support him.

Sandra's answer was, "I know your time is valuable; however, I do not want to have a regular affair. When I feel I need you I will be glad to call you." By saying, "I know your time is valuable," Sandra indicated that she was willing to pay Allan. As she put it:

> My feeling is that no man is interested in me for myself, alone, but just for money. If I was in a night club and a handsome man came in and started paying attention to me, I would feel that it was only because he knew what I did and expected to get money from me.

After spending the night with Allan, Sandra gave him a hundred dollars. She felt guilty about taking another woman's man and wondered why she had done it.

When we explored the matter it became clear that in many ways Terry had represented her sisters. Again Sandra had felt the same ambivalent feelings that she experienced about her sisters. It was again a mixture of attraction and jealousy. In connection with these feelings Sandra showed new insight about her own seductiveness to the first foster father. She realized that she had made an attempt to get close to this foster father, to make herself as close to him as his own daughter had been, perhaps even closer. When despite her having performed fellatio with this foster father he still continued to show preference for his natural daughter, this had first made her feel that men did not appreciate what was done for them.

Similarly, she now saw that the feelings of jealousy she experienced when the second foster father went to the other girls were in certain ways similar to her feelings about Terry. Now, as then, she felt a conflict between feelings of relief and the wish to make the man prefer her to the other girl.

In having this affair with Allan, she had been paying back her own sisters and the other girls in the first and second foster homes. The money had to be given to Allan because she did not believe that it was possible to accomplish this otherwise, that she was better or more attractive or more desirable than any other girl, except in her capacity to earn money.

Another factor that became clearer at this time was Sandra's great fear of success. There had been opportunities for Sandra to live with some of the men she met professionally; there had been other opportunities where Sandra could have taken a well-paying job as a beautician; but she could accept none of them. She felt guilty and felt that to accept any kind of success, to achieve in any way, was wrong. As she put it one time: "My feeling is—who will be watching when I catch the brass ring?"

Her fear was of the hostility she would arouse if she achieved anything. To understand this feeling we must remember her earlier life. Feeling rejected by her mother, she had turned to her father. Here she felt that her mother had the advantage; her mother's sexual behavior had succeeded in seducing the father away from Sandra. Sandra had then tried to turn to her sisters. Mingled with her feelings of rivalry and anger for the sisters was a wish not to lose them. Her feeling, therefore, was that if she were to become successful in any way she would arouse the enmity and anger of her sisters and lose them irrevocably.

Underneath all her other problems was Sandra's feeling that she had been deprived of mother-love. Therefore she had first turned to and then against her father and her sisters because they could not compensate for her feeling of deprivation. Rather, they were rivals for the warmth and nurture she was seeking. Later when men sought her because of her sexual attractiveness she tried to make them give her the warmth and nurture she desired; instead she received only money. Since the money could not satisfy her emotional hunger, she threw it away contemptuously on Phil. At the same time there was the contradictory hope that if she gave to Phil, he would in turn give to her. When finally Phil left her she was again filled with rage at the additional betrayal. She tried again to win her mother now that her father was dead and the other sisters married, but still she was not successful. Sandra then returned to the racket in another desperate and doomed effort to be nurtured.

After some of these matters were dealt with, Sandra began for the first time to explore the problem of how to act as a woman, how to be more feminine. It seems paradoxical that a girl who was earning her living by supplying female gratification should need advice from a man on how to be feminine. But it must be remembered that because of the early rejection by her mother and the feeling that her mother was cold and unloving, she had been unable to use her mother as a consistent model of femininity. Also, owing to the feelings of rivalry with her sisters, she had been unable to use them as models for femininity. Therefore Sandra had patterned her behavior on the only ones with whom she had any relationship— the men who had entered her life and had shown her some kind of warmth because of their physical desires for her. This was one reason why Sandra acted out the part of a John with Allan, Terry's pimp, calling him when she wanted him and paying him off. Her wish was to have relations with Allan and pay him just as her clients paid her. However, as Sandra began to understand her previous attempts at masculine imitation she became interested in finding out how to act as a woman.

She described one incident involving a man who had asked to meet her. This man had seen her in the company of one of her girl friends and had thought that he might like to make her his mistress. As Sandra told me, "I'm not interested in having him keep me but I would like him to ask me. I would like to feel that he wanted me and yet I don't know what I have to do to make him want me."

I pointed out that her approach was still essentially a masculine one, that by thinking she had to be the one to make the man want her, she was really approaching the problem as a man. She felt that she had to do the courting.

Sandra was now able to see this and went out on the date with a different attitude. She returned to the next session and reported: "Of course—it worked very well. I let him court me. He's called me three times and wants to take me out. He doesn't want to take me out in the same way as Johns. When we go somewhere he opens the doors for me; he opens cab doors for me; he treats me like a lady and it feels good."

Sandra slowly began to build new kinds of friendships with men who differed from the pimps and paid lovers she had known previously. She began to have social relationships, at first temporary ones, and then as she began to improve in her understanding of what is expected of women in our society, her relationships became more lasting. The men she went with were professionals: two doctors, a writer and an actor. With one of the doctors she succeeded in having a relationship that lasted for several months before she went to bed with him. This was a great surprise to her. "You know," she said, "he seems to like me for my company. He takes me out just to talk to me and he's happy if he kisses me. To think that I used to believe that I not only had to go to bed with a man, but to pay him for this privilege."

About this time Sandra left her profession, became a full-time beautician and, after many detours, set out to try to be a normal woman in her relationships with men. When last I saw Sandra (1969) she was about to marry.

In my practice as a therapist I have never had the experience of a dramatic revelation that immediately caused the patient to change. Usually it takes many hours of slow, careful work before changes, dramatic though they may be, begin to take place. Hollywood and some of the more sensational writers on the subject of psychoanalysis have made it seem a *tour de force*—producing a sudden break-through into health. Perhaps it is possible to do this. I haven't had that experience.

It is true that the rewards are great but the work itself is slow, long and sometimes tedious. Still I never found my work with Sandra tedious. It was always exciting—always a kind of walking-on-eggs operation.

It will of course be clear to anyone acquainted with psychoanalytic technique that the methods I employed with Sandra were far from orthodox psychoanalysis, in which the analyst acts as neutrally as he can. With Sandra I was constantly partisan and pro-Sandra. I felt that she had been so deprived of normal human warmth that she needed this above all. Much of my work was therefore supportive. Fortunately there was so much in Sandra I could genuinely like and respect that this task was not an onerous one.

4. STELLA

IT WOULD BE DIFFICULT to find two early environments that contrasted more sharply than Sandra's and Stella's. Sandra had been raised in poverty at the very margin of existence; Stella had been raised in a solid middle-class home. Sandra's parents were uneducated immigrants; both of Stella's parents were well-educated, cultured persons. But both girls became call girls and suffered from similar problems. What was the tie between them?

Usually an analyst first meets a patient as a voice on the telephone. When the patient appears at the office, it is usually with a guarded attitude—against revealing too much of himself to what he imagines is the penetrating eye and mind of the psychologically trained person. My meeting with Stella was of a different nature. I had gone to a party celebrating the opening of a Broadway musical comedy. I knew very few of the people present and was wandering around the room when a slim, pretty redhead came over to me and said: "You seem lost. Can I get you a drink?" She was bright, friendly and witty. She asked me what I did and seemed interested to learn that I was a psychologist. While we were talking, some other people mentioned that my brother is Michael Kidd, the choreographer and director. The fact that my name and my brother's are not the same was not mentioned.

Several weeks later I received a telephone call from Stella, who opened the conversation by saying, "Why didn't you tell me your name was Greenwald? I've called every Dr. Kidd in the phone book, and it was only by accident that I found out your name and was able to call you. I've been wanting to see you ever since we talked at the party." We made an appointment and she came to the office.

I asked her how she felt I could help her. She told me that several months before she had swallowed about twenty sleeping pills and had awakened in the hospital thirty-eight hours later sick and miserable. She related that when she came home from the hospital she was struck by the beauty of the grass, the sky, the trees, and she decided that she wanted very much to live. Recently she had become afraid that she would make another suicide attempt. She also said, "Since I'm such a bungler, I'll probably bungle it again and wind up in Bellevue. I don't want that to happen to me."

In addition, she described periods of depression during which nothing seemed worthwhile, the world nasty and against her. She seemed to feel that there was no possibility of happiness for her, and she was hoping that with analysis she could find a way out of her depressions.

It was only after several further sessions that I discovered that Stella was earning her living as a call girl.

Her background was almost diametrically opposed to Sandra's. Stella was born in the state of Washington. Until the age of six, she had lived in a small city where her father was the leading accountant and a respectable citizen. Her parents were quite comfortable, had a large home and two servants. Stella was an only child and she first reported her mother as being completely devoted to her and having always been keenly interested in her welfare.

The first few months of the analysis consisted of a strange kind of contest in which Stella seemed committed to an attempt to convince me that she was completely bad and I tried to indicate that she had some mitigating reasons for her behavior. She attempted to refute me by recounting misdeed after misdeed, trying to prove that there was some inborn devil in her, some innate defect of character or personality. She tried to prove that although she had devoted parents, she had still acted badly in every situation.

One of the incidents she recounted to prove this was the following: When Stella was a child both she and her mother took piano lessons from a man named Harvey. He was married; Stella's parents and Harvey and his wife were very good friends. In addition to the professional relationship, the two couples often went out together socially. After a while Stella began to suspect that Harvey and her mother were more friendly than is usual between music teacher and pupil. She started spying on them and on several occasions saw Harvey and her mother embracing. One time her mother left the house saying that she was going on a shopping trip. Stella suspected that her mother was going to meet Harvey, and when Mrs. Harvey called up and asked to speak to Stella's mother the girl said, "She's out with your husband." Mrs. Harvey's suspicions were aroused and she found out that the two had been having an affair. Stella's mother came home that afternoon and said to her, "I could kill you." The discovery of the affair caused a scandal, Mrs. Harvey spreading the story that Stella's mother had been pursuing her husband.

Soon after this, Stella's parents moved to Chicago, where things became more difficult for the family. Stella's father had to take a comparatively poorly paid position with a large accounting firm, and they moved to a small apartment. The family's mode of living was very different from the one they had enjoyed on the Pacific coast.

Another proof that Stella offered to demonstrate her intrinsic worthlessness was her early sex experience. As she put it: "Other girls were seduced by the boys. I did the seducing." On one occasion she lured a little neighborhood boy into her garage, and when the boy was shy about exchanging views of each other's genitals, she urged him, "Come on, show me yours—I'll be glad to show you mine."

She looked up and saw two other little boys from the

neighborhood looking in through a window in the garage. For weeks thereafter she was frequently followed home from school by the boys, who taunted her with, "Come on, show me yours . . . come on, show me yours."

She remembered a time when a friend was visiting her mother and brought her baby son. Stella, who was then three years of age, picked up a knife and found herself outside the baby's crib ready to kill the little boy.

While these last two experiences are not highly unusual, Stella felt they demonstrated her great abnormality even as a child.

At school Stella was a bright student. In addition she was busy taking dancing lessons, singing lessons and piano lessons at her mother's insistence. Her mother would schedule her from class to class and from day to day. She stated that her mother was always patiently sitting by, watching her and making helpful suggestions no matter how long the classes lasted.

When I raised any question about whether she felt her mother loved her, Stella insisted that she did. She said:

Look at how much she sacrificed for me. Even when we moved to Chicago she would take money that could have been used for her clothes or for the home and spend it on me—on my music—on my dancing. Also Mother would always tell me how beautiful I was. When we'd walk down the street she would say to me, "Look how everybody is watching you. See how attractive you are. You're such a beautiful child!" Mother was very close to me, loved me and was proud of me.

When Stella was sixteen her mother died. Here, again, Stella presented a proof of her general worthlessness:

What did I do? Did I cry?—no. The first thing I did when I came from the funeral was to move my things into Mother's room. She had her own room and didn't sleep in the same room with Daddy. I started to try on all her dresses and shoes. I couldn't wait to take over. Her body wasn't cold yet, and here I was already grabbing her things. That's the kind of a person I always was.

Stella continued her musical studies for a short time after her mother's death. She started going out with boys, particularly with a young man five years older than she who was working as an assistant to her father. The boy had had a fine career at college and many people prophesied that he would become a highly successful accountant. He fell in love with Stella and asked her to marry him. She didn't think she really loved him, but he was so bright, spoke so well and was so intelligent that she consented.

The marriage seemed to be working out well at first. This first husband, James, was a dedicated pacifist busily engaged in attempting to mobilize public opinion for peace before World War II. James tried to educate Stella and she said:

Many nights when we should have been in bed making love, he would sit up with me explaining various things. I was interested and it would have been fine except that our experiences in bed were so unsatisfactory. I would get stimulated and excited sexually, but I would never have any release. I never had an orgasm in my relations with James and I would be left excited, irritable and angry.

This continued for several months and Stella decided to leave him.

Her father had remarried by this time. Stella disliked her stepmother and decided to go to New York to pursue a theatrical career. In New York she met many aspiring actors, actresses and entertainers.

Stella managed to find a job singing in a small night club. At this night club she began to meet people who were quite unlike any she had ever known. They drank heavily, smoked marijuana and spent a great deal of time discussing and experimenting with a variety of sexual experiences. In general, they were completely indifferent to the dictates of conventional society. While working at the club she met a young dancer named Paul.

By this time Stella had begun to be promiscuous and would go home with a different man almost every night. Paul was unlike the other men and she found him more interesting. He didn't pursue her sexually or praise her beauty, seemed quite indifferent and sometimes acted hostile. She described him to me and said:

It was amazing. I always thought I liked big men, but Paul was slim. His waist was so thin I felt I could put my arm around it. Yet he was the one man I was interested in.

She finally succeeded in persuading Paul to live with her. One day she realized that she was pregnant. On that day she packed her belongings and moved out of Paul's apartment without leaving any forwarding address.

Stella explained that she didn't want to have anything more to do with Paul. She felt that she couldn't rely on him, and if she was going to have a baby she wanted the baby to be all hers. She started to go out with another man, Ted, and convinced him that he was responsible for her pregnancy. Ted didn't want to remain with her, but agreed to marry her so that she would not have an illegitimate child. They were married but never lived together. Stella had the baby alone and told me, "That was the way I wanted it."

After her baby was born Stella made arrangements to board her with a family in New Jersey and then went back into show business. At that time Ted was making some financial contribution to her expenses, so between what he was giving her and what she could earn working in small night clubs, Stella was able to live. However, she found it difficult to keep her jobs in night clubs because she was always getting into arguments with the proprietors of the clubs, with various customers and with other performers. She often felt that they weren't paying enough attention to her and that they were creating many difficulties for her during her performance—the musicians didn't rehearse properly or the lights weren't used properly or she wasn't given the proper introduction. Her social life continued with the unattached, promiscuous marijuana crowd, the same as when she first came to New York. It was within this group that she first met call girls and made good friends of several of them. Even within this group she didn't quite feel she belonged. After all she still was a "legitimate chick." Also her education was better and her interests wider, and this difference only depressed her.

One evening the owner of the night club where she worked came over to her, bought her a few drinks and said, "There's a fellow I know who would like very much to meet a girl like you. He doesn't want a regular hustler. He'd like somebody like you and he'd like to go to bed with you, and he's willing to give you a hundred dollars." The money was very attractive to Stella but the idea repelled her. She had a few more drinks at the urging of the owner and finally agreed reluctantly.

That night Stella started out on her first professional call girl job. When she came to the man's hotel room, she found him both repulsive and exciting. Physically she found him revolting, but he was an intelligent man, an important government official, and she enjoyed his conversation while they had a drink. When he suggested they go to bed she started to cry. As she later explained, she cried in sheer terror and disgust with herself. The man said, "I'll make it another fifty dollars." She cried harder. By fifty-dollar steps he raised the offer to three hundred dollars. In bed with him she felt angry, disgusted and detached as if she were an onlooker at a "sordid exhibition."

The next morning she thought of committing suicide, but felt she didn't have the courage to carry it out. Instead she started to drink early in the morning and then got someone to give her marijuana. She remained "high" on either alcohol or marijuana for the entire week, spending all of the money she had earned her first night.

The next time she found it easier. She was less disgusted, less angry and more detached. Soon Stella, like many of her friends, was a practicing call girl. For a year and a half she did little else but work as a call girl. Even as a call girl she felt that she wasn't really conscientious at the job. She would waste time on "tricks" (paid sexual intercourse) and, as she explained it, "I would get into long conversations with the men." One of her special problems was that she frequently got into fights with the Johns. She would ask for a certain sum of money, and if the man refused to pay it she would revile him bitterly.

When an opportunity came to go back into show business she gave up being a call girl and worked in a television series for about a year. In this series she played the second female lead and constantly found herself furious with the girl who played the lead. Stella felt that she herself had more talent but that the leading lady knew a variety of ways to ingratiate herself with the producer, the director and the sponsors, and that was the reason she had the better part. Finally when Stella was given a larger part in one script which was comparable to the leading lady's, she thought to herself, The hell with them. They've treated me so badly up to now—now they need me they can go and whistle. She quit the job.

After she left this job she secured a few small parts on television and had just enough money to get by. It was at this time that the people with whom she boarded her daughter called and told her that they knew a childless couple who would be happy to adopt her daughter, with the understanding that she must never try to see or communicate with the child.

Feeling that she was not in a position to provide her daughter with a proper home and that she was the wrong kind of person to rear the child, Stella agreed, because the people seemed to love her daughter so much and wanted to give her a home. Two weeks later she regretted her agreement and called the family in New Jersey who had made the arrangements. They refused to tell her where her daughter was, pointing out that she had signed an agreement and that she had waived her right to see the child again.

At the same time she was carrying on a love affair with a man named Fred. She went to Fred and asked him whether he would help her find her daughter. Fred refused. She cried and was bitter and depressed. That night she called Fred again and said, "I must see you. I feel so desperately lonely."

Fred said, "I'm sorry, I'm busy."

As he was talking on the telephone she thought she heard a woman's voice in his apartment. After hanging up the phone Stella went to the bathroom and swallowed a bottle of sleeping pills.

She woke up two days later in a hospital, with her father at her bedside. He had been notified about the attempted suicide. For several days she was ill and finally the day came when she walked out of the hospital. That was the point at which the sun, the trees, the sky and the grass in the park looked too beautiful to lose; she decided that she didn't really want to die. She made another attempt to get into show business and was finally hired for a small part in an important television show.

When she appeared for the first day's rehearsal she was terrified because she recognized the director as a former client. This man, whom she had known only as Bert, had never had intercourse with her, but used to come to her apartment, sit in an armchair and ask her to put on as much clothing as she could. Then she would slowly remove her garments one by one in strip-tease fashion with the lights dim. He asked her never to speak while she was disrobing. As she was taking her clothes off he would satisfy himself.

However, Bert gave no sign of recognition now, and their relationship during the six months she was with the show was an impersonal one.

Again she had difficulties with the various members of the cast and with the producer, difficulties punctuated by romances with some of the men in the company. One girl in the company became her close friend. One day the girl asked her to stay at her home. Stella was pleased because she admired and respected this girl. When they went to bed that night the girl put her arms around Stella, drew her close and started to caress her. Stella found this pleasant and exciting. She returned the caresses and soon found herself making homosexual love with this girl. However, she said, "I find sex with women great, but just sex. I can't form any attachment to a woman." After this initial relationship she had a number of other homosexual experiences.

Her difficulties with the people in the show grew worse and eventually she was discharged.

Stella, like Sandra, had great difficulty in speaking freely about sexual matters. Still she was determined to get as much assistance as she could from her analysis, and she started writing about her problems. The following is the first piece she wrote for me, which describes one of her difficulties.

July 3

Lying here in bed as I am slowly coming into consciousness and the new day—I stumbled into a free association matter that I think may be important.

I remember in the early days of my first marriage lying in bed giggling and twisting in my husband's arms and he was teasing me in a playful but determined way.

"Go on, now, say it!"

"I can't," I giggled and pushed my head even further into the pillow.

"It's only a word—say it!"

"I can't, I can't." I began to want to say it, and there came an edge of panic to my voice because I was embarrassed and couldn't say it. Finally I buried my head, hiding my face against his neck and with my arms tightly clutching his neck, I whispered "fuck".

At his promptings I repeated the word over and over and then he made me say it without hiding my face and my giggles became laughter freed, triumphant glee at my mastery over shyness—he said:

"You see—it's only a *word*. Nothing to be afraid of."

This memory became recalled to me as I lay here in bed thinking of my last session on Harold's couch where I endured a somewhat similar sensation of being unable to describe the affair between myself and Tony in graphic terms. I then felt the same desire to speak, but was bound by embarrassment and shame. Now the flood gates of memory open and I ponder and delve back—why was I so shy? I was passionate and daring in my actions but the word was impossible for me to even whisper without hiding and cringing with fear.

My next association from that jumped to my father and I remembered the fact that I had never heard him curse, using anything stronger than an explosive, "Jesus Christ!" or "God damn—" even "hell" was a word seldom exposed in anger. I then think of other households and children's backgrounds I've heard or read about where fathers exposed their children to violence, fury, drunkenness, beatings, sexual sights and foul words in anger. My father (and mother) were terribly refined. Their arguments never climaxed into violence in the presence of their daughter. Their affection never manifested itself more intensely than in a forehead kiss or casual embrace. I never saw my father unpleasantly drunk or at a loss of dignity. Only once did I see him racked by emotions and vulnerable enough to almost cry and that was shortly after my mother's death and his suffering must have been unbearable to allow even this degree of emotional exposure. I realize in these reminiscences the fact of the excessive sheltering I endured from life's "seamier" side in our house. Everything was hidden from me that suggested the bad words.

As I remember my girlish timidity in bed with my husband during my seventeenth year—I cry a little for the sweet young thing that died in my youth.

Some months later she was able to write the following much freer expressions.

Dec. 5

Ode to Analysis

Every day is new crap. Crap to me is more than describing the feces. Crap is the word I use to describe frustration, anger, revolt, irritation, calamitous events, even tragedy in its way contributing its share of crap into my life. When experiencing any of the above described emotions I will very often expel as an epithet this nasty, vile, revolting sounding word—crap—why?

Fuck is another word I frequently employ in anger, passion and revolt as the expression "fuck you" is so violently challenging in fury.

Why?

I have just had occasion to use both these words while determinedly trying to write this crap—during which period I exhausted the possibilities of two refills for my ball point pen, and a second fountain pen (ball point). None worked and I had several immediate reactions. I wanted childishly to throw the pen viciously against the wall—quietly drop it and in injured withdrawal refuse to put my thoughts on paper, or the third alternative of searching diligently with controlled frustration and find a pencil. This I did—however by now I've forgotten what I had to write about.

Jan. 21

I have finally arrived at the unpleasant realization that I am profoundly inhibited in your presence and so am resorting to this cowardly device to expose aspects of our relationship—and my reactions to it, with as much honesty as I am capable of. I realize these repressions on my part are hindering my progress in analysis so I am overly anxious, (perhaps too aggressively so as is my usual problem) to eliminate them.

There is a twofold advantage for me in writing. I can express myself more clearly and honestly and say the things I want to say the way I want to say them, rather than the fumbling, censored ramblings on the couch. I will not attempt to analyze this, merely report.

There are so many questions and comments that never become expressed when I am with you and when I am alone I meditate on this to such an extent that I think I must employ whatever means possible to get them out.

I feel rather like I am constipated mentally and with great effort forcing a movement. Here I hesitate because automatically I wonder why I left out the word "bowel" which is the movement I associate with constipation. This form of free association is easier for me on paper than in person.

Now as to the WHY regarding my reluctance to expose myself and be completely natural with you I don't know, I must confess to both you and myself that at times I adopt a polite social attitude to our sessions. The intrusion of too great an intimacy is (which completely unrepressed confidences necessitates) something I am either afraid to accept or unable to give. I am in a sense holding you at arm's length saying you may help me just so far but no further. What I fear is an unknown quantity to me at this time. It is a feeling which asserts itself only in personal contact. I do not consciously wish to retard our progress and I realize that my resistance to you is irrational and contrary to my logical acceptance of our relationship. Perhaps I am afraid of it assuming a man-woman aspect which in my confused mind and frightened unconscious seems the logical emotional result of complete exposure and the intimacy pertaining to it.

In meditating on my reluctance, even resistance to free discussion of my sex life, I have wondered if I am afraid I may change my impersonal attitude towards you (although—without wishing to wound your masculine vanity, which even a psychologist must have—I must say I feel no element of physical attraction to you)—There now immediately I say to myself your analytic reaction to this will probably be to interpret that because I say I have no desire to wound that must be the underlying motive. You see how twisted up I'm getting—I seem to be seeing the pieces behind the pieces of a jig-saw puzzle.

To say I am confused at this point is an understatement. I am totally befuddled and being brutally pummelled by conflicting desires. I want to eliminate my self-conscious deception, I want to be able to release myself from the bondage of the shell enclosing my emotions and give up the precious privacy of this nonsense yet I can't let myself go.

The bravado I employ extends only as far as the use of four letter words, an occasional vulgarism and a forced boldness at times. I do not feel relaxed with you nor do I feel I have the right to presume beyond the limits of the time allotted me for each session (which occasionally by telephone after hours, I feel is an infringement on your privacy and an imposition on my part—*there is the polite side of me at work again*). I think this polite side may very well be the fly in the ointment (forgive the cliché, the writer in me rebels!)

Perhaps a composite of all these repressed urges may be the answer to why I am tense and reluctant and frightened. I don't know—but at least I am saying them now on paper. It is of course my wish to be able to express and expose as honestly during our personal sessions as when I sit down and write—almost to myself you might say. The fact that I will give these pages to you somehow is not as real as words spoken up into the air or face to face.

1st Day & Introduction   *Analytical Entry*

My psychoanalyst suggested I write for a half an hour every morning on arising—even before coffee and toast. I applied the time and more every day to this endeavour—but *after* coffee and toast.

Well, whether or not the following entries are interesting analysis-wise is not my main concern. Something even bigger has materialized out of this experiment—I made a fascinating discovery which will be exposed when I introduce the following entries.

Feb. 26

I think I have met the man I am going to love. There have been so many unsuccessful auditions for this role in the past few years, I was begining to think it would remain uncast indefinitely—and a life of auditioning lovers is sadly frustrating. There have been too many "inadequate" or "miscast" men in my roster. The results have made me like a play that keeps running on hope for the right replacement—but the current performance is bad entertainment with no message and inferior results.

This morning being Thursday is my day at Unemployment Insurance at 9:15 A.M. It is the first morning in many months that I exerted sufficient will-power to do so.

Also, just now, for the first time in my lazy life I employed the use of a dictionary, instead of scribbling a mis-spelled word (exert) with the usual off-handed excuse of—"I'm a miserable speller"—after all there is hardly any reasonable excuse for bad spelling where one has the intelligence to use words advanced enough to confuse the writer's knowledge of spelling. In future my dictionary will always be in close proximity so that my negligence will not be repeated.

But back to unemployment. Every Thursday I have goofed. This is $30 weekly that I cannot afford to ignore. Why I have not the self-discipline and incentive to get up and collect this money (even if it were seven A.M. instead of nine) is a question I am unable to answer. If I understand that, maybe I would understand many other indulgences on my part that are reluctant, but happen!

I attribute it to laziness, but I suspect it goes deeper than that—for what is laziness, but a restraint of energy over action, and then we come to the core of the question—Why desire to restrain oneself from an action—What suppresses the energy?

Anyway, although I don't know the basic cause, I today resolved to change my policy of procrastination and neglect—and in the future *pressure* myself, if necessary to attend to pressing responsibilities and obligations. This *defiant, rebellious* lack of discipline, even if discomfort and worry result, is debilitating.

The Discomfort of a Messy Home

Unattended washing and ironing, closets and drawers in confusing disarray, dirty dishes and sticky droppings on kitchen surfaces, to say nothing of unpaid bills piling up like myriad warnings of disaster. Disorganized manuscripts and music arrangements, unanswered mail—neglected wardrobe and social obligations—these are a few examples.

Eventually the total disorder causes a guilty disre-

gard of responsibility (a childish revolt) and a violent
hatred of the ensuing discomfort of living thus. How I
wish I could overcome my inertia regarding these matters. Staunchly I frequently resolve to do so by getting a
disciplinary grip on my "lazy" self and try to mend my
mouldering structure both physically and mentally.
Then for a day or two I try to function constructively
with moral integrity and reparatory attention to my
problems. This flame of high resolve too soon splutters
and dies, and I lapse back into the old familiar pattern
of slovenly disinclination to adhere to discipline. . . .

Evidently this self-abusive dissertation must have
sparked some deeply embedded desire to reform into
action.

I have just completed laundering several pairs of
panties and stockings that were on the verge of rust from
old-age dirt. Also dishes and ash trays that have lain in
muggy accusation for days now sparkle like a TV ad
for soap. Next I will attack the glass tops and carpet.
They both have developed peculiar designs which only
surplus filth can paint. Tonight my house will chuckle
with warmth and charm and cleanliness.

I hope my new lover will be here to see and enjoy its
comfort with me—but if he isn't, I still will have
cleaned my house, shampooed my hair, written my
poetry, practiced my singing, as well as attending to my
household and personal duties and thus found temporary surcease from the pain of yesterday.

I now terminate the entry for Thurs. Feb. 26.

I wonder whether I write faster in pen or pencil.
Half hour to write. Pencil I don't like. Too much like
school Wrote an M like Dad used to. Handwriting is
like Dad. Wish I was he. How silly. This is nonsense
must get a pen. The pencil I don't like. Can't get the
hang of free association. By trying to write quickly I
write with tension and arm gets tired. Wish I had a tape
recorder to talk into instead of write. Writing takes too
long. If only had some money! But I'm not smart at

"Con." All I want to do is indulge myself. Write, read, sew, sing, make love and have a ball with life. I hate inconveniences like needing money. Why is money so important. Screw money or screw for money. Same thing.

Can't write fast enough, The clock ticks in rhythm. Can't write fast enough. To free associate should lose myself. Maybe if I think slower—the clock ticks too fast—Tick, tick tick tick—uneven. My nose is itchy and used to be large. I edited that sentence—Fred— Can't remember his name the writer I am reading now. Why can't I remember his name. It's Fredrick[1] some- thing—Reik—just remembered by spelling it wrong— Why do I forget name, why his name I just finished reading him two minutes ago. Must learn to listen with third ear—money—oh how I want some. But how to get it. Psychoanalysis will teach me . . . Think right . . . make money . . . work and have fun . . . sing—act— play—love. All so distant why not now? Patience must learn patience. Can't. Mind stopped for a moment. Went blank. This is hard. Doesn't seem to say anything with importance.

Masturbation fantasies. Sadism—Male being pun- ished. His body caressed then whipped. Have him tied and helpless. Other female used to stimulate him. I watch. Pull her away from him by force and cruel grab of her hair. He cries whimpers. Body is purple with agony. Face contorted by lust convulsions. When he begins to droop and he quiets down—make her caress more and bring pitch up to agony. Get her caressed in same way. No relief for either—the whip to both. Spread her on table—open legs. She screams writhes in terror. Hold her down by force (others hold her) I then whip thighs. She is in terror and she knows I'm going to whip her again soon. She pleads cries, twists—I stand erect whip comes down—she screams incredibly like animal I laugh—whip again goes down she writhes, convulsive sobs, wonderment—he caresses himself— then he is helpless, spasmodic—unhappily in agony—

---

[1] [Theodor Reik.]

no sense—all sex—mind is polluted I'm dirty—no
sense. Why? dumb, stupid. I hate what is it ever who
know why what where who what am I. Can't write fast
enough can't go fast enough.

No life, troubles, defeat, misery crowds dreams too
lazy should but can't, hiding what who where I am.
Nuts. What will they say if they found this nonsense.
Need a dictograph or tape. Writing doesn't make sense
too slow, tedious. In a hurry but where am I going.
Never be able to read this back—Half hour is long time
(clock ticks)—must do it got to finish experiment. I'm a
psychologist want to be a psychoanalyst better than
singing; singing for kids, analysis, science, medicine,
life, work, grown-up. Child helpless, stupid. Nuts.

Where, why, what—these words keep coming back,
what do they mean. Where am I going? Who am I?
What is my secret guilt?

I don't know, Harold will find out. No, no! Why no?
I mean yes, subconscious hiding from me and Harold
but no good, must find out, want to be psychoanalyst
but subconscious repressed, please let me go—lose repressions, drop inhibitions, sanity is waiting, help find
clues get answers slowly, takes time but its coming. I'll
have the Psychic orgasm yet—Yes Yes Yes La La La
La—Half hour soon up writing like a fiend. I am
determined I'll master any damn thing I want, alone if
I have to, but I won't be suppressed by unconscious.

Mother & father two people I hate. Yes hate! They
are demons in one. Closing of liberation. Must free
myself free association that will do it. Will be like
Freud, analyze self. He did it with no help why can't
I—with books, Harold, and a science to study.

Thank God for Freud and others like or approximat-
ing him Reik, & Harold. I wonder if Reik analyzed
Harold—

I must ask him. Reik loved Freud. Who did or does
Harold love? —Is he happy, does he feel insecure too, is
his wife good to him, does he love her? What is his sex
life like? All from the unconscious. These last thoughts.
Everything is from the unconscious.

Half hour up.

I did it—

Hooray—
I love *me*

Dream No. I   *Beach Scene*

Slowly, reluctantly dreams are breaking through my forgetful consciousness. I awake with vague, nebulous memories. Last night and the night before they went, scattered and kaleidoscopic like this—

I was at a summer resort. But didn't go out into the sun. I remember saying (in the dream) "I can get a beautiful tan if I stay in the sun." But I stayed out of the sun. One day while I scoured the beach with a friend, formless and nameless, looking for a man for company (she, or he, the formless friend) pointed out an attractive man sunbathing that I had overlooked as being eligible. I looked again and was pleased.

I remember another segment of opening a door to a hallway containing several other doors leading to separate private rooms. I opened each door along the hallway looking for someone familiar. The one I sought had his room taken by someone else—had checked out. This had happened in reality the night before when I called a man by the name of Carter who had checked out and his room was occupied by an unknown woman—(the phone was used as contact in this instance)

The next adventure in the dream was at dinner time. I entered the bar still with an imaginary friend and passed several groups. Happily and with relieved anticipatory pleasure I recognized a tall friend in a group of people. I no longer felt lonely and unfamiliar—I tugged at his arm in passing, wanting him to invite me to join his group, but he warningly frowned me away, indicating by facial contortions and directive eye glances the tall blonde beside him—I indicated back that I was innocuous and meant no harm—but continued on. There were no tables and the hostess (or someone as indistinct as my spiritual feeling of a friend by my side) led me to the crowded bar and introduced me to three unattractive unescorted women. I was reluctant to join them. Feeling I would become like them, or would be seen and evaluated as such because of being with them, until one woman (of the group) with friendliness and welcome smiled at me. She I recognized with surprise and enthusiasm as Elsa Lanchester and immediately I became ingratiatingly warm, introducing her to my friend (still unknown) as a fine actress who would be remembered for her work opposite Charles Laughton. Later I remembered she was also Laughton's wife but I neglected to mention this—Her own position being sufficient recommendation and introduction.

Dream No. II

It is a great struggle to recall the kind of a dream that gives no clue except a feeling of having become aware of something—yet no picture, event or people are left in the mind on awakening. Such is the case now as I try to understand the following enlightenment.

I learned that slow, methodical analysis and study can create a finished product of beauty and firm strength. In my dream (singing or studying something) I worked slowly and painstakingly with minute attention to detail and careful development—the result was knowledge that far surpassed the flamboyant dynamics of a rushed, too quickly finished product of virtuosity. I know this to be so in reality, yet my subconscious seems to have also at last agreed to this procedure.

The last segment of this dream cycle occurred as I watched and listened to a singer who in a way reminded me of Marian, although she didn't look or sound like Marian, and sang with exquisite beauty and feeling, a song from some musical (I think *Finian's Rainbow*). I remembered in the dream the words and melody and the sound came effortlessly and beautifully. I watched, and felt tears in my eyes at the beauty of it all—both feeling and hearing the rich, solid soprano as if I were singing in my head silently and emoting along with the girl who sang with her face pure and musically transfigured before me. I think in this dream, as in several others, I was both women.

I am suddenly, concretely sure that my dreams expose the duality of my personality. Frequently I am both the observed and the observer—The do-er and the watcher, the sufferer and the physician. The criminal and the redeemer, the wanderer and the companion (as in the dream of the invisible friend).

Much of this material hardly needs analyzing. Actually Stella does a pretty good job of analyzing herself. However, there are several points to note because they bring out again in the case of Stella, as in the cases of all the twenty girls who were interviewed for the social psychological study, some of the most pertinent aspects of the kind of personality found in the call girl.

Again we have examples of the difficulty in establishing close relationships and the difficulty of trusting any other human being. In the first piece of writing Stella shows one of the problems she had in the analysis—the difficulty she had in trusting the analyst. This was an example of Stella's general difficulty in human relationships. In fact Stella states explicitly that she is afraid that if she were to drop the barriers the relationship might become closer and she would find this too uncomfortable and too doubtful a situation. She feels she has had little experience with such relationships in the past.

Another aspect demonstrated is the difficulty Stella had with internal controls. She states that she had been advised to do her writing in the morning before having breakfast. She explains that she did the writing but stopped to have breakfast first. This may not seem like a very important point but she was anxious to analyze herself, to establish the optimum conditions, and yet she was incapable of any sacrifice.

One of the problems Stella faced was her feeling that she had been damaged in life; that she was not going to permit any kind of pain to bother her again; that she was not going to make any further sacrifices. Linked with this attitude was her rebelliousness. A person who feels hurt and injured frequently searches for revenge. Stella searched for such revenge by demonstrating her rebelliousness in most situations. It was for that reason, among others, that I had suggested the writing—so that she would feel she was analyzing herself. Since she was unable to trust me I thought it might be easier for her to work at home. I think that some of this material indicates the progress Stella was able to make in her self-analysis.

Another point that has been mentioned previously and of which we have an example here, is Stella's rejection of female identification and her obvious wish to identify with the father rather than the mother when she states: "I wish I was he."

In her process of self-analysis one useful factor of identification is present. In the effort at free association, Stella breaks through and identifies first with Freud, then with Reik, and then with her own analyst. Apparently she was able to utilize the positive aspects of the authors she had been reading and of the work she had done with the analyst in order to form a picture and to internalize a personality that was less destructive than hers.

In the sexual fantasy that Stella describes we have many of the elements that are frequently found in the call-girl personality. First we have the reversal. Stella had never been able to achieve an orgasm during normal heterosexual intercourse. She longed for it, hoped for it, even had sexual relations with women in the hope of finding it, but had never been able to do so. The tantalizing aspect and the torture of this experience are demonstrated in her fantasy. Only this time it is not Stella who is suffering but others. Each participant almost reaches climax, but at the last moment she stops it as, in actuality, part of her own personality had stopped her.

The defense that Stella uses against the feeling of deprivation is to fancy herself in the grandiose omnipotent role. She stops the man; she stops the woman; she beats both; she is completely the master. She is trying to compensate for the lack of mastery she felt in her personal life.

Because Stella came from a "good family," secure, intelligent, educated; because she never experienced the kind of material deprivation that Sandra had suffered, and because Stella's life seems more similar to that of the average girl growing up in our predominantly middle-class society, it may be helpful to pay some attention to the factors that crippled Stella's development as a human being.

The first factor was her feeling that she was exploited by her mother. This feeling is frequently found in persons less disturbed than Stella.

As she put it: "Mother valued me for my pretty red hair, for my ability to sing, for my brightness, never for me alone."

Children, valued for such external, superficial factors frequently feel just as deprived as if they had been completely neglected. They feel it is not they who are being valued but something outside themselves. Apparently Stella felt that her mother was cold and indifferent and could accept her only for her talents. What she wanted was the close warmth which is given just because one is oneself. Unconsciously then, Stella had a tremendous need to pay her mother back for this deprivation—to revenge herself. The problem with this revenge was that it was tied up with great fear. One aspect in which this fear stood out most clearly was the fact that Stella was afraid that if men, for example, found her attractive, her mother would be angry with her.

She had had one such experience. Harvey, the mother's lover, had been quite attracted to her. In part her homosexuality could be explained as a defense against the avenging mother. Angry at her mother and afraid that her mother would punish her, she protected herself against this punishment by being very kind and attentive to her mother. Later she acted similarly with other women who she felt might possibly punish her. Therefore in her homosexual relations she found herself attracted to women who were hard and strong—the kind of woman who might be punitive. If we substitute Stella for one of the women she describes in her sexual fantasy we can see that the fantasy was not one of kindness and tenderness but of punishment.

The need she seemed to feel to debase herself is then partly explained as an attempt to see whether she could be loved for herself. Another component in this is that she seemed always to be saying: "See, Mother, this is what you did to me," avenging herself on her mother by being exactly the kind of person her mother did not want her to be.

Side by side with Stella's need to debase herself was her constant search for power. She was really searching for the power to control her own impulses. In this search she would frequently over-react. For example, when she started to take constructive steps toward helping herself she did so in an obsessive manner. She would write down long lists of things to do and would then do them one by one. When she became the kind of person who could clean her apartment she scrubbed it scrupulously and thoroughly. As she mentions in one of her entries, when she started to write, she secured a dictionary and looked up the spelling of every word about which she was doubtful. All of this was an attempt to control herself and her impulses.

It was helpful to Stella to move from complete lack of control to extreme control. Because of this extreme control, she was able to build a new career and eventually to become a successful performer.

The crucial change Stella had to make was to stop punishing her mother by coming to peace with the memory of her mother. She had begun to understand her mother's own difficulties and frustrations and inability to express herself; that her mother's anger, which Stella had interpreted as anger at her, was really anger at her own position. Stella was finally able to make some identification with her mother and to understand her actions.

A dramatic incident occurred at the time that Stella worked through the problem of accepting the memory of her dead mother. It will be remembered that when Stella first became pregnant she could not accept the fact that a man had caused the baby and she left the man who had been responsible for the conception to take up with a man who had not been responsible. (This is not an unusual pattern for girls who become call girls—the need to rob the man of this sign of virility; the wish to imitate the men who "lay 'em and leave 'em.") During the time that Stella was in analysis, and fortunately just at the time that the problem of identification with her mother was being worked through, Stella got word that the woman who had adopted her daughter had died and that if she wished, she now had the opportunity to get her daughter back. Not hesitating for a moment, Stella welcomed her daughter back, and made strenuous efforts to give her the love and attention she would have liked to receive from her own mother but felt she had never known.

It was at about this time that Stella started to change her standards of the kind of man she found interesting. Instead of the ne'er-do-wells, the hangers-on, the barflys, she began to be interested in other types of men. It was interesting to note that, as in Sandra's case, her first subsequent affair of any consequence was with a physician. This doctor was an intelligent and cultured man, and she had a real relationship with him. In the early period of this relationship she had many difficulties, of a kind that seem strange in view of Stella's background. She complained that he was too physical. As she put it: "I wanted him to value me without this nonsense of sex." Once when she was out with him she told him that there had been many men in her life but didn't specify that she had been paid by any of these men. She also told him that since he meant so much to her she didn't want to spoil their relationship by making it only physical right at the beginning.

To women this may sound like a reasonable point of view. To most men, even to a man as understanding as this physician, this was a difficult point of view to appreciate. Most women feel accepted only when a man loves them for themselves without sex. Most men feel accepted by a woman only when they are accepted sexually. He agreed to her wish for a platonic relationship, but as soon as they got home he insisted on kissing her. Stella broke out of his arms and told him to leave the house.

Stella, who had gone to bed with hundreds of men, became upset because one man, whom she liked and who liked her, wanted to kiss her. Stella's explanation was that here again was someone who didn't understand her. She had wanted this relationship to be different. By forcing his favors on her he was acting like all of the other men—like all the Johns.

She was ready to break off the relationship and not see him again. We discussed this attitude and when Stella began to understand how difficult it would be for most men to acquiesce in her point of view she continued to see him. She talked the problem over with him, explaining how she felt and what made her feel the way she did. Fortunately he was an understanding person, accepted the explanation and patiently wooed her as if she were a frightened, inexperienced young girl who had never been close to a man.

In a sense Stella never had been close to anyone; most of her previous experiences with men had been so impersonal that being emotionally close was a new experience. She had never previously experienced a combination of tenderness and sex. She had known sexual feelings and had attempted to gratify them directly with no control. Having both tender and sexual feelings for the same person was completely new to her. At the beginning of her relationship with the doctor she had felt that sexual feelings appearing in a situation such as this would destroy the tenderness. In this respect Stella was not unlike a great many other women in our society.

Stella began to learn that there were men who were capable of meeting some of her needs, which were tremendous because of her long period of emotional starvation. It was necessary to remind Stella repeatedly that no single individual could ever satisfy all of her needs and that she was fortunate to have met a man like the physician who was willing to try to meet as many of her demands as he possibly could. Unfortunately, he was married, but Stella had known this before their relationship began. When he began to speak of leaving his wife, Stella refused to permit him to make this sacrifice. He had children and she felt keenly what would happen to the children if the home was broken.

Stella moved to the West Coast when the show in which she was starring moved there, in order to make it easier for them to separate. She was unhappy about leaving the man she loved and apprehensive about leaving analysis; depressions still plagued her occasionally. But by this time she had acquired so much strength, was able to do so much self-analysis about her more serious difficulties, was able to put so many of her feelings into her acting, that she was willing to take the chance.

She left New York hopeful that she would be able to establish a relationship with a man who could be helpful to her. She was now well established professionally and felt confident of her ability to build on her two years of success and not destroy herself.

Underneath all her problems Stella, too, felt that she had been deprived of love and warmth. She had reacted to this feeling of deprivation with intense anger which she usually kept bottled up. On a few occasions this anger broke out: when she wanted to kill the little boy; when she told Harvey's wife of her mother's affair with Harvey (who was a rival for the mother's attention); and when she took her mother's clothing immediately after her death. In her fantasies, too, she expressed the wish for vengeance.

Usually, though, she turned the anger in upon herself and suffered from intense depressions and self-destructive urges. Her mother had told her that she was bad, and to the child it was safer to feel that she was bad than to express anger at her mother. This fear of expressing anger openly was generalized so that as she grew older she strove continually to repress the rage that seethed within her. Consequently Stella had not dared to get too close to any human being for fear that her hate would erupt and possibly destroy her or the other person. Perhaps this is why Stella at first permitted her own daughter to be adopted; so that she would be safe from the rage she perceived within herself. Before Stella could become a mature, disciplined human being, she had to come to terms with this internalized rage and its source in the early feelings of rejection.

Only after she had relived her hatred of her mother and understood its source, was she able to love her mother and to love herself and other human beings, only then was she able to realize some of the creative potential with which she was endowed.

5. ROSE: THE HYPNOANALYSIS OF A PROSTITUTE[1]

The case of Rose was added to illustrate some of the problems of a "house" girl as distinct from a call girl and to demonstrate what I have on occasion found to be a highly successful adjunct to therapy, hypnosis. It took me a long time to overcome my own resistance to the use of hypnosis because my training as a psychoanalyst was opposed to it. Rose helped convince me of the value of hypnosis both as a timesaver and as a source of information about the deepest levels of unconscious material.

Because hypnosis can be so effective when it is indicated by the specific needs of the patient, it can be dangerous to the practitioner. Many hypnotists tend to develop even greater grandiosity than therapists in general. Also the easily learned knack of hypnotizing is no substitute for thorough training in psychology or psychiatry. It should be used only by a thoroughly trained person in one of these disciplines.

When I opened the door of my office that morning the phone was ringing. I lifted it off the cradle and said, as I usually do, "This is Harold Greenwald."

The voice at the other end was hesitant, shy and

---

[1] New material for this edition.

seemed to be that of a very young girl. "Are you the Dr. Greenwald who wrote the book?"

By now I was accustomed to questions of this type and so I replied, "Do you mean the book about the call girl?"

The voice at the other end said, "Yes, that's the one. I read your book and I came to New York from Arizona just to see you. Could I come and see you, please?"

I happened to have a free hour the next day and so I replied, "If you're free you can come to see me at nine tomorrow morning. What is your name please?"

There was hesitation and then the voice said, "Rose."

"Rose," I repeated, with a questioning note in my voice so that she would give me the second name. There was no reply. "Rose, who?" I asked.

The voice at the other end lost some of its fright, became slightly angry, and said, "Rose, isn't that enough? Do I have to give you my whole biography on the phone? Rose will be enough for now."

"I'll see you tomorrow, Rose," I replied.

The next day at nine o'clock when I went into my waiting room I was surprised to see that the girl waiting for me—Rose, that is—looked older than her voice had led me to expect. She was rather plump, dressed in clothes that made her look like a caricature of a small-town prostitute. The dress was much too tight, made of some shiny material, her face was heavily made up, with a fur piece around her neck. I was arrested, though, by the expression in her eyes. They were frightened, pleading and yet somehow also rebellious. There was a strange mixture of anxiety, a wish to please, covered by an angry look. It was an expression I had observed frequently in prostitutes all over the world.

I asked her to come into my private office. She did, sat down, and I asked, "How can I help you Rose?" Her mouth started to form words, but she couldn't quite utter them. I saw that I would have to ask an easier question. "How did you hear about me?" I asked. This seemed to help and she started with a rush of words:

"You see the landlady in the house where I worked, gave us your book to read. She gave me and the other girls this book to read. She thought it would make the joint more high class if we read a book about call girls and learned the kind of things they do. I read your book all day Sunday. When I finished, I packed my stuff, said goodby, got on a bus, and rode for five hours to Phoenix. There I caught a plane and came to New York. When I got to New York I looked you up in the phone book and I called. The first one I called was a different Dr. Greenwald, but they told me your number so I called you."

While I knew the term "landlady" from previous experience, I still wanted to make certain and I said, "By landlady you mean the madam?"

She replied, "Yeah, sure, the madam. You know the word, you used it in the book. The madam of the joint where I worked. I was a hustler; I've been a hustler since I was eighteen; I'm twenty-eight now. Ten years I've been a hustler working double shifts, making seven and eight hundred bucks a week. Ten years; that's all I know. That's all I've done. Now do you want to take me?"

I said, "Well, tell me more about what you want."

"I want to quit. I want to kick the racket. I want to get out. I want to be a real person. I don't want to be a whore no more. I want to get a job, get married. I don't want to be a whore no more."

I asked her why she needed me for that. "If you want to do that," I said, "Why don't you do just that?"

"How can I do it?" she answered. "What do I know? I don't know nothing. Since I was eighteen I've only had one square job in my life. Once I worked as a helper taking care of kids for a lady. I don't know anything about jobs. I don't know how to get a job. I don't know how to live, but I've got some money. I'll pay you. How much do you want?"

I told her what my fee was and she took out enough money to pay for ten sessions. I said that she didn't have to pay me in advance. She insisted: "Oh, please take it. If I keep it I might spend it. Already I've been spending money—see—" She held out two books of poetry which she had bought immediately upon coming to New York. I asked her if anything else bothered her.

Before she answered that, she had to make sure. "You mean," she said, "you're going to take me? You're really going to take me. You don't care what I did. You're really going to take me?"

I said, "Of course."

"Okay," she said, "I'll tell you. For one thing I like to booze too much. Yeah." It was a habit she had I was later to discover, of frequently reinforcing a statement by saying, "Yeah" that way, almost naively, like a young girl. "Yeah, I drink too much. When I used to work, I'd work and work for four, five months, save up my dough, rent a car, go to Dallas and drink it all up in a week. I can't drink when I work. Whenever I would take a rest I'd spend all my money drinking."

"Is there anything else?" I asked.

"Sometimes everything blacks out. I can be walking in the street and suddenly everything gets black. I went to the doctors. They don't know what the hell it was. Paid them lots of money and they never knew what it was."

"When did it start?" I asked.

"I think it started when I had my second abortion. Yeah, that's right. I was knocked up and a girl told me you could get one in Mexico so I went to Tiajuana. Two hundred bucks it cost and then I was sick for three weeks. I didn't feel good. I fainted a few times then. Since then I think I faint a lot."

To determine how strong her wish was, I asked: "Tell me, why do you want to leave the racket. You seem to be doing well; you say you make seven to eight hundred dollars a week. You'll never be able to make that kind of money in a straight job. Why do you want to quit? After all, you can take your vacations and go out and get drunk. You can live it up. You won't be able to do that if you have a square job. You're living in a house, there are a lot of girls; you must have some fun there."

"Yeah, sure, we have fun, but I hate it. I hate it and I'm afraid of it. Once I used to be a call girl. I was working in Dallas. I went to this big hotel. I met this John at the bar, tricks we call them down south. I met this trick and we went up to his room. I took my clothes off and the first thing I knew, he started to beat me. Yeah, that's right, beat me. I didn't even say nothin'. I didn't do nothin'. He started to beat me. I thought he was going to kill me. I ran all over the room. Finally, I got to the door and I ran out into the hall buck-naked, without a stitch of clothes on screaming and he after me. The elevator operator and the bellboys got a hold of him. I got my clothes on and I left. After that I didn't want to be a call girl no more. I was living with this pimp then, Fred. He wanted me to do it. He had good connections. He knew everybody in the big hotels, the managers, the fellows who ran the conventions and he wanted me to continue. I had a sister-in-law, another girl, who was also giving him her dough and he wanted the two of us to keep hustling for him. I said I wouldn't so he beat me. So you see, who wants that kind of life? Who needs it?"

I said, "How about in the house where you worked? You didn't have that kind of trouble?"

"No, the landlady had her old man. He was a big guy. He would take care of any tricks that made trouble. But you never knew. You never knew when you'd get some kind of a kook in there, some kind of a nut, a freak, who would want to beat you, or kill you, or something. And then having to go to the doctor all the time and be examined, every week, yeah, every week we had to go. Who wants to get all those things? I don't want it. I want to quit, but I don't think I'll ever be able to. You think you could help me?"

I said that I didn't know; that I would have to know a great deal more about her. Would she tell me the story of her life? I found that Rose had great difficulty in telling the story in any kind of organized way. Therefore, I didn't ask that she do that. What she gave was a far from chronological account. She would give pieces of her most recent experiences, pieces of her past life, all interwoven, wherever her associations led her. For analysis, this is frequently the most useful way to obtain the patient's history. However, even in presenting these bits and patches, she had great difficulty and constantly had to feel that I was still interested. I had to ask her questions frequently. There were sessions when she was not able to tell me anything about her life, but would just aimlessly discuss things like the weather, or where did I get the pictures on my wall, or show me drawings she had made in a bar. She had a facility for drawing and frequently carried a pad with her on which she would sketch people and things. Sketch them in a sort of primitive abstract form, but with definite skill and a feeling for line and shading.

Rose was born and spent the first six years of her life in a small Texas town. Her father and mother separated when she was three. Her father wanted her, he wanted her to come and live with him. The mother wanted Rose to live with her and the grandmother wanted her there, so that the three of them were after her. She stayed for a while with the father who put her in a boarding school and used to come to visit her every week, would take her to nice restaurants, buy her pretty clothes and toys. Then she stayed with the grandmother and her grandmother sent her to school. Then her mother took her. Her mother had moved to New Mexico with her new husband Frank. Frank was rather strict. He used to make Rose study. When she didn't, he would hit her with a strap. "Yeah," she said, "hit me with a strap." She didn't like school much. She didn't like the other kids. They didn't talk to her. She had trouble talking to them. Her mother had three children with Frank and she had to help her mother take care of them. She didn't mind taking care of the kids, but she didn't like having to help with the housework. She was very good in music. She used to sing very well and once she won a prize for being the best singer in the school. Then she was entered in a contest for the whole county but they didn't tell her what happened. A week later they called her up in the assembly and they gave her a prize. She had won the contest for having the best voice in the county. But then she got into trouble. About the time she finished high school, she didn't know why, but her mother and stepfather didn't want her around any more. She couldn't go to her father because he had died so she got a job as a baby sitter. She went to work for a woman in Santa Fe taking care of the children and at the same time she was going to music school. She had a teacher who liked her and helped her a great deal with her singing and she was also studying piano. But the woman for whom she was working scolded her once. She started to go out with boys and one night she came home very late. The woman said, "I don't want a girl like you in my house who stays out so late. I have a little daughter." So Rose got angry and left. That night she took her things, left Santa Fe and went to Phoenix.

In Phoenix she got a job for two days working in a store. They fired her. She met a man in the store who told her she could stay at his place. She stayed there for a while and then she left him, stayed with another man; then she was broke. One day she had a fight with the other man. She was hanging around with a wild crowd. She met them at different bars. There was a large wild crowd at that time in Phoenix. Through them she met a great many hustlers, girls who were working as call girls and working in houses, joints. She decided to turn out. She became a call girl. At that time she met Fred. Fred was her first pimp. He introduced her. He taught her the ropes and she used to give him all her money. She started to make a lot of money, five, six hundred dollars a week. She would give it all to Fred and he would give her a few dollars for expenses. One day she was arrested. She had gone to a bar where she usually found customers and one of these customers turned out to be a vice-squad policeman. After she solicited him, he went up to the room with her, told her to take off her clothes. She took off her clothes, and after, as she said, "He had a good look, he flashed his badge and told me I was under arrest." In the jail she was thrown in with many girls who were more experienced, knew a great deal about the racket. One of them told her about a house in a town near Phoenix where she could go to work.

She liked it better in the house because it was steady and protected. She worked there until the police decided one day to clean up the town. The town had a bad reputation, there were five houses there. The police came and arrested all the girls and threw them into jail, all of them from the five houses into this one jail, about forty girls. Finally they were brought before the judge and were told that they could go free if they would promise to leave town immediately.

Rose left town and went to Texas. Here she worked in several houses and then she went back to Phoenix and worked for a while as an outlaw. By this she meant someone who didn't have a pimp. Working as an outlaw was better because it meant she could keep all the money for herself, but what could she do with the money? She couldn't spend it fast enough so she would stop working and go on a binge and drink it all up. The first time she became pregnant was in Phoenix. She found a doctor in town who performed the abortion for six hundred dollars. Then she went back to Texas, worked in another house. She said this house "was like legal" because "every week we'd go down to the police station and there'd be a doctor there and he would examine and the boss had to pay a certain amount of money and then we could continue working. "Once" she said, "I even went up to Nevada and worked in a real legal house. It was not against the law in Nevada and it wasn't much different; just the same. Still the drunks and the tricks and having to work all the time. They were waking you up in the middle of the night because some trick would arrive. It was the same with all of them. It doesn't make any difference whether it's legal or it's illegal. They are all lousy."

Finally, she went back to Texas and it was at this last house that the landlady had given her my book to read, and that she had decided after reading the book to quit the racket.

While she was telling me the story of her life, she was also describing the difficulties she had in living in New York. In many ways Rose was like a girl who had been educated in a convent. For example, when she first went for a job, they asked her for her social security card. She had no idea what a social security card was. She asked me what it was and I explained it to her and also told her how to go about applying for one. She had managed to find a room near Columbia University where the woman rented rooms to students. Rose lived in that apartment but found it quite expensive. Meanwhile, she was slowly pawning and selling her furs and her jewelry. She said she didn't want to go to work as long as she had any of that left. As she put it: "I think I want to get rid of everything that reminds me of the racket. I don't want to have anything of it. I don't want to be reminded in any way. I'm going to make a clean break. It's like the addicts, the drug addicts. The only way an addict once told me you can really quit is to quit cold turkey, to get rid of all the hypos and all the junk and all the connections and all the people you know. That's why I came to New York where I don't know anybody and that's why I want to get rid of anything that had anything to do with the racket, including clothes and jewelry, especially the trick clothes." She explained that the trick clothes were the costumes she normally used while working. In order to be able to get in and out of them quickly enough, they were made ingeniously with one zipper so that you could just pull down the zipper and quickly get out of the dress. She was finished with all that she decided, and she wanted to get rid of it.

Rose had trouble in the furnished rooms she found. In one she felt the landlady was too nosy, always trying to find out her business, asking her what she did, what kind of a job she had. She didn't know what to say to such questions. At one place she got so angry when the lady persisted in her questions that she answered, "I was a whore. I've been a whore all my life and you'd be one too if you weren't so goddam ugly." With that she took all of her belongings and moved out even though she had paid for a week in advance and had only lived there for three days.

Meanwhile, she slowly began to make friends. It was quite painful to her and she asked me how to go about it. I told her I didn't know, really, but she, herself, found that if she went to bars she could make friends. It was interesting that she gravitated toward the kinds of bars she had known all her life. Even though my office was just a few blocks away from one of these bars, I had never known of its existence until Rose told me about it. It was a bar where all the people, in one way or another, were part of the rackets. "Even if they have square jobs, they still have something to do with the rackets. Like there's one fellow, he's a manager of a supermarket, but he also makes book. So he's in the supermarket watching sales and deliveries and at the same time guys come in and give him money to bet on the horses. So he's a manager and a bookie. That's a good combination.

"It's great at night: they turn on television and watch all the gangster programs but they always cheer for the gangsters. When the cops or the F.B.I. show up, they boo and they hiss and sometimes when the guy is pulling a heist or a stick-up, they yell, 'No, that ain't the way to do it' because they know much more about it than the guys on the T.V. It's a great place." At this place she made several friends. One of them offered to introduce her to a nice fellow. This fellow, Antonio, turned out to be a pimp and he wanted her to work for him.

She told him, "Listen, I don't want to have anything to do with you. If I had wanted that I could have stayed back home in Texas. I came here to get out of the racket and I'm not getting into it for a jerk like you."

Finally the time came when Rose had very little money left and she decided that she had to get a job. She found that among her new friends, several of them were working as waitresses and they told her how to go about getting a job and the places to apply. The first few places she left, frightened when they asked her about her past experience. She was sure that they knew she had been a prostitute and because of that, she didn't want to go any further. She felt that by the way they looked at her, the way they spoke to her, they knew what she had done and been. Painfully she continued trying and finally she got a job. She worked for two days and then she was fired because the man said she didn't know anything about the restaurant business. It took her about three weeks before she felt courageous enough to go out and try to find another job. She found one and here she lasted for three days. The third job she lasted one day. She was very discouraged and thought it would be impossible for her ever to make it as a waitress.

"I'm just too goddam stupid. I don't know nothing. I don't know how to make out a check. I can't write an order. My hand starts to shake when I have to write the check."

It was while she was deeply discouraged and she was describing her discouragement and desperation, that she called me one day in a spirit of excitement. Up to this time in talking to me in the office she had been rather polite, rather formal, rather distant. On the phone she sounded different, angry. Her opening words were, "You son of a bitch, you did it to me. I couldn't do it."

"What couldn't you do?" I asked, puzzled.

"I couldn't turn a trick. I went up to this place. The man said he had a job for me. I went up there. I said I wanted to work, he said he had a job and when I came up there were three guys and they wanted to have me go to bed with them. I couldn't do it. I couldn't screw them. You did it. It's your fault. I don't know how you did it but you did. I could have made enough money in an hour to take care of me for three weeks, but no, on account of you I have to go and be a waitress."

Finally she got a job as a waitress working nights. It was on the edge of the Bowery but she liked it. She said, "This is the world I'm used to. It's a place where hustlers come in. I like working nights. I hate working in the daytime. There are only squares around. At night you meet people you can talk to." She worked steadily at this job for about six months from twelve midnight to nine in the morning. She learned about the business, she made friends with people at the job, she began to go out, go to parties. She found other bars where she could make friends. She settled in a furnished apartment but every now and then things would get too difficult for her. She would find herself going on one- and two-day drinking bouts. One time after such a bout of drinking all day and having no sleep, she went to work and reported: "The first customer who came in started to give me a hard time. He didn't like the coffee and then he didn't like the sandwich I brought him. I told him I was sorry. That was the only kind of food we had. He started to yell and scream and I told him, 'If you don't like it, you can go some place else to eat.' Then he backed down." She became more and more irritated with the customers. As she lost her fear of the job, she became angrier more frequently.

Then she ran into difficulties with the manager of the restaurant. "He's always trying to get me down in the cellar. I told him if he put a hand on me again, I'd chop it off with the cleaver. That's what I told him. I said, 'You put your dirty hands on me again, and I'll let you have it. I'll cut your Goddamn hand off.'" He was constantly finding fault with everything she did. He would bawl her out in front of the customers. Finally she got into such a serious fight with the manager that he had her fired. At this time she was so angry, that she couldn't seem to find any other work. She went from place to place and was unable to get any job. She liked the first place, she said, and if the manager hadn't been such a jerk and if there hadn't been so many screwy customers, she would have been able to continue there, but no, she had to run into these kind of jerks.

Mixed with her attack on the manager and the customers, there was also a great deal of self-blame. She felt that she was no good, that she would never be able to get another job, that nobody wanted her and that the only thing she was really good for was hustling.

Also her speech, which had never been too easy, became more and more diffident. She found it harder to talk. Frequently an entire session would pass with Rose just saying a few words. It was at such a time that she began to ask me if I couldn't hypnotize her. She told me that after all, she had read about hypnosis, read about doctors who use hypnosis when a patient can't speak freely. I was very reluctant, as I explained at the beginning of this chapter, to use hypnosis. However, countering my reluctance was the feeling that usually a patient knows what type of treatment is most useful in her case. I tried, however, before using hypnosis, to explore the resistance as to why she couldn't speak. It was impossible to get any material from Rose which would explain the great difficulty she was experiencing in speaking. Finally I decided to try hypnosis, but to try it in a very limited way, to see if it were possible to explore the reasons for her inability to talk.

Customarily, hypnosis is used in psychotherapy to remove the resistance. Since I believe that Rose's resistance, the reluctance to speak, was connected with many of her deeper problems, I felt it was very important not just to by-pass this resistance, but to study it, so that in understanding why she couldn't speak to me, it would perhaps be possible to understand some other aspect of her character. And if I could understand this and somehow convey that understanding to her or have her become aware of it, I felt that this might not only solve the impasse in the therapy but might help her with some of her other problems. I therefore finally decided to try hypnosis. Rose is one patient with whom I have never regretted this decision.

With hypnosis and as I began to learn more about its use, and specifically to help her, I was able to get a much deeper and more meaningful impression from Rose of her life and her problems than I think I have been able to get with any similar patient.

In the first session where I introduced hypnosis I made no effort to elicit any information from Rose at all. What I did was induce a trance state, let her rest in it for a while, and then bring her back to full consciousness. Carefully I questioned her about her experience and she said, "It feels great. It's like taking pot, you know, marijuana. Yeah, I felt very relaxed, very calm, floating. In fact I feel much better. Did you ask me any questions?"

I explained that I hadn't but only wanted to see how she would react.

"You can ask me anything you want. I think I can talk that way."

At the next session, as soon as she came in she said, "Well, aren't you going to hypnotize me this time?" I agreed and again she went into a trance, this time much easier than the first time. The first attempt had taken about twenty minutes. The second time it took only ten minutes to induce the trance. I woke her and then helped her go back into a trance two or three times. When I say helped her go back into a trance, I should really explain that all I did in this case (as in other cases where I have utilized hypnosis for psychotherapeutic purposes) was to facilitate her going into a trance. In common with most people who use hypnosis from time to time for purposes of psychotherapy, I have never used and feel that it should not be used in an authoritative way at all. It should merely be used in helping the patient achieve the state that he or she would like. Since Rose was quite willing, all I had to do was make the suggestion to her for the trance and she at all times, as I made clear, had the right to accept or reject the suggestion. I also made it clear that if at any time during the trance there was anything she didn't want to say, she didn't have to. However, I induced the trance several times and then explained to her that it was better to go into the trance on a very brief signal in order to save the time taken for induction. At first I used just the Greek letter *Alpha*. I would say "Alpha" and Rose would immediately go into a trance. However, I found that this seemed to cause a shock to her nervous system and so I lengthened the procedure with a "go to sleep, Rose, go to sleep, one, two, three, four, five. You are asleep." In this way, going into the trance was a gentler procedure and yet one which did not take too much time.

I then proceeded to follow my original plan which was merely to study her resistance to communication. I felt that perhaps this resistance was also connected with her resistance to working and to getting a job. And so after two sessions of training in trance induction, I asked her when she went into the trance at the third session why she was having trouble talking. Her mouth tightened and through almost tightly clenched teeth she said, "I don't know. I can't tell you." I asked her why she couldn't tell me. She said, "I don't know. I don't know anything about it. Don't ask me these questions." I think this is a very important point because many therapists, especially psychoanalysts, object to hypnosis because they think it removes resistance. I never found this to be so with Rose or with any other patient, perhaps because this was not my intention. Unlike other psychotherapists who use hypnosis for removing the resistance, I was interested in understanding it.

However, I still was curious about the reason for her inability to speak and so I said, "Rose, perhaps you would like to have a dream. Perhaps you will let yourself go and have a dream, a dream which will tell us why you have so much trouble speaking. I'm going to let you dream now. I won't say anything. If you do have a dream when you finish, move your right hand and I will know that you have finished dreaming."

For several moments Rose remained silent on the couch. There was no movement except for the occasional flickering of her eyes and working of the throat muscles which is frequently characteristic of dream activity on the part of the sleeper or hypnotized subject. Finally, there was a small movement of her hand and I asked, "Would you like to tell me the dream, Rose?"

"There's this girl walking some place. She's walking on a path and it's next to the river. She walks alone. There are people. When the people see her they turn away. They don't want to have anything to do with her. She's going to go to the river and she's going to jump in."

"Do you know why those people are turning away?"

"Yeah. It's the same reason she's going to jump in. She's no good. She's just a goddam whore. That's why they don't want to have anything to do with her."

It seemed to me that here Rose was expressing her problem. She felt such a keen sense of worthlessness that she felt it was no use talking; that talking would only make her feel worse; that it would expose the worthlessness. It reminded me of a comment she had made once. She was telling me about going to the beauty parlor and she told me, "There are lots of girls there. You know, hustlers. Yeah, they come to the same beauty parlor."

I asked, "How do you know what they are?"

"Oh," she said, "you can tell. They come late all the time."

I said, "That's true. I found the same thing when they come here. Most of them come late all the time. Why is that?"

"Oh," she said, "You're putting me on. You know why it is."

When I assured her that I didn't know the reason, she told me, "Don't you see, when you're hustling, the last thing in the world you want to do is come here and look at yourself. So that's why you're late because you don't want to look at yourself." Incidentally, Rose was late only two or three times in the three years of therapy and then her latenesses usually coincided with periods of intense resistance.

When Rose came out of the trance, which was shortly after telling me the dream, she started to speak spontaneously without any urging from me and without my discussing what she had told me in the trance. I believe that even when the patient does not directly remember what he has said in the trance state, he becomes aware of it at some higher level of consciousness than previously because he has said it. So without any direct questioning from me, she told me about her fear of speaking, her fear of interviews, of talking to customers when she worked as a waitress for fear that she might reveal the kind of life she had lived. She felt that people would then know that she was "nothing but a tramp" and she also told me that she was sure that I too must feel that way about her sometimes. For several sessions thereafter, she spoke more freely than she had in the past and so we didn't use hypnosis again until once more she had difficulty speaking. Again she started asking for hypnosis.

This time she said, "Please, hypnotize me so that I shouldn't drink any more."

I said, "If you don't want to drink, why do it?"

"I can't help it. I just go to bars and I start drinking. There's nothing I can do. Put me to sleep and help me not to drink any more." I told her that I didn't think that would be useful to our relationship because I didn't want to use the hypnosis to force her to do anything she didn't want to do.

She said, "But I do want to stop. I do want you to hypnotize me out of drinking. You're not forcing me. You never told me to stop drinking. I want to give it up myself."

Against my better judgment, but as an experiment, I hypnotized her and made the post-hypnotic suggestion that she would not drink again; that she would go to a bar but that if anyone asked her if she wanted a drink she would order soda or ginger ale.

A few days later she called me and in a very loud, boisterous voice, announced, "I'm loaded. I'm real drunk." Then with great triumph added, "You see, it didn't work. Ha."

Here was another example of the resistance. Rose had unconsciously asked me to make the suggestion about not drinking in order to test whether the hypnosis was robbing her of her will completely and when she discovered that this was not so, she was able to trust the hypnotic state much more.

One impressive by-product of hypnosis was Rose's ability while in a hypnotic state to interpret dreams. She could interpret her dreams at such time in a manner as skilled as any analyst I have ever known and far more skilled than most. Certainly she understood her dreams better than I could.

Another interesting by-product of the dream work during hypnosis was that frequently she would tell me the dream in the waking state. When I hypnotized her and asked her to repeat the dream, it was generally much fuller, frequently the most significant details were the ones she omitted in the waking state. In such situations I would attempt to investigate why certain details had been omitted in the waking state since they would be clues to understanding her resistance. Several times I tested her ability at interpretation, tested it in the waking state and then in the dream state. In the waking state she could make very few statements about her dreams but in the hypnotic state she was able to explain them far more thoroughly. After about a year and a half of hypnotic work she began to develop the same facility in her waking state. But at the beginning I found the differences were remarkable.

For example, Rose came in and reported the following dream: "I was trying to clean the mirror and I couldn't get it clean."

While she was still awake I asked her what it meant. She answered with two words, "It's here."

I said, "What do you mean?"

"It's here," she replied. She wouldn't elaborate, but just repeated, "It's here."

When she went into the hypnotic state, I asked her again about the dream. I asked her to repeat the dream. She repeated that she was trying to clean the mirror but no matter how hard she tried, no matter what she did, she couldn't get it clean.

I asked, "What does it mean?"

She said, "It's just that I don't want to face myself. When I'm here, I don't want to face myself. You're trying to make me look at myself and I won't do it." The awareness of the resistance to the analysis seemed quite clear but I asked, "What is it you don't want to face?"

"I don't know."

I asked, "Does it remind you of anything?"

She said, "Well when I was a kid I used to take baths with the boys, my half brothers. I felt ashamed against the boys because they had pricks and I had nothing. I didn't want to look at myself. I didn't want to see that I had nothing." Apparently while one aspect of her resistance was her refusal to face herself because she felt worthless for having been a prostitute, at a deeper and more primitive level, it appeared that these feelings were grafted onto the earlier and more primitive conviction that to be lacking a penis was the original cause of such feelings, that she was incomplete. In fact, my later work with her, as with other girls in her profession, indicated that one of the many reasons that led her to the choice of profession was so that she could attach such feelings of worthlessness to the prostitution which was her own choice rather than to the lack of a penis over which she had no control. Here is an example of how much deeper and fuller the interpretation of the dream was in the hypnotic state than in the waking state.

There were other dreams which I shall recount later on where the differences between what she remembered in the waking and in the hypnotic state as well as the differences in her interpretations in these two states are even more marked than in the above example.

At about this period in our relationship, Rose started to ask me whether I would ever write a book about her, or if I would ever include her in a book as I had other girls, the ones that I had described in my book on the call girl.

I asked her if she would like that, and she said, "Yeah, I would."

I asked her how she felt about my describing her being hypnotized and she said that would be all right with her. At about this time, a class I was teaching asked me if they could see a living example of analysis with the aid of hypnosis. I asked Rose if she would be willing to be hypnotized before such a group, all of whom were practicing analysts who wanted to learn something about hypnosis.

She answered, "You're putting me on. You're trying to tell me they could learn something from me."

When I explained that I thought they could learn a great deal from her, she seemed very pleased at the prospect and asked me several times when the class was going to meet and when I wanted her to come. There was some delay about a date and during this period she began to have some difficulty again in speaking, even under hypnosis. By now our procedure usually followed a pattern: she would come in, tell me about the happenings of the week in her waking state, then go into a trance with my assistance and discuss dream material and perhaps some of the problems she had raised in her awake state but on a free association basis—that is, my suggestion to her would be "Say whatever comes to your mind," the same as might be said to a patient who was not under hypnosis. She still had some difficulties. I wasn't sure how much the session would reveal to the audience about hypnoanalysis, but since it appeared to mean a great deal to Rose, I agreed and arranged for her to come to the class. I was aware that there was a wish for exhibitionistic gratification in her desire to appear in a book or to perform before a class. However, I believed that the exhibitionism here might perform a useful service in furthering the analysis. It turned out to be perhaps the most crucial and important session in the entire analysis.

She had no difficulty going into the trance despite the fact that there were ten other people in the office, all of them interestedly observing her. Once she was in a trance, I assured her again that the people listening were all professional people who were interested in learning from her some of the advantages of the particular kind of therapy she was engaged in.

Rose spoke first in a general way about some of her problems and then when one of the members of the audience asked me if I had ever used regression with her and could I demonstrate it for them, I asked her to go backward in time. First I instructed her, "You are now twenty years old. Where are you?" She responded, "I am hanging around a bar waiting for my old man [her pimp, that is] to come in. I've been working and I've got some bread [money] for him. I don't know where he is. I don't know what's happened to him. I'm getting pretty mad waiting around." Then I told her she was fifteen and I assumed the role of her mother. In regression it is often important that the therapist be someone who was known to the patient at that time, so I said, "This is your mother. What did you do today?"

Her answers were angry and curt. "Nothing."

"Did you go to school?"

"Yeah."

"What did you do in school?"

"Nothing." She was completely uncommunicative. I then took her back to the age of five. Again I was the mother and I said, "Where were you today?"

She replied, "In school."

"What happened in school today?"

"Oh, nothing. On the way to school I saw some flowers. They were very pretty. I stopped and picked some. When

I got to school I gave them to the teacher. She said, 'Where did you get these flowers?' I said, 'I picked them.' She didn't believe me. She didn't believe. She kept saying, 'Where did you get the flowers?' She didn't believe me. She didn't want my flowers. She threw them into the basket."

The latter part of this recital was told with considerable excitement and anger. Then I said to her, "We'll go back further. You're now three years old. "How is your mother?" I acted as an indefinite person, perhaps as an older person whom she knew.

She answered, "Mother is fine. My mother is very nice. I like my mother very much. She's good. I like it when she holds me. I like to kiss her. My mother is sweet. My mother is very good."

"How is your father?" I asked. She started to cry. "What's the matter?" She told the following story while crying and in a state of considerable upset:

"My father showed me a gun. He said he was going to shoot my mother. He came to the house and he called. He called my name. I wasn't at home. My mother came out and he shot her and wounded her. He wanted to shoot me. Why didn't he shoot me instead of mother? I want him to shoot me. Why did he have to shoot her? He should have shot me." She broke into violent sobbing.

I helped her go into a deeper trance, returned her to her present age and asked her while she was still in trance if she remembered the shooting.

"Yes," she said. "My father had planned to have me come out. He was going to shoot me and then as I was lying there he expected my mother to come running out and he would shoot her too." She repeated the same cry. "Why didn't he kill me? He should have killed me. I would have been better off if he had killed me. He never should have shot my mother. I was the one who should have been shot." And then she continued, "They used to send me down in the cellar. They never threw anything out in that house. The clothes were there. I went down to the dark cellar and I saw the clothes. I saw them soaking in a pail. It was all bloody. Why didn't they throw it out?

Whenever I looked at it, I thought he should have shot me. Why did he shoot my mother?"

At this point she was quite upset. I made a few calming suggestions and told her that if she didn't want to remember any of this, she didn't have to and then awakened her. She looked at me, then looked around and asked, "Was I all right? Did I do what you wanted? Did I tell the people anything?" I assured her as did the others present that she had been very interesting and that what she had told us was very valuable indeed.

From that time on, Rose's resistance to talking, at least under hypnosis, decreased. She requested the hypnosis because as she explained, it was much easier for her to speak then, but she rarely fought the wish to talk. Often she didn't agree with me. Often she fought with me. Sometimes even in the hypnotic state she would attack me and would say I wasn't interested in her. She would resist certain things but never again was there as serious a problem of being unable to speak while in the hypnotic state. At least that problem was diminished.

Now Rose began to give a different picture about her early life than the one she had first described. She began to describe her feeling that she had been shuttled back and forth between her parents. First she had gone to live with her father and then he had pushed her into the boarding school. Then she had gone to her grandmother and her grandmother tired of her and sent her to her mother. After she had been with her mother for a while, she sent her back to the father. So that what had first been presented as the picture of each one wanting her, now changed to each one not wanting her, and sending her back and forth with no one particularly interested in her.

One thing that became clear at this time was that the fainting spells were connected with the early incident, particularly the bloody clothes soaking in the pail, since she had not actually seen the shooting. Rose had up to then found it impossible to ride in the subway without becoming faint. In the restaurant where she worked she refused to go down to the cellar and while at first, for all that she still had some problem about it, she was eventually able to use the subway, she never got to the point where she didn't use a bus or a cab if one was available to her rather than the subway. However, it was no longer compulsive and she could, if she had to, use underground means of transportation.

Shortly thereafter she was able to get herself a job in a much better restaurant than the one she had worked in previously, and even to be able to work days. This job she was able to keep for a year. The job required that she join the union. She did, and announced that she had even gotten up to speak at a union meeting. She was at a large union meeting and had disagreed with a report given by one of the officials and felt very good about being able to get up and speak at such a large gathering.

One day she announced, quite unexpectedly, "I have a boy friend now." Her boy friend was a married man and she asked, "What do you do on a date? I don't know how to go out on a square date. But one thing I like very much. I like making love to him. It's very different than it was with tricks. When you have lots of tricks, it's always the same but with one guy it seems to be different each time. It's fun having one boy friend instead of tricks. I wish he could give me a baby but I don't think he can. He's no good at making babies."

After the relationship with the married man, which lasted for a few months, she came into the office one day rather excited and told me, "I have a new boy friend. He's not married. He wants to take me out. You know with Joe [the married man] I didn't really go out because he was worried about being seen. We used to meet at a bar, have a couple of drinks and then go up to my room. But with Andy [the new boy friend] it's different. He wants to take me out. I don't know how to act. I don't want to go to bed with him yet. What should I do? How do you stop him? What do you say?" She was completely ignorant of the patterns of dating. She didn't believe that it was possible to have a relationship without direct sex. I asked her why she didn't ask any of her girl friends about what to do.

She replied, "Most of them are as bad as me. They don't seem to know anything about it."

I said, "Why do you have to know? Why don't you leave it up to Andy?" She dated Andy for several months until he became seriously interested. He took her to meet his family and started to speak of marriage. Apparently this frightened her and she didn't want to see him any more, and explained that she really thought he was a jerk, that she was not interested, and then asked why it was that she was not interested. I told her that we would have to know more about her entire life and suggested under hypnosis one day that she think about her entire life and tell me whatever she thought was important. She said, "I feel nervous."

I told her, "Go with it. Feel more nervous." In order to understand what was making her nervous, I had suggested that she intensify the feeling so that the associations connected with the nervousness might come to the surface.

As she became more nervous she suddenly burst out, "I wonder if you want to get rid of me. Every time I like somebody, they want to get rid of me."

I asked, "Who wanted to get rid of you in the past?" She answered, "My mother got rid of me, my grandmother got rid of me, my Aunt got rid of me, and then my father got rid of me, and then after Fred, the pimp, I decided never to like anyone else. Pimps can all go to hell. I'm not putting up with their shit ever again. When I was an outlaw, I was the best-dressed whore on the floor. I was good for seven, eight hundred dollars a week. I couldn't spend it fast enough. I didn't know anything else to do until I came here. That was the luckiest thing that ever happened to me. The other day some son of a bitch who lives in my house came in to the restaurant where I work and as I was taking his order, he patted me on the ass. I told him to keep his hands off me or I'd spill hot coffee on his balls. You see I like you so I think you're going to get rid of me. I think you're going to be like all the rest of the men, that's why I don't want to like you and I don't want to like my boy friend. I don't want to like anybody."

Then followed a period of some difficulty as she struggled with this feeling of liking me and the opposing feelings that because she liked me, I would probably get rid of her. At the end of the spring, I left on vacation and during the vacation she saved enough money to pay back her debts which had accumulated during part of the time when she wasn't working. Shortly after I returned, Rose reported a dream. She was counting windows in a house and when she came to one window she looked in and saw a double bed. She didn't like it and decided not to count any more but to make up a number to tell her mother.

When I asked her for associations to this dream, she couldn't give me any in the waking state. Under hypnosis, I asked her again if she had any ideas about this dream, and she said, "It means I don't want to come here any more because I have to give you money and I decided a long time ago not to give money to a man." At the end of the session, I asked her again if she wouldn't dream next week and remember the dream; maybe that would tell us some of the other problems that she had with me.

The next session she told me she dreamed that she threw a newspaper at me, a rolled-up newspaper. When I asked her what she thought it meant, she told me, "It means that I want to throw a penis at you, mine. I don't want it any more." I asked her what her penis was like and she said, "It's a big, pretty one. It's bigger than yours, it's bigger than anyone else's except, maybe, my stepfather's. It's almost as big as my stepfather's." Then she went on to say that now she didn't want it any more and she was ready to get rid of it, but that she had once seen her stepfather's penis and after that decided she had one just like it.

At this point I suggested that she go into a deeper trance and using a method of intensifying the hypnotic stage, asked her again about the dream, whereupon she added, "You said something I didn't like and I threw the paper at you. You acted the same way you always do. You thought it was funny. There was somebody else, another woman. There was another woman, and you said, 'It won't make any difference,' so I threw the paper at you. I didn't like her. I didn't want anybody else to have you. I always thought that talk about one thing changing your life is a lot of bullshit. I read your book and I came here and it changed my whole life. That's why I like you so much, I'm willing to throw my prick away and I don't want you to have any other patients. I hate your other patients like the girl I see coming out of your office before me. The other woman looked like that girl."

At the next session, she reported the following dream while awake. "I wanted to move a television set or a suitcase. You were lying down and talking. There was a big window facing the terrace and a man came in through the window with a gun. You jumped up and went after the man with the gun. I locked the window and went out into the hall where I saw a girl covered with blood putting the television set or the suitcase on a cart. The man with the gun and you were coming after me. I ran outside and was in a park and I felt I couldn't get away so I started to fly. I thought a bullet would hit me so I woke up. The girl in the hall told you and the man with the gun where I was running."

She remembered while awake that the room looked like the room she had at boarding school. She also remembered the time her father showed her a gun and bought her a Shirley Temple doll. The doll was in a box with paper on it and she couldn't get it unwrapped. Her father told her he was going to kill her mother with the gun.

After she had finished the associations, I hypnotized her and told her to rest for a few minutes and think about the dream. Then I asked her if she now remembered any part of the dream she had failed to tell me before.

She replied, "When I went into the room, the other girl wasn't bloody, but the blood was spattered all over her when I came out. She must have been shot when I was in the room with the man."

"How come you left that part out before?" I asked.

"I guess I didn't want you to know I was in the room with the man, that it was my fault the girl got shot," she answered.

"Who was the other man?" I asked.

"He was a light man, real young-looking. When you went after him, he gave you the gun and you both came after me. You came after me because of what the other man told you. He told you I was no damn good. He told you that something I did was really bad, evil. He told you that I was really bad, I slept with too many men. I gave somebody the clap, you know, gonorrhea. I had something before I turned out, before I became a whore, but I'm not sure it was the clap or something similar.

"A guy I was going with said I gave him the clap. He took me to the bar where all the hustlers were. He quit me and I was upset. After that I turned out, I started to hustle."

Further associations indicated that Rose felt that the man that had the gun was her father, and that the reason she had wanted to have him shoot her instead of her mother was that as a child she wanted her father to give her a baby, and the Shirley Temple doll he did give her made her feel guilty and deserving of death because she felt that it was his baby. The later sins she committed were, as she put it; "I copped a plea—like when you murder somebody and you plead second-degree, they shouldn't get you for first-degree. That's the worst thing of all to want your own father to give you a baby—that's worse than hustling or giving somebody the clap."

A month later she reported the following dream: "I was in a garage trying to sweep the floor. The more I swept the dirtier it got. One of the girls I work with was eating in a booth. I was in a town without sidewalks and there was somebody taking care of a baby and the baby messed its pants. She couldn't open the pins to change the diaper. A girl was eating comfortably right out of a box."

Again she wasn't able to say anything about this dream until she was hypnotized. She had no associations to anything in the dream. Under hypnosis, however, she said, "Things were clearing up but the home is not clean yet." She was coming to analysis but she was not finished as yet. She wasn't clean yet. She had a lot of stuff to get out of her yet. She wanted a baby but if she had one it would be dirty because she didn't know yet how to take care of one properly. She didn't want to live someplace without sidewalks, that's not even civilized. Going back to her life as a prostitute would be like living in an uncivilized manner.

I asked her, under hypnosis, why she was able to understand this dream so well in the hypnotized state but not in the awake state. She had made it clear in discussing her dreams under hypnosis that she was still concerned that there was more work to be done in her analysis and that therefore she wasn't ready for marriage, wasn't ready for a permanent relationship, but that she was increasingly ready to be a female and was giving up the fantasy penis. That she was concerned about expressing anger at me because it didn't have sufficient results, didn't provoke any answering response from me, but that she was still dirty. She couldn't attain this kind of understanding when she was awake. I asked her, "How come you understand this dream when you're hypnotized but not when you're awake?"

She answered, "I'm not on the outside when I'm hypnotized. I'm all inside." Apparently she was referring here to the heightened consciousness that hypnosis makes possible. Some people who are familiar with hypnosis or think they know something about hypnosis are disappointed the first time they go into a trance because they expect to be unconscious, not realizing that actually hypnosis is a state of heightened consciousness, particularly of one's self. This is what Rose meant by being on the inside. She was able to exclude external stimuli of all kinds and, therefore, concentrate on what was in her own mind to a greater extent and deal with the material. The recognition of her feminine wishes and the discarding of the pretense of being like a man, giving up the notion she had a penis, giving up going around and sleeping with many men made her realize that she no longer could block out from her consciousness the fact that she wanted to be a woman like other woman; that she wanted to be married and have a man of her own; and that she wanted children. For a while these feelings made her feel quite depressed until, at one session, she described the fact that when she was a child and at school, at the boarding school where her father had placed her, her father acted toward her as a boy friend might. He offered her presents, he would take her to dinner and once he asked if the stepfather ever beat her, and told her that if he did, he would come and kill the stepfather. He would be happy to come and kill the stepfather. He would be happy to come and do this, and this memory gave her considerable pleasure.

Sometime later she had the following dream: "A man grabbed me but he couldn't have intercourse with me because I was wearing pants. Later on I was walking along the river and I saw colored eggs. They looked like Easter eggs." Again she was unable to give any associations or meanings of this dream until she was hypnotized. Then I asked her to tell me the dream again. This time she was able to describe the dream in much greater detail. "I was walking down the river. I was going to have a party and I was hiding the eggs. Somebody I didn't like grabbed me from behind and threw me down. He was trying to have intercourse with me and he couldn't because I had my pants on. Then I was away. When I came back, there were hundreds of eggs. I said they had been there for years. There were kids playing in the water. They broke one of the eggs and it was rotten and some of it splashed on me. They found silver in the water. It was right in a courtyard. A man gave a girl five hundred dollars of his money and she should keep it for him. I told the girl it was stupid to have the money."

She was able again in the trance to explain this dream in a meaningful way. She explained that "the eggs are my eggs, the eggs that make me a woman. I was always a woman but I didn't know it. It was hidden from me. The man doesn't really want to have intercourse. He's a trick, a John, a customer. The other man stops me from having intercourse with the trick and that's you. But the eggs are still there and I'm still a woman. There's something left to go into and I'm afraid."

It is interesting to point out again that under hypnosis, resistance was still present. She knew "there was something left to go into" and she also knew that she was afraid and therefore couldn't. The difference between the trance and the waking state was that in the waking state the patient usually is not apt to express the resistance so openly. Hypnosis merely made resistance more available, rather than eliminating it. Her resistance was in the open and could be studied.

A few days later she came in and said, "I had an important dream, I know, but I can't remember it." When she went into her hypnotic trance, she was able to tell the following dream:

"I was walking along and came to a waterfall. There was a body circling round and round and, perhaps, it's going over the waterfall. Then I'm looking through a book or a magazine and there's a picture story of a kid teaching dancing to older people and it seems silly to me."

In her associations, she explained that she likes to masturbate in the bath by lying back in the bath tub and letting the water flow on her. She thinks it feels good and sometimes she thinks it would be nice to make love with somebody who would be clean like the water. Her association to, and understanding of, the second part of the dream was that the analyst was writing a book about her and it seemed ridiculous to her that anyone would write a book about her, or that anyone could learn anything by reading about her. "It's a pretty miserable story to put down," she said, "but really I like the idea if you wrote a book about me but I couldn't tell anybody about it."

At the height of her feeling about me, which ended sometime around the spring, she began to have difficulties again in her job and began to complain about the people she had to work with, about the customers, and just at the point where she was entitled to a week's vacation and was beginning to discuss how she would spend this vacation, she got into a serious fight with the manager of the restaurant and was dismissed.

And now she made it clear that she was having great difficulty getting another job. She neglected her appearance, she spent a lot of time in bars, she didn't want to look for a job, she didn't want to have anything to do with the problem of finding a job. She recognized the part she was playing in this situation and knew that she was doing something. In fact, she presented a dream in which she was with a girl who was turning tricks—that is, taking on clients—in a trailer camp and there was a chicken coop there with miserable chickens. She had her home on a crest of a hill. It was a nice house but it had cracks in it. She complained to the landlady that if she didn't do something about the house, there wouldn't be any more houses on the hill. I asked her what was wrong and she said, "I didn't have the house. The house was similar to another house. From the hill, the house looked like a circle and inside it looked like a studio apartment."

When I asked her what this dream reminded her of, Rose replied, "Whatever I was complaining about wouldn't get fixed. It's like what's happening here. I'm complaining about having to work and you haven't fixed it. I loused my job up and you didn't do anything about it."

The same day she reported another dream. She was visiting someone who had a place with a courtyard. She had a chicken. Two of her girl friends were playing a game, Herta and Georgine. She left and went to the apartment where they were cooking eight chickens. They didn't want her to stay so she became very angry and left. From the stoop she saw Tony, who was a waiter in the last job she had. Tony was there and they were cooking the chickens for others. In the next scene of the dream, Tony was in jail. She got him out and he didn't meet her where he was supposed to. She went to the apartment and he was there. In her associations she told me that Tony had quit his job at the restaurant and had gone to Bertha's apartment. Bertha was keeping him. The only reason they were cooking chickens was for work. It was like in the restaurant. They were doing this for somebody else.

I asked her why she had wanted to be thrown out of the house since it was her dream and in the dream she had arranged to be thrown out and she said, "I didn't like the people there. I didn't like the people I worked with. I didn't like the customers." So that apparently she found something about her work unpleasant, something difficult, and she didn't want to work.

This was the first part of her story. As we went further on, it became clear in the next few weeks that she was doing two things. She had decided to test me to find out if I really liked her and what I would do for her. She began to have difficulty about paying her rent and began to tell me that she was going to be thrown out of her apartment and be out in the street soon. It was clear to me that what was happening was that when I said that maybe I would write a book about her and her experience, if she wanted me to, she had at the same time become angry and decided that I, too, was exploiting her. However, she was unable to express this anger directly, and because she couldn't express it, she was turning it on herself. I tried to discuss this at several sessions while she was awake and then I asked her in another session why she couldn't express her anger at me, to which she replied that she didn't feel angry with me.

About this time she made three minor suicide attempts. She did not consider them serious and they were told to me each time as if she were testing me to see what my response would be. First she took a plastic bag used for laundry and put it over her head. She said, "I just wanted to see what would happen." Then she took a knife and slightly slashed her wrist. She said, "I didn't cut real deep. I just wanted to see what would happen." And then she told me that she would start drinking so heavily that she would just drop dead from the booze. But still she wouldn't express any anger.

At her urging, I had been planning to present Rose to another class of mine because she had asked me many times if I wanted her to appear before a class again. I told her that I was planning to present her shortly. As I didn't want her to be anxious about it, I waited until one specific afternoon, when I asked her if she was free that evening to appear before my class. She said, "All right I'll come there but maybe I'll make an asshole out of you." This was the beginning of her ability to express anger at me. In the class, she again went into a very rapid trance, and I asked her if she was going to make an asshole out of me in front of the whole class.

She laughed and said, "No, I won't do that. I would rather make an asshole out of myself."

I asked, "Why? Why can't you say if you're angry at me? Why do you have to hurt yourself rather than tell me that you're angry with me?" As a matter of fact, in this simple statement of hers, she had expressed one of the basic aspects of masochism, a wish to punish the other person, originally the parent, and then whoever one is involved with, by hurting oneself to make the other person feel guilty. I have found that often the first step in curing such masochism is for the patient to learn to express this anger at someone else rather than hurting himself. I was, therefore, trying to get Rose to express this anger. She wouldn't do this and I asked her why she couldn't and she said, "They said it would be okay for me to be angry but when I said anything they threw me out. My father threw me out; my mother threw me out; my grandmother threw me out. Even the pimp threw me out when I told him that I didn't want a sister-in-law, that I didn't want to share him with anyone else. You're not going to be any different. If I say anything to you, you'll throw me out too."

As so frequently happens when a resistance is expressed, its expression makes it lessen. Once having explained why she was afraid to express her anger, Rose began to berate me more and more. She began to find fault with the way I had treated her, with the appearance of my office, with the way I dressed and looked. She felt that I had let her down and what was the use of her wanting to get married and have a baby. She could never do either because her life had been so miserable that all I had accomplished was to make her more depressed. She pointed out that previously she at least had the racket which kept her busy and kept her mind occupied all the time. She didn't have to think about so many things. There were so many things to bug her. She had to go out and find a miserable job with managers and customers and people working with her, all of them bugging her, all of them making demands on her. What did she need all of this for? What good had I been to her? She began to speak about my approaching vacation and how it was a bad time for me to leave. When I left for vacation she still wasn't working. She told me she didn't think she would ever get a job again.

When I returned from my vacation, two months later, she called me, made an appointment, came in and said, "Well, I got news for you. I don't know if I need you any more." She had found a job during the summer, she had decided that it was no use, I wasn't going to support her, that she needed to work for herself, that she needed to establish herself, and that she felt that now she might make it on her own. She was planning to work and since she owed a good deal of money, she wanted to pay off her debts. After she paid her debts she would come back, if she still felt she needed me. But meanwhile, she didn't think she needed any more treatment. I told her that was all right with me, that it was quite possible that she didn't need any more treatment, but I wanted her to understand that I wasn't trying to get rid of her, that this was her decision, not mine. She assured me that she understood and that it was her idea and that she was going to try it.

Two weeks later she called me and said, "Can I come and see you?" I asked her what the trouble was, because she told me that she would only call if she got into any kind of trouble. She explained, "Well, I just want to come and talk to you just like this." I told her, "Then don't make a regular appointment. Why don't you come around lunchtime and we can have a cup of coffee together."

When she arrived, she seemed quite pleased and told me that she was very glad that I had just told her to drop in for a friendly visit instead of as a patient; that maybe I didn't dislike her so much. Again she asked me if I would write about her. I told her that I would see how she did. She left in quite a good mood and three days later called me and announced, "Harold, I have a suitor and this is serious. I have a real suitor. Now I think I can make it with a straight guy." Since then she has continued to improve on her own and reports frequently on her progress.

I have often consulted the notes I took on this case

because Rose explained so many things about herself and her problems, so many things which are common not only to prostitutes and call girls, but to many women growing up in our society. It is true that Rose had special problems and deprivations and traumas of a kind that one doesn't usually come across. It is true that compared with her early life, the lives of most neurotics seem happy indeed. In Rose's case, deprivation and danger and rejection was on a scale so grand that it is difficult to understand how she was able to make any kind of adaptation to life and why she hadn't long since taken refuge either in a complete break with reality as in serious mental illness, or in suicide. It is very difficult to understand this, and the surprising element was not Rose's problems, not Rose's turn to prostitution, but that Rose was able to come out of it, that Rose had as much strength as she had; that despite the kind of life she led, she was able to deal with her problems. As a matter of fact, Rose was able to make quicker strides in her analysis than any other girl with the background of a call girl or prostitute that I had ever treated. She was the only one who never went back into the life, into the racket world once she left it. She was the only one who established a position for herself and learned an occupation and stayed with it through all the years without any serious backsliding. Others were able to get out of it but usually only after considerable backsliding. In fact I asked Rose once how she was able to do it and the only thing she was able to figure out was that she was able to save some money and felt that with this money and with me, she might be able to make a break. Also she said, "Maybe because I was at the worst end of the racket, I got tired of it. The others may still like it. There was nothing about it I liked. I had had it, and I didn't want any part of it any more."

In telling the story I have perhaps eliminated certain elements that should be explained. One of them was after the experience in regression in which Rose went back to the age of three and remembered loving her mother and thinking her mother was kind and good. Shortly thereafter, she called her mother long distance and spoke to her for the first time in several years. At the next session she reported in great excitement, "You know what? My mother said she loves me. Who would have believed it? She said she loves me. I still remember that time when my father sent me some money and she had me put it in the bank and then I took it out, and went with a girl friend for a trip to the city and we had a lot of fun. We went to the movies and we spent ten dollars. When I came back she found out about it and beat me. She took my dress away and made me stay in the house for two days. It was my money but she did it to me, and yet she says she loves me. Here all the time I was really hoping that you would write about me so I could send her the book and say, 'See, your daughter was a whore.' That's how I was going to fix her."

Again the strong masochistic trend is noticeable. Her anger at her mother was so great and she still felt herself to be a helpless child incapable of hurting her mother except by hurting herself.

One of the reasons she chose to be a prostitute was a wish for revenge on her mother. Her anger at her mother seemed to stem from the feeling that her father's wish to kill her and the father's wish to kill the mother was originally occasioned by Rose's wish to have her father's baby and her mother's standing in the way; that the mother refused to permit her to enjoy her father's gifts like the money.

A more puzzling aspect was her constant iteration whenever she thought of the incident, either under hypnosis or out of it, of the feeling that her father should have killed her instead of her mother. Exploration of this indicated first that she felt this way because she felt guilty about her later life and would rather have died than live as she did. And secondly, because she had at times actually wished her mother out of the way so she could be alone with her father. Rather than face the realization that she wished her mother dead, she preferred to believe that she wished she had been killed for her murderous feelings toward her mother.

But at another level, her wish turned out to be somewhat different. While Rose was under hypnosis one time, I said, "All right, your father did kill you. You walked out and your father did shoot you. See what happens next." She said, "I walk out. My father shoots me. My mother comes running out, throws her arms around me, my father shoots her and we both remain lying together." So if her father had shot her, she would have remained together with her mother instead of facing the unhappy periods of rejection by all members of the family. To the infantile unconscious, unaffected by later developments because it was not accessible to her, it was preferable to remain dead with mother than to be alive and separated.

In any analysis that goes deep enough, I have found that one of the aims of neurotic behavior and of antisocial behavior is frequently the same—namely, the child's wish to be close to mother. In a sense it is difficult to explain because people expect the unconscious to be logical, not recognizing that the unconscious is quite capable of contradictory attitudes. It is very much like the story of the man who borrows a pot and when he is asked for the return of the pot by his friend, says (1) I didn't borrow it, (2) it was broken when you gave it to me and (3) I returned it to you. The same kind of contradictory defense existed with Rose as it does with most people so that (1) her prostitution was an effort to revenge herself on mother, (2) she was convinced that her mother was a bad woman; she was involved with another man when she was still married to Rose's father so that she, too, would be a bad woman like her mother, and (3) that by being so bad, she would earn the wages of sin, death, and be killed as her father had wanted to kill her mother and thus rejoin mother and have her all to herself.

This was also the reason she gave herself a fantasy penis. If she had a penis like her stepfather, she could sleep with her mother, the way her stepfather did.

Then, of course, there was the other factor; that it seemed to her that she had only received attention when she was bad. This is the factor that frequently operates in many delinquent children. Their attitude is that the only time they received attention was when they were bad; otherwise they were neglected.

Rose, too, explained that the only time she received attention was when she was bad, as when her stepfather used to beat her for not doing her school work, which she felt was a sign of love. At least she was getting attention because someone was concerned with how she was doing. This also showed up in her relationship with me, as when she lost her job to get attention from me.

Her life as a prostitute then, seemed to present to Rose a method of solving some of her problems. First it appeared to be a way of receiving attention because she was bad and second, as a means of obtaining a man of her own. On one occasion during the course of therapy, in order to test her determination to stay out of the life of a prostitute, I said to her, "Why don't I give up this racket [meaning analysis] and go off with you? You'd work for a while (lots of people call and ask me if I know the name of a call girl) until we could save up some money. Then we could go off and buy a motel together and just take it easy." It was difficult for me to carry through this role because of the yearning with which she looked at me, the wish for this kind of life.

She explained, "There's one thing about a pimp when you first go with him and he's courting you, you feel that finally you're going to have a man of your own. You feel that finally someone is going to take care of you. You're going to have what the others have. You'll be just as good as anyone else. You will have your own man. And if he had remained true to me, I would have been glad to give him all my money. What did I need money for? It would have meant that for the first time I would have somebody who belonged to me and nobody else."

Another factor in her wish to be a prostitute was that although she had been a good singer at school, she had never done very much with this talent, and had been discouraged from pursuing her studies in that direction. She felt that she had learned a skill as a prostitute and that, as she put it: "I was a damn good whore. I worked hard." So that in a strange way she was aping the goals of respectable society by having a skill and by proving that she worked hard and earned a lot of money. But most of all she seemed impelled toward prostitution by the feeling that she was bad and that no one wanted her. As a prostitute, she was wanted and paid for. Men proved they wanted her by paying her. As a prostitute, she repeated the early childhood experience of going from one client to the other.

It is strange and difficult for the layman to understand that the neurotic, the disturbed person, frequently repeats the most painful aspect of the very situation that contributed to the disturbance in the first place. For example, the woman who as a child was frequently subjected to severe beatings from her father, will frequently provoke such beatings later on from her husband. In part she does this because she is accustomed to such behavior, but there are other reasons. The other reason in Rose's case seemed to be that she wanted to repeat the situation which had originally been traumatic, and this time handle it properly.

One dramatic thing happened. One time Rose called and asked to see me as soon as possible, the only time she ever asked for an emergency session in her three years of therapy. She asked if she could come to see me because something had come up.

She came to the office and said, "I was going home yesterday from work. It was about one o'clock in the morning. As I came to the corner near my house, I heard some shots. I thought it was a car backfiring or something. A man pushed me behind the mailbox. I went home later and I went to sleep. I must have gotten up in the morning, I must have gone to work, but I don't remember anything about it. At eleven o'clock I stopped work and I was going outside to get something for the boss. I put on my coat and the boss asked, 'What have you done to your coat?' I looked down and there were bullet holes. I started to shake then, and I rememberd what happened. I still don't know how I got to work. I just had blacked out all that time."

Here the repetition of the early trauma when her father

shot and wounded her mother had been so disturbing that Rose had absolutely no memory for that period of time from one A.M. when she heard the shots until eleven o'clock the next morning, a period of ten hours.

There was one other strange mechanism at work in Rose's case. She was determined to prove that she was the bad one because, as she said: "If I was bad, then my mother wouldn't be so bad. I don't want to have a bad mother." Again the masochistic attitude of preferring to feel that she was the bad one, she was the wicked one, rather than to accept that her mother was bad or wicked.

While Rose still has many problems, she nevertheless did make remarkable advances. From the girl who had known nothing but prostitution from the age of eighteen to twenty-eight to a woman who was able to hold a job and work for (now) five years, to maintain herself, to have friends, including a relationship with her suitor (as she called him) is considerable advance. Also, her drinking became much less compulsive. She was in control of it and no longer had the need to engage in regular bouts of drunkenness. Beyond this, she had won the ability to withstand the problems of her life and not to return to the apparently easy way out of prostitution, the complete disappearance of the symptoms of fainting, the ability to overcome the claustrophobia; all of these symptomatic improvements, in addition to the complete change in her way of life, plus the regaining of sexual feelings. Throughout the time she had been a prostitute she had never experienced orgasm. After two years of analysis she was able to experience and to enjoy sex in a completely different way than she ever had before, and was able eventually to give up masturbation which, until that point, had been the only gratifying outlet for her. All of these things amount to substantial improvement in a person with such serious problems as the ones Rose presented when she first came to me.

Frequently I asked her what were the factors she felt were helpful to her. At various times she told me many of them. There is also a certain amount of theoretical explanation as to why Rose was able to make the gains she did.

In the first place, she was similar in many ways to some of Freud's first patients. Fortunately she knew very little about psychoanalysis when she came and therefore that knowledge which is frequently used by patients as a means of resistance, did not exist in Rose's case. Not having such knowledge, she was able, with the aid of hypnosis, actually to relive many of her early experiences rather than just intellectualize about them. She was not an introspective person and so, not having bothered to think much about her past life and the reasons for her behavior, all of them came to her fresh during therapy and frequently laden with the original emotion. She relived her experiences but relived them now in her adult self which was able to handle these experiences better than she was able to as a child. Secondly, she developed remarkable understanding for her motivations, for her unconscious drives— a drive to be like a man, a drive to revenge herself through destroying herself, a drive to be one with her mother, even if it required death.

These insights she utilized not only to understand *herself*, but found that she was better able to understand her friends. She did become friendly with a number of girls who were still in the racket, still working as prostitutes, and could see fairly clearly what they were doing and why they were doing it. This helped her further in her own understanding. One factor which she ascribed more importance to than I do was that she felt I knew all about her and, as she says, "didn't throw me the hell out. I expected you to throw me out as soon as I told you what I did. Even though you wrote the book, I still didn't believe that you wouldn't throw me out. When you didn't, and when I saw that you were really interested in me, I became less of a hater or maybe I didn't become less of a hater. I used the hate to cure myself. Instead of hating everybody around me, I began to hate some of the things I was doing and I wanted to change."

I feel that one reason why she felt my interest so keenly, unlike many other similar patients, was that the special kind of relationship we established as a result of the hypnosis was different from the other relationships she had had. One could say that the hypnosis impelled her to give up her rebelliousness, forced her to give up her refusal to do what was asked of her. I would rather say that it didn't compel, but that the relationship was such that for the first time in her life she was able to do what was asked of her. Up to that time, she was so angry at the world, she was so convinced about the justice of her grievances, that she was fixed in the pattern of rebelliousness, of refusing to do what was asked of her.

With the aid of hypnosis, she was able to respond to the demands made on her and not feel that she was violating her own code, because the code of many people like Rose is one which calls for them never to do what is asked of them. It was almost as if she used the hypnosis as an alibi for doing what was being asked of her. I think also that the demonstration and the recognition of the intense interest of the ten or so analysts who heard her during these demonstrations made her feel perhaps as though she were someone of worth. It helped lead to a decrease of her feelings of inadequacy. I think Rose took great pride in her ability as a subject; while I never told her so, she was certainly the best subject I ever encountered up to that time. Some of this was owing to the excellent concentration she was able to display and which was required in order for her to be such a good subject, and some of it was because of the abilities she developed in the understanding of symbolic material, like her dreams, which evoked genuine admiration on my part. Again, while I never voiced it, I still think that Rose was aware of the fact that I admired and, I must admit, sometimes envied her ability to understand her dreams as well as she did.

I think also that the experience of appearing at these demonstrations was to her a gratifying one in the sense that in front of these other people she belonged to me, and had a closer relationship to me than any of the others did. And that while the others were my colleagues, she and I obviously had a more emotional involvement than they had and that to her amazement, these others, instead of attacking her for this, as her earlier experiences had led her to expect, admired her. They admired her because she had achieved depths of insight in her own therapy which professional analysts had not been able to achieve. My own feeling was that she re-experienced the early infantile hatreds and love and demands and the things these did to her personality as few other patients have had the opportunity of experiencing. It was impossible for the other analysts not to appreciate and indicate this to her, and for her not to be aware of this.

It seems to me that all of these things helped in the situation. Also the fact that the hypnosis was never used to obliterate Rose's defenses helped her to feel independent, helped her to feel that this wasn't something that had been done to her, but was a collaborative effort in which she and I joined against a common enemy.

After saying all this about Rose, I still must in all humility point out that time alone will tell how stable her gains will be. Bitter experience has taught me that what seems like magical progress one day becomes defeat the next.

Perhaps the claims of remarkable cures for hypnosis which did not hold up have led to the strange history to which this field has been subject.

6. PSYCHOANALYTIC SUMMARY

IN ADDITION TO SANDRA, Stella, and Rose,[1] who have been described in detail, I also had the opportunity of seeing several other girls for therapy. There were striking similarities in all of the cases. Of the six girls seen for psychoanalytic therapy, five eventually left the profession. As described, Stella became an actress; Sandra eventually found other work; Beverly married (a letter from her opens and closes the book); and a fourth girl became a restaurant manager. Etta, the fifth girl—she was only a part-time call girl who usually worked as a singer even when she was functioning as a call girl—eventually concentrated exclusively on her singing. Unfortunately the sixth girl left therapy at too early a stage. I have not been in touch with her and cannot say what she is doing at the present time.[2]

In arriving at a summary from the psychoanalytic point of view, let us first examine what some other psychoanalysts have said about the problem of prostitution. While

---

[1] Rose finally became a waitress in a first-class restaurant and when I spoke to her recently was engaged to marry a successful veterinarian.

[2] Since then I have treated about twenty other girls. Of the eighteen who remained in therapy for longer than six months, all but two left the racket.

143

there has been relatively little attention paid to this problem,[1] I did succeed in finding at least five psychoanalysts who discussed prostitution. Several of these psychoanalysts were writing about prostitution in cultures other than our own—that is, not in the United States. There may be some difference in the personality dynamics leading to the choice of prostitution as a profession because of the different standards of other societies. However, none of the psychoanalytic writers mentions the possibility of the dynamics varying with different cultures. They seem to be describing what they consider a universal prostitute type.

Karl Abraham,[2] one of the founding fathers of the psychoanalytic movement, said:

> Frigidity is practically a *sine qua non* of prostitution. The experience of full sexual sensation binds the woman to the man, and only where this is lacking does she go from man to man, just like the continually ungratified Don Juan type of man who has constantly to change his love-object. Just as the Don Juan avenges himself on all women for the disappointment he once received from the first woman who entered his life, so the prostitute avenges herself on every man for the gift she had expected from her father and had not received.

Apparently Abraham saw prostitution as an act of hostility directed against the father. It is true that all of the call girls studied evinced marked signs of hostility toward men.

The following authority wrote about this problem twenty-three years later. Apparently he had made a more intensive study of prostitution than Abraham. In an address before an international meeting of the Bureau for the

---

[1] The otherwise excellent psychological library at Columbia University has only one entry on the subject of prostitution— Geza Roheim's paper on the dreams of a Somali prostitute.

[2] Abraham, K., *Op. cit.*, p. 36.

Suppression of Traffic in Women and Children of the
League of Nations in 1943, Edward Glover[1] stated:

> Although the prostitute has apparently broken away
> from the family at an unusually early age, this some-
> times ostentatious and rebellious independence is only
> skin-deep. Under the surface there exists a strong
> "fixation" as it is called, to the Oedipus phase.

Glover apparently felt that actually the prostitute was
demonstrating her independence of her father, even though
she was still tied to him, and that prostitution was a way
of denying her attachment to her father.

Helene Deutsch[2] reported an attempt to deal analyti-
cally with a prostitute, but mentioned that she did not
have much success in getting an honest report from the
patient. Dr. Deutsch mentions several possible causes of
prostitution arising from the personality of the girl. They
include, first, having high ideals for herself that are threatened by sexual feeling, so that when she experiences sexual feeling the girl says to herself, "You are a prostitute,"
and when this ideal does not win—that is when the girl
does not give up her sexual feeling—she turns to prostitution. Dr. Deutsch's explanation makes clear the prostitution fantasies of many respectable women. (I worked
therapeutically with an unmarried woman of forty who
had had no sexual experience. When her sexual feelings
expressed themselves in dreams and in associations, she
said to me, "I guess I'll have to become a prostitute now."
There seemed to be no compromise possible to her between rigid rejection of all sex and acceptance of all sex as
prostitution.)

Also Dr. Deutsch states that many girls in learning that
their respectable mothers have sex lives reject them com-

---

[1] Glover, E., "The Abnormality of Prostitution," in Krich, A.M.
(ed.), *Women*. New York: Dell Publishing Co., Inc., 1943, pp.
247-273.

[2] Deutsch, H., *Op. cit.*

pletely and therefore experience feelings of intense hatred and rage. They use the prostitution fantasy as a way of getting even with their mothers. On finding out that their fathers are in a sense unfaithful to them because they are having relations with their mothers, some of these girls retaliate for this faithlessness with their own faithlessness: all men instead of one man. "She lowers herself to the sexual role that she formerly assigned to her mother."

Agoston[1] recognized the felt bi-parental rejection on the part of the prostitute, with the resultant fear, isolation and the frozen quality of her emotional development. He also recognized that the money was used as a defense to conceal her indiscriminate sexuality.

Caprio,[2] places greater emphasis on the factor of homosexuality. He discusses the Lesbian practices among prostitutes in various parts of the world and he feels that prostitution represents a defense against homosexuality. He is in agreement with earlier investigators on this point, such as Lombroso, Moll and Martineau. In summing up his findings Caprio states:

> I am further convinced that prostitutes, by and large, are victims of unresolved bi-sexual conflicts and their flight into sexual intimacies with many men, rationalized by profit motive, is symptomatic evidence of their fear of their own unconscious homosexual desires. As one might surmise, the majority of prostitutes invariably come from homes where there has existed parental incompatibility. Having been deprived of a normal love relationship during childhood with mother and father, their basic feelings of insecurity unconsciously inspire them to seek out the affection of both sexes via intimacies with both men and women.

---

[1] Agoston, T., "Some Psychological Aspects of Prostitution— the Pseudo-Personality." *International Journal of Psychoanalysis,* 1945, 26, pp. 62-67.

[2] Caprio, F. S., *Female Homosexuality.* New York: The Citadel Press, 1954.

While some of these findings may appear contradictory, with Abraham stressing the importance of frigidity, Deutsch the restrictive ego ideal and the revenge motive, Glover, Agoston and Caprio all recognized the lack of early adequate family love. Thus in writings from the British, French and American point of view respectively, we find the stress placed on the lack of early family love as it is placed in the present study.

My own interpretation from the psychoanalytic point of view is based on the developmental history of the individual girls. On the basis of my experiences with the call girls, particularly those in analysis, I believe that the first and most serious cause of their later difficulties was the intense early feeling of deprivation because of rejection by the mother, the feeling that the mother did not want to nurture them, feed them, take care of them. It is true that this lack of early nurture was sometimes caused by immediate economic problems facing the mother, but more frequently it seemed to arise from the fact that the mothers were inadequate individuals, immature and unable to give their daughters the love they needed. At a primitive unconscious level, the girls seemed to see their mothers as withholding the breast from them, withholding the warming, relaxing milk of love.

There are a number of reactions possible, even to a young child, to such deprivation. The girls reacted to this withholding with rage and desperation: rage at the deprivation and desperation in their efforts to compensate for the initial loss. Because of this desperate need they were never able to progress to the later differentiating stages of emotional development and searched unceasingly for warmth and love from men and women alike. Therefore they were never truly differentiated sexually.

When the girls found their mothers inadequate they turned to fathers or father substitutes, hoping that they would compensate for what the mother had not supplied. It is this turning to the fathers or father substitutes which made some of the analysts quoted feel that this was an Oedipal relationship. It seems to me that what the girls were seeking from their fathers and later from men in general was not sex so much as actual nurture, feeding and being taken care of. When this search too was unsuccessful, they attempted to gratify themselves in every whim and need. They could not make sacrifices because they felt they had sacrificed enough, that they had been deprived of so much that nothing more could be asked of them.

Because of early deprivation and their rage at this deprivation the girls also turned to self-abasement and self-degradation. By degrading themselves, by lowering themselves, they punished their mothers for what they had not done for them, mothers who had repeated at various times: "I don't want you to be a bum. I don't want you to be a whore." Their mothers had actually taught these girls how to hurt them most.

More important than the motive of revenge and the acting out of their rage was the search for someone who would take care of them in the way that they had not been cared for originally. For that reason it was extremely difficult for the girls to mature emotionally and become independent human beings. If they became mature and independent, they felt unconsciously, they would never receive the infantile love and attention they still wanted. Money became a symbol for the warmth and love they had not received. The money represented the food they had craved but had not received.[1] However, the money turned out to be an unsatisfactory substitute and because it was so unsatisfactory they vomited it up—by giving it to the pimp or squandering it.

In the relationship with the pimp, money served a double function. The girl could rid herself of the bad, poisoned milk (money) and at the same time attract the pimp with it. The hope was that here was somebody who would satisfy the desperate craving for oral gratification. When we discussed this, Sandra remarked, "Bad tit is better than no tit."

In the early stages of the therapeutic relationship it was

---

[1] It is interesting that their slang word for money should be "bread."

extremely important for the analyst to be aware of the girls' feelings of deprivation. They were therefore treated differently from other neurotic patients. If the girls arrived late, this was accepted. The analyst substituted his acceptance and also his appreciation of their abilities for the mother who had not fed them. The feeding was thus done on a symbolic level. Also because of their early lack, the girls had to find a source of identification, someone with whom they could start to identify and start to build a self-image other than the diverse, diffuse and contradictory ones that they had known. In helping them to build this self-image, it was necessary first to stress their attractiveness as women. The analyst did this by responding when they came attractively dressed, by mentioning how well they looked, by noting their seductiveness and by indicating that while he found it interesting and challenging, it would not be to the advantage of the therapy situation for him to respond in kind. (This seductiveness was also a test by them to determine whether the analyst, too, wanted them for sex alone.)

Other steps were taken that were departures from traditional psychoanalytic therapy. For example, early in the analysis when it became clear that Sandra had an ability to analyze dreams, I frequently shared other patients' dreams with her: first, because it was a helpful, ego-building experience; second, because it helped Sandra recognize that other people had problems; and third, because frequently her interpretations were quite helpful. Similarly, both Stella and Beverly found the task of interviewing other girls helpful in making identification with the analyst.

One interesting example of how identification developed came about by accident. A patient of mine, Frances, a woman in her late forties, was having difficulties with her husband and realized in the course of therapy that one of her problems was that she did not know how to behave attractively with a man. Since there had been some mention in the press of my working with call girls, she asked me whether she could meet one of them who might advise her how to behave in a more feminine manner. Although

I pointed out that call girls were not the most wholesome models of feminine behavior, I arranged for her to meet Etta, after discussing it fully with both of them.

They met in a restaurant. At first Etta could not believe that any woman was as naïve as this married woman. When she recognized that Frances was sincere and did not know how to deal with men, Etta gave her a number of practical suggestions. For example, she noticed that Frances held her cigarette in the corner of her mouth, letting it hang—in the style of a movie gangster. She pointed out to Frances the unfeminine look of this habit and suggested that she hold the cigarette in her hand instead or at least place it in the center of her mouth. When Etta took out a cigarette and Frances lit it for her with a lighter, Etta made another suggestion. Rather than use such an efficient lighter when there was a man present, she advised Frances always to fumble in her bag for matches. "Get the man to help you. In that way he will feel that you are feminine."

As they got up to leave the restaurant Etta dropped her handkerchief. A young man saw it, picked it up and hurried after Etta to return it. Etta stood and waited for the young man to return it instead of rushing forward and getting it for herself.

On their way out, Frances walked ahead to the door and held it open. Again Etta pointed out that this was not feminine behavior—that it was important for a woman to learn to stand near a door until a man opened it.

The importance of the incident for Etta was that it gave her an opportunity to identify with me, to be helpful, to advise someone else on how to be feminine, and to become more aware of her own problems in this area.

It should be made clear that while five of the girls left the profession subsequent to therapy, this was not a direct goal of the analysis. Like other people who come for analysis, they came because they were depressed or lonely or had fears. Thus the goals of therapy were to help them with their depressions, loneliness and fears. They stopped being call girls because they found another kind of life more satisfying, but the success or failure of their analysis cannot be measured by their change of profession; it must be measured by what happened to the symptoms from which they desired relief. While they experienced some amelioration of these symptoms, I do not wish to appear to claim that analysis solved all their problems.

PART THREE

Social Psychological Study

7. METHOD OF OBTAINING INFORMATION

I BECAME INTERESTED GENERALLY in the problems of the call girl through seeing the aforementioned girls for psychoanalytic consultation. I became curious as to whether the similarities I noticed among patients like Sandra and Stella were similarities that would be found among the entire population of call girls. I wondered whether certain difficulties of those I knew arose because they were girls with serious emotional problems or whether these problems were characteristic of call girls in general. I therefore decided to attempt to study a sample of call girls who were not coming for consultation. In studying this group I decided not to proceed as most investigators who had made previous attempts had done—that is, to study girls who were under arrest or in jail or who had to answer questions because the questioner represented authority. Rather, I decided to select only individuals who were operating freely, who were not part of a prison or any other institutional population.

To find twenty call girls who were willing to be interviewed was not as easy as I had thought it would be. It took a lot of time and presented many difficulties. It would not have been helpful to my relationship with the girls I was seeing for consultation to ask them to recommend others to be interviewed. However, I was fortunate

155

in that each of two girls that I had formerly seen for consultation recommended another girl for interviewing. I was fortunate, too, in that I had a friend who knew a great many call girls (I have never inquired as to his relationship with these girls), and he introduced me to three girls who were willing to be interviewed. One of them, Marie, with whom he arranged an interview, became very interested in helping me. She arranged for me to see two other girls. Also, while visiting some of the bars frequented by call girls in an effort to get some of the background material for the study, I met a girl (Paula) who apparently thought that I was a prospective client. In the course of our conversation, she suddenly stopped, looked up at me challengingly and said, "What are you, a psychologist or a psychiatrist?"

At this point I fell back on a standard defense, to try to bring out what was behind the question, and said, "Why do you ask?"

She answered, "I had too much experience with you people not to be able to recognize one." It turned out that she had been in the Federal Hospital at Lexington, Kentucky, in an attempt to cure her addiction to heroin, and there she had had experience with psychologists and psychiatrists. When I explained why I wanted to talk to her, she cooperated quite willingly.

Another girl I met at a party. In the course of our conversation I began to suspect that she might be a call girl, so I mentioned my study. She showed a great deal of interest, admitted she was a call girl herself and volunteered to act as a subject. Another girl was recommended by her former husband, whom I had also met at a party. He arranged for his former wife to be interviewed.

In order to make certain that I was getting accurate information, I had decided as a result of a suggestion by Professor Lorge of Columbia University to divide my group into two parts of ten each. Ten were interviewed by three call girls whom I had trained to do the interviewing and ten by myself. The volunteer interviewers obtained their own subjects.

The volunteer interviewers were Stella, Beverly and

Marie. Stella was described in Chapter 4. She interviewed Anne and Ethel.[1] In the interviews she took full notes.

The second interviewer was Beverly, who is about thirty-six, tall, slim and brown-haired. Intelligent and extremely well-read, a high-school graduate, Beverly was born and raised in Texas. She came for therapy because of a phobic fear of surgery. Actually there was no obvious reason for her to fear surgery—no surgery was indicated at the time that she came. Beverly had such a gift for colorful description that it was often difficult for me to help her concentrate on the meaningful story of her own life. She was the product of a broken home and had been both a call girl and a madam. I had the opportunity of working with Beverly for only six months but she has kept in touch with me through occasional lengthy and lively letters. In addition to working with me, Beverly also consulted two therapists in Texas. She is now happily married and lives in a middle-class suburb of Houston, Texas. Beverly interviewed Frankie, Georgia, Helen, Irene and Jane.

Marie is described in the Appendix, in the report of my interview of her. She interviewed Betty, Carla and Diane and these interviews were tape-recorded.

Originally I had planned to divide the group of twenty into two parts in a more or less random fashion. For statistical reasons this would have been better. That is, I would have interviewed the first girl available for questioning, one of my investigators the second, I would then have taken the third, and so on. Unfortunately, this was impossible. The girls who were the subjects of these interviews had great trouble in making and keeping appointments. When I made an appointment with a girl it usually didn't work out. I learned that when an opportunity came to interview a girl it was best not to delay in taking advantage of it. If, for example, I talked to a girl on the telephone and she said, "I'm willing to see you," I would

---

[1] Excerpts from all twenty interviews are included in the appendix.

grab my notebook, get into a cab and go to see her immediately.

It is interesting to examine the reactions of the subjects to these interviews. All the girls who were interviewed by me seemed to enjoy it, and despite the popular belief that call girls are motivated only by the love of money, not one asked payment for her time, although a great deal of time was involved in several instances. Sometimes it was convenient to interview them in a restaurant or a bar, in which case I might buy food or drink, but they didn't consider this as payment. They regarded it as part of the normal social pattern between a man and a woman in an eating or drinking place.

Nine of the girls who were interviewed by me seemed to feel that they received a certain amount of therapy or help out of it. As they were talking, they would ask such questions as: "Why do you think I did such and such a thing? How do you think I should act? What should I do now?"

Marie, who guided me to some of the bars that call girls frequent, introduced me to a number of people as "my psychoanalyst," although she never was a patient in the formal sense of the word. (Both Marie and Rhonda telephoned me later, after the interviews were concluded, to ask advice about personal problems. Marie, on several occasions, recommended patients to me.)

The procedure of the interviews varied greatly according to the way in which the interview was arranged. For example, the two girls Marie introduced me to were interviewed in her apartment. A large part of one of the interviews was conducted in a taxi as it circled around and around New York's Central Park. Other interviews took place in my office, in restaurants, in bars and in night clubs.

The girls seemed to approve of the purpose of the study. Four of them stated they hoped somebody would finally tell the truth about them. In eight of the sessions, despite the fact that I wanted as much of their time as possible, they became so interested in being interviewed that it was I who had to terminate the interview.

I found my familiarity with their language (which I had acquired from analytic sessions with call-girl patients) useful in the interviews. For example, one of the girls, Karen, started by talking very elegantly in broad generalizations which weren't particularly useful for my purposes. I found it helpful in such a case to repeat her statements in the kind of language that I knew these girls used among themselves. For example, when she said, "Then I acquired the horrible habit of drug addition," I answered this by saying, "What did you go for—'horse' or 'M' (heroin or morphine)?" As a result of my continuing to reflect her remarks in this kind of slang she dropped her affected speech and spoke in a more natural manner.

Most of the interviews were what psychologists call the "open-end" variety; that is, questions were asked in such a way that they could not be answered in a few words. For example, I might say, "Tell me about yourself," or, "What has your life been like up to now?" rather than a specific question such as, "How old are you?" or, "Where were you born?" By asking these broad questions, it was much easier to get information, particularly information that the girl might not consciously have wanted to give.

I prepared an interviewing guide which the girls and I followed in asking questions, but usually that guide was followed only to see that all the material was covered. The only time specific questions from the guide were used was when a girl had trouble getting started; then it was sometimes helpful to ask, "Where were you born; how much schooling did you have; what kind of famly did you have?" before proceeding to general questions. However, this was rare; most of the girls responded to the broad general questions and spoke very freely and helpfully, after their initial resistance had been overcome.

The interviews lasted from two to six hours. In some cases there was one interview and in one case four interviews, but most of the interviews required two three-hour sessions.

Two of the volunteer interviewers had experienced psychoanalytic therapy and the third had herself been interviewed by me, so they were familiar with the technique of asking broad general questions. However, I went over this with them and the advantages of this method were explained to them. In addition, each of the three girls had a copy of the guide and followed it to see that she got the information required. The girls' manner, as far as I could tell from their reports, was even more informal than mine. I felt that if I had used questions as direct and searching as theirs it would have interfered with the relationship. This may be owing to the fact that as an analyst I have been trained to use broad questions because they are most useful in therapy, and also that I was a man and a psychologist, but certainly there was no evidence that the girls who were interviewed by the volunteers had any difficulty answering their questions. For example, Stella in interviewing Anne asked direct questions about masturbation and sexual experiences in a way which Anne might have considered censorious and threatening if I had asked them. Anne didn't seem to mind being asked these questions by Stella and answered them freely, as far as I could tell.

Of course the girls had another advantage. They understood the background of the persons being interviewed, and they spoke the same language—a phrase which, in this context, has very special meaning, as the language of many of the call girls is often quite direct and idiomatic. Beverly, when she interviewed Irene, asked her about the racket, and Irene answered, "I wouldn't have the vaguest idea, never having been in the racket." Beverly then told her, "Irene, let's face the facts. If you go to a man's hotel room and have sex with a man for money, if that doesn't make you a whore, please straighten me out!" Apparently because of this directness Irene then responded much better to the interview.

My interviews took much longer to get the required information than those which the three girls conducted. There was a great deal of initial resistance; at first they didn't want to talk freely, they didn't want to tell me about certain aspects of their lives. In some cases, of course, they wanted to be sure that I wasn't a potential client before speaking freely. If I had been a prospect, they never would have admitted the fact that they had no sexual feeling during intercourse with clients because many of their clients had the illusion that the girls responded to them sexually and liked the girls for this reason. The girls all pride themselves on their ability to act as if they were highly responsive sexually to their clients.

Then, of course, since I represented respectable society, the society that they disliked and were in rebellion against, they seemed to have less confidence initially in me than in the voluntary interviewers. Three of the girls whom I interviewed in my office, for example, noticed my recording machine; they stopped and checked to make sure that their conversations were not being recorded. Even my note-taking—I tried to take verbatim notes of the conversations—couldn't be introduced at the beginning of each interview. I had to act as though we were just having a friendly conversation; then I would introduce the paper and pencil gradually. Stella, on the other hand, was able to make a very lengthy recording of one of her interviews and Marie was able to record all three of hers: the girls made no objection, though they knew the recordings were being made. However, so far as I can tell from the material gathered, once I had gained their confidence my subjects seemed to be able to speak about as freely as the others did to the volunteer interviewers. There was practically no difference. I even tabulated how often such things as sexual fantasies, homosexual experiences, masturbation, hatred of men, absence of sexual feeling, and drug addiction were discussed with me and with the volunteer interviewers. There was no significant difference. These are matters that most people don't talk about freely and which, in some cases, might actually have been dangerous to discuss, yet the girls did discuss them with me apparently as freely as they did with the volunteer interviewers.

One advantage of volunteer interviewers was that they were able to interview girls whom I probably could not have reached. One girl, for example, Anne, broke three appointments with me but spoke freely to Stella. Another one, Carla, told Marie that she refused to speak to any man. These interviews were interesting too because of the insights they furnished into the attitudes of the volunteer interviewers. For example, when Beverly wrote of her interview with Georgia, she remarked, "The only prostitute I know of who has not attempted suicide (except daily); the only one who likes the racket"—an expression of Beverly's own feeling that to be a prostitute was really a slow form of self-destruction.

The most dramatic effect of the interviewing was on two of the volunteer interviewers, Stella and Marie. Beverly had decided to leave the profession before she started the interviewing and had already made the change. On the other hand, Stella had drifted back into it whenever she was depressed or things were difficult for her financially or emotionally. But after she held her two interviews she told me that she was determined, more than ever, to get out of the racket for good. Shortly thereafter she started on a tour of managers and agents and found a very good role in a television series. To the best of my knowledge she has never again worked as a call girl.

Marie, when I first interviewed her, was not only a practicing call girl but was also acting as a madam for call girls. That is, the new-style madam previously mentioned (p. 17). Marie did not maintain a house. In the course of her interviews with me, Marie decided to leave the profession and try to make more normal social connections. First she tried to buy into a restaurant, then she took a job with a public relations firm as a secretary.

DESCRIPTION OF SAMPLE

Now that we have examined the methods by which the interviews were conducted, let us describe the girls who were interviewed.

All of them were working as call girls at the time of their interviews. This was their chief source of income. They ranged in age from nineteen to forty-three years, with the average at twenty-nine. They had very different educational backgrounds, some of them with only eighth-grade education and others with as much as two years of college. The average was a high-school education. In addition to formal education a number of the girls had some other kinds of education; one had gone to art school, one had gone to telegraphy school, two had had music lessons.

Six of these girls had never been married; seven of them had married once; six had been married twice; and one had been married three times. None of the girls was married at the time they were interviewed. Thirteen of these girls had no children; two had one child each; three had two children, and two had three children.

The facts about the socio-economic backgrounds of these girls were a surprising revelation. Many people think that all prostitutes come from extreme povery. Three of the girls came from upper-class parents, fourteen from middle-class parents, and only three came from lower-class parents—that is, from the kind of poverty usually associated with prostitutes' beginnings.

Most of the jobs they held before becoming call girls required little skill or training, and even the girls who were in show business usually had jobs as show girls, dancers in small night clubs, or strip-teasers, all jobs that required little training and experience.

In this chapter I have described how the information was gathered for the psychological study and also some of the salient points about the girls interviewed. Earlier, in Chapter II, I gave an over-all picture of the social and professional life of the typical call girl. Now let us examine the results of the study.

8. PSYCHOLOGICAL AND SOCIAL FACTORS INFLUENCING THE CHOICE OF THE PROFESSION

AFTER THE TWENTY GIRLS had been interviewed, I found I had amassed a large amount of material relating to their early lives, their feelings and their attitudes. The problem was how to organize this material so as to give a meaningful picture of their personalities and their lives—to make understandable why they had made the choice they did: to become call girls.[1] I decided to organize this material into three parts: first, to deal with their developmental patterns—the way in which they grew up, particularly their relations with their families; secondly, to indicate the symptoms that their particular experiences had caused them to develop and how these symptoms may have contributed to their choosing their profession; and lastly, to show the variety of ways in which they tried to defend themselves from feelings of anxiety and guilt.

While I believe that most call girls will show some of the symptoms and some aspects of the kind of personality development described in this chapter, it is possible that in different societies the individual forces that go to make up the prostitute's personality may be different. The emphasis

---

[1] Ackerman, N. W. & Jahoda, M., *Anti-Semitism and Emotional Disorder,* New York: Harper & Brothers, 1950, was a helpful model of how to organize material dealing with social pathology.

164

in this chapter will be placed upon the individual personalities and the forces that molded these personalities. I
have always tried to keep in mind that this does not mean
that social forces do not have any influence on these girls,
but rather that the social forces express themselves in the
actual personalities of the individuals.

I know that others may come to different conclusions
from the same material, depending upon their points of
view. Much of the material illustrates more than one
aspect of personality; I have deliberately used longer quo-
tations than might be necessary merely to illustrate the
point under consideration so that more of this material
will be available to people who are interested in allied
problems and to people who want to reach their own
conclusions.

A. Relationship Between the Parents of the Girls

There is an amazing similarity among the family atmo-
spheres into which these girls were born. Of the entire
group of twenty, I found not one example of a permanent,
well-adjusted marital relationship between the parents.
Not one of these girls reported growing up in a happy
home where her parents got along well together. In fifteen,
or three-fourths of the cases, the girls' homes were broken
before they reached adolescence. This contrasts with
about one-fourth of the general population which comes
from broken homes.[1] In the five cases where the home was
not broken by the time of adolescence, where there was
some attempt to maintain the home, the girls never saw
any evidence of sympathy or affection between the parents. In most cases the girls saw relationships that were of
a very transitory nature. Two of the girls came from
families where there were three divorces; three from
families where there were six divorces; six of the girls saw
their mothers living with men to whom they were not
married. This absence of warmth and permanence be-

---

[1] Kuhlen, R. G., *The Psychology of Adolescent Development.*
New York: Harper & Brothers, 1952, p. 366.

tween the parents made it difficult for these girls to form any kind of attachment to the family. When a girl cannot form an attachment to her family, does not feel close to them, there is no way in which she can absorb the values of our society, which most of us generally absorb from parents to whom we feel close.

When Stella asked Anne whether she would like her parents to take care of her children, Anne said:

> That's the one thing I would hate more than anything in the world. I don't want my children ever to be like them. The way they talk and live is revolting. I would never want my children to fall into their hands.

Carla in discussing her family, said, "I never knew Pop, and Mom never had time for us."

Beverly, after interviewing Georgia, stated:

> Mother took subject to California and then returned to Texas, where father resided. Put subject in convent and private schools until she left the father, taking subject with her to California. Got a divorce and remarried six weeks later. Told subject the reason she left father was because of subject's asthma and that Houston was not climatically advantageous for her. The following marriages (five in all) were to ne'er-do-wells.

Ethel knew that her mother had lovers and saw them in the house constantly. Marie's mother was never married to her father and he left when she was quite young. Much later Marie discovered that he had had six different wives. Helen's parents were divorced when she was two years old.

In the five cases where both parents remained in the picture, the children saw open hostility between them. Since there was so little love in the girls' families and since most of the families were broken, the arrival of children was not regarded as fulfillment but as an unwanted additional burden. The attitude of the parents toward the children seemed to be one of complete rejection. Again and again they were rejected by fathers who left home and by mothers who reminded them what a burden they were and what sacrifices had been made for them. Karen's mother was married six times; she often went away and left Karen with various relatives. Nineteen of the girls reported feeling rejected by both parents. This double rejection helped give them the feeling of worthlessness that was so characteristic of the entire group. The open rejection caused them to feel unwanted and unloved and unworthy of being wanted or loved.

In the cases where there was any discipline or control in the home, it was extremely uneven. Three of the girls passed from family to family; three from foster home to foster home; four lived in a succession of boarding schools. There was very little consistent pattern to their lives.

It was in the context of neglect and rejection that ten of the girls had a special kind of experience in the form of early rewarded sex—that is, they reported engaging in some form of sexual activity with an adult for which they were rewarded. They discovered at an early age that they could get some measure of affection, of interest, by giving sexual gratification. Here, too, a pattern began to be set: in giving this sexual gratification they were rewarded by overcoming, no matter how temporarily, their feelings of loneliness and unworthiness, and at the same time expressed hostility toward the parents.

The case of Frankie shows many of these features. Beverly's account of Frankie stated:

Born London, England, and went to India with father and mother. Was illegitimate. This used to weigh on subject's mind. Identified herself with and romanticized grandmother, who was also illegitimate. Father was in the service of the Crown. Economic factor different than here. Subject had personal amah and tutor and the family had many household servants. In India where poverty is prevalent, they would have been on a high economic scale by comparison. Was taught by mother and by mother's lover who was real father. Husband left mother after discovering pregnancy.

At the age of four, she has the recollection of a servant who told her his penis was a little black doll and wanted to make a little house between her legs, which she permitted. Subject related experience to parents and showed mother where the doll had spit on her. Father was furious. Threatened to kill servant and boy ran away.

At the age of five, subject frequently went by the office of an elderly man where she would allow him to kiss her mouth and fondle her, at the conclusion of which he would give her the equivalent of ten cents or so, in American money, for sweets.

Another early recollection of a man who was like a grandfather or uncle to her, not directly related, who took her into the library of his home during a party at which the family was present (parents) and held her on his lap while fondling her and asking her to display herself.

At one time she remembers being locked in bathroom at father's request as punishment or disciplinary action. There was a tarantula in the bathroom. Cries and screams were construed as childish rebellion and father refused to allow amah to unlock the door.

Here we have the factors mentioned previously. First the unstable family relationship. The mother was separated from her husband and was living in an extra-legal relationship with the man Frankie called her stepfather but who was actually her real father. As a result the family relationship was an extremely confused one. Frankie was entrusted to the care of servants for her upbringing so that in addition to the confused relationship there was a lack of close contact with her parents. She saw her father as a punitive figure, if the memory of the bathroom episode may be regarded as a typical memory. She must have felt that sex relations were wrong because of the early relationship with the servant boy, and yet she gratified her wish for gifts and for friendliness with the older two men and at the same time was able to gratify her hostility toward the parents for depriving her of a more stable family life and for her father's cruel punishment.

The following is another example that includes an early sexual experience:

Olive was born in Pittsburgh of an unknown father, and her grandmother took over her upbringing. Her mother never publicly acknowledged that she was her child. She lived with the grandmother and aunt throughout her upbringing, part of the time with the grandmother in Pittsburgh, and part of the time with the aunt in Cleveland. She went back and forth from one to the other, never knowing when she was going to stay with one and when with the other. She attended school sporadically in both places. Because she kept changing and because both her grandmother and her aunt moved around so frequently she never had any regular group of friends in either city.

Olive stated that when she was about six years old a cousin, who was then fifteen, got into bed with her one night and started caressing her. She found this quite exciting. He used to give her toys and bring home candy for her frequently. She loved candy, her aunt never gave her much, and this was one way of getting it.

Here, again, was rejection; the first rejection by the father she never knew; the second rejection by the mother who never acknowledged her; and the third rejection by the grandmother and aunt who shipped her back and forth. The cousin, who got into bed with her, gave her some candy which was, to her, a tangible sign of the affection that she received nowhere else.

The subjects seem to have recognized early in life that sex was a commodity which they could barter for some form of emotional contact in a family situation empty of that kind of contact. Against such a background, they acquired skill in acting seductively.

While there is evidence that women often fantasy such early sexual experience, the consistency with which this pattern appeared in the girls' stories makes it probable that these were actual rather than fantasied experiences. Even if we concede that there are fantasied elements here, there is rather a special quality to the fantasies: namely, that they had sex and were rewarded for it.

It is not surprising that out of such backgrounds the girls carried over intense feelings of hostility to their parents of both sexes.

Stella said, in writing about Anne:

She describes mother as mercenary. "She's always trying to figure out ways to milk me for more. She came up with the scheme to look after the children for the summer for three hundred and fifty dollars, even gave me a flat fee, but I wouldn't send the kids there. I would never want my children to fall into their hands."

Perhaps perceiving that her mother was mercenary was one factor that made it easier for Anne to become a call girl.

Diane illustrated the wish for revenge against her mother's failure to provide early security. In her interview with Marie she said:

You know, I'm sorry Mother knows what I'm doing, but hell, if she'd ever married a rich sucker and stayed with him, I wouldn't be doing this. Actually it's her own fault, so what can you do? Can't fight City Hall.

Karen, the only girl who reported being arrested, stated:

I was arrested only once. I lived with a girl in Florida by the name of Helen. This girl did me dirt but when a friend needs me, I'll be there. When I lived with Helen a detective came along and arrested us. I was charged as the madam. We were booked and fined and then freed. It was in the paper and I showed my mother the write-up.

Karen and her mother fought constantly. Showing her mother the story might be interpreted as an attempt at revenge, since the arrest happened in a city quite distant from her mother's home and there was only a slight possibility of her mother's ever seeing the story otherwise.

Beverly reported that Helen felt:
Great antipathy toward her mother. Mother predatory and aggressive; very interested in social work, women's organizations, etc. Subject only child of this mother. Half brothers by mother's previous marriage very cool toward subject due to the fact that [their] mother ran away with [Helen's] father [leaving first husband and sons].

Again there is the lack of any model of good relations; the disturbed marital relationship and Helen's great hostility toward her mother robbed her of a stable home life.

Beverly, of her interview with Jane, reported:
Great antipathy for the father. He has contacted subject but she refuses to have anything to do with him. Feeling that he deserted her and her mother, any need he might have of her is a little late materializing. It pleases her that he is rather old and alone at this time. She feels it is retributive.

The image of one or both of the parents is usually incorporated into the personality of an individual, and it is this image that is frequently the source of knowledge of what is right and what is wrong. However, the feeling of rejection that nineteen of these girls reported experiencing from both their parents made this process of identification incomplete and distorted. Their blunt expression of hatred of their parents and the feeling that their parents were out to manipulate them made it difficult, if not impossible, for them to incorporate parental images as sources of identification, of internal control.

The lack of identification and consequent lack of internalized controls, plus early rewarded sex experiences, made ten of these girls particularly susceptible to a life of prostitution. In all twenty cases there seemed to be few controls. Since the only ties remaining were ties of hatred and anger, prostitution could be used as retribution.

B. Symptoms

What were the behavioral symptoms, and what kind of personalities did these girls develop as a result of their experiences and their family relationships? Since I believe that diagnostic labels are frequently confusing rather than clarifying and because I am more interested in trying to trace the internal dynamic forces rather than in putting the girls into categories, I shall make no effort to assign such labels. However, those who are so trained and so inclined may find some of this material adequate if they wish to make their own diagnoses.

In presenting the symptoms I shall try to describe, first, the ways in which anxiety showed itself in these girls; second, the confused sense of self that the girls showed; third, the kind of relationships that they had with other people; fourth, their attempts at conformity; fifth, their problems with reality; sixth, the results of their lack of inner control. In pointing out the emotional factors that I think predisposed the girls toward drifting into the call girl's profession it will be necessary to isolate these factors and to present them one by one. However, I do not believe such factors exist as separate, independent traits but that, as in all people, these traits are interrelated within the personality. Also let me make it clear that these symptoms may frequently be seen in other girls who had similar backgrounds and who did not become call girls, so that the existence of such symptoms does not necessarily mean that one becomes a call girl.

1. Anxiety

All of the girls interviewed showed open, undisguised signs of anxiety in varying degrees during the course of the interviews. The ten girls interviewed by the writer could be divided into three different groups according to the way in which they expressed anxiety.

One, Karen, attempted to mask her anxiety with an air of smoothness, with a superficial charm that made her sound like an actress in an English drawing-room comedy.

After the first interview, as she began to realize that I was well acquainted with the conditions of her work, which I demonstrated in part by my use of the special idiom which call girls employ, she dropped the superficial mask of politeness and spoke in the tough argot more characteristic of her world. The words she used to describe intercourse and various perversions and bodily functions were simply four-letter words uttered with hostility and contempt. During the third interview she dropped her air of superficial toughness altogether and expressed her fears, her insecurities and her anxieties.

The second group, consisting of seven girls, made no effort to mask their toughness with any air of politeness, but immediately (unlike Sandra and Stella) used the idioms and the four-letter words so characteristic of their world. It was only after considerable discussion that they dropped the toughness, particularly when the discussion turned to their early familial relationships. Then they too began to express their fears, anxieties and insecurities.

Two of the girls—call girls for one and two years respectively—made no effort to appear tough but from the beginning behaved in a manner that made clear their anxiety and insecurity. While anxiety and insecurity are not uncommon in our culture, the inability to repress this anxiety and its relatively quick manifestation in the cases I interviewed—and in the cases interviewed by the three volunteers—were marked. In the interviews with me this anxiety was shown in the way the girls spoke, in their restlessness, in their continual observation of me to discover my reactions to what they said. The fidgety restlessness most of them displayed was much more pronounced than that usually observed in psychological interviews.

Marie, who had attempted to mask her anxiety with an air of superficial hauteur, received a call during the first interview and asked if she could be excused while she went to see a client. When she returned she looked at me searchingly and demanded, "What are you looking at? How have I changed? Do you expect to see something on my face?"

The anxiety also manifested itself in a great degree of

social discomfort. Also many expressed fear of becoming
or already being insane. All of these girls had attempted to
find relief from their anxiety in alcohol, marijuana, or
other narcotics. In social relations these girls felt constantly vulnerable. They felt that the world was ready to
laugh at them.

A few further illustrations of the various types of
anxiety may clarify the matter:

Anne reported:
My speech used to be awful. With my first husband
I used to drive him crazy the way I pronounced words. I
used to read and write poetry so much but the words I
learned I never heard spoken so how could I pronounce
them—like canapé. You know how I pronounced that?
—kan apes. Well, one time my husband had a big dinner
party and in front of everyone I kept mispronouncing.
At first they thought I was joking but it wasn't funny
when they realized I was for real. At least my husband
didn't think it was funny at all. He used to laugh at me
and ridicule me when we were alone but it embarrassed
him when it happened in front of people. Oh, you
should have heard how bad I was then. I got so self-
conscious. I started talking real fast to glide over the
pronunciation. I was never sure whether I was saying a
word right or not, so I'd rush over it. That's why I
speak so fast now.

Another example of this anxiety may be noted in the
case of Karen:
It makes me feel sad to think that most people are so
selfish. It's more than sad. I feel very annoyed, like the
feelers on a spider's legs. I spent six years looking
around for what I needed to make myself complete. It
always seemed to me that there was something lacking
in my life and I was depressed.

Beverly, who interviewed Jane, had the following to say
about her:
Also I have noticed that she frequently sighs. She
often has a frowning expression that's difficult to ex-

plain but I get the feeling of not frustration, but more like wistfulness, a sort of lost expression.

A good deal of this anxiety expressed itself in feelings of loneliness and isolation. Betty, a white girl who had been married to a Negro attorney, had the following to say in her interview with Marie:

> Doug and I were happy as long as we were alone. His friends disliked me and my so-called friends treated him like the janitor of their building or worse. But since Doug had plenty of money and his practice was good, we got along fine, with his friends [Negroes]. Then after a while they began to accept me into their society. They even asked me to work with the local chapter of the Society for the Advancement of Colored People. Since the family had completely disowned me I did it. But every once in a while I'd get lonely for my own kind. Remember I'd call you and get you to drive me over to Cincinnati so we could lunch and take in the Saturday matinee? You felt so sorry for me, the sick one, and you tried so hard not to show it.
>
> It became unbearable when I couldn't get a reservation in any decent hospital to have my baby. I made Doug get me an apartment here and believe me I'm staying here [New York]. I want after I get the apartment fixed to start various savings accounts in the baby's name. I also want to get some insurance.

Although she was extremely attractive, Ethel showed anxiety even on that score:

Until I became a call girl I never thought men found me attractive. Only when they were willing to keep me, did I begin to believe I was desirable.

Marie, who read this portion of the study, said:

That's so. Being a call girl helped me overcome my inferiority complex. I used to feel very unattractive to men but since so many of them want to pay me to go to bed with them, I guess I can't be all that unattractive.

Ten girls expressed anxiety about sex; six seemed to feel that sexual expression could cause physical damage.

Anne said:
Every time you have an orgasm it takes a fluid that is drawn from the base of the spine. The loss of that fluid drains off energy and slows up your brain and makes you physically tired.

2. Self-Image

In order to function, each person needs to know who he is; he needs to have an image of himself. Nowhere was the inner confusion of the girls more apparent than in the vagueness they all shared in their images of themselves. They all seemed to have doubts as to who and what they were and seemed to be in search of hints from the outside to tell them what role to play. For example, in the sexual role most of us act like men because we imitate our fathers or like women because we imitate our mothers. These are the people who most often act as models when we assume our sexual role. Because of the severe emotional deprivation suffered by the girls and the resulting anger they felt toward their parents, they could not choose either parent as model. Therefore, in their sexual role the confusion showed up most dramatically. Fifteen of the girls admitted having had homosexual relationships. Even in such relationships there was considerable confusion. Many homosexuals choose a specific role. Among female homosexuals the "femme" acts the role of a woman and the "butch" acts the role of a man. Most immediately recognizable Lesbians are "butches." They tend to dress like men in suits, ties, flat-heeled shoes; they wear no make-up and try to assume hearty voices. "Femmes," on the other hand, dress as women. In the case of those call girls who engaged in overt homosexual behavior, they usually could not choose either role consistently, but alternated between the "butch" and "femme" roles. In the course of their work they had to dress like women, but in their off-hours they seemed to be undecided. One of the girls, when interviewed, was wearing a frilly, lacy blouse, dungarees, high-heeled shoes and earrings. The confusion was mirrored even in the choice of clothing—part man, part woman—in not knowing which she wanted to be. In a few cases the girls even lived with homosexual pimps. Instead of having male pimps, they had female pimps and gave money to these pimps in the same way they would have given it to male pimps.

Beverly reported Georgia's relations with her boy friend:
She told me that he has become to an extent a transvestite. She went over to his apartment early in their relationship [after working hours] and he was in bed. She got in with him and he had on long silk stockings, a garter belt, panties, a bra with falsies. She didn't make any reference to it and they had sex, with her playing the masculine role, assuming the male position as it were. Even before their affair began, he had mentioned to her previously that this was his inclination and had begged her to take him along on one of her tricks in "drag" [women's clothes]. He always had women's clothes in the house when the two of them were living together. He had shoes that he bought in a woman's shoe store by saying that they were for his sister.

In some cases the confusion about sexual role was compounded by early upbringing. Marie reported about her childhood:
Grandfather was very interested in me and by the time I got to know him well he was retired and didn't have much to do. He loved to hunt and fish and was disappointed that I wasn't a grandson and so he made the best of it by training me in all these things. I knew how to shoot as well as any man. I could fish, tie my own lures, and when I went to school I would more frequently play with the boys than with the girls. I worshipped my grandfather as a child. I thought he was wonderful and I hoped in some crazy way that I could grow up to be like him even though he was a man.

Paula asked me if I knew of a psychologist who would take her as a patient, saying that she thought it would be helpful to have a woman therapist. When she was given some names she asked:

Are any of them butch? I have found that most women who are lady doctors and things like that are big dykes [homosexuals]. If they start anything with me they'll be surprised. I've had lots of them come to me and say, "I'm a man, I'm a man," but I turn them. I make them all into femmes. When I'm with a woman I'm the man.

Similarly Karen said:

For a period I supported a man because I was lonely and I needed someone. He was the woman and I was the man. He resented this often because I used to be very curt to him. Later I put him to work because I wouldn't give him any money.

The pimp had the double function of assuring her she could have a man and still play a part in acting out the attempted reversal roles.

Role confusion, particularly sexual role confusion, manifested itself not only in overt homosexuality, but in the promiscuity that almost always preceded the girls' entry into the professional call girl's life. This promiscuity was often caused by great fear of homosexuality. Before they openly recognized their homosexuality or permitted themselves to be involved in homosexual relationships, many of the call girls rushed into large numbers of relationships with men in an attempt to prove to themselves and to the world that they were not homosexual. Such a pattern is frequently found in promiscuous people of both sexes. However, it would be a mistake to regard all of these girls as truly homosexual. What seemed to have happened was that early deprivation or trauma made it impossible for the girls to develop a pattern of adult sexual differentiation, and they remained fixed at a level of development before such differentiation could take place. These girls were not examples of regression but rather of arrested development.

At birth infants do not act as either male or female. They learn their sexual role through identification with the same-sexed parent and by the responses their behavior evolves. Even as a very young baby, the little girl is usually greeted pleasantly when she shows feminine activities and, similarly, the little boy when he displays so-called masculine attitudes. However, if the child has no one who is interested in his behavior he consequently has no reliable guide for his behavior. The call girls, having no such clues, had great difficulty in making a sexual differentiation.

All of these girls seemed prey to feelings of worthlessness. Georgia in describing how she got into the racket, told Beverly:

A couple of men asked us to go out after the show. I was tired of men always making passes so I told them, "Sure, we'll go to bed with you but it will cost you a hundred dollars."

Beverly added:

When they acquiesced it seemed pretty easy and so stage-door Johnnys became stage-door Johns. As the Johns became more prevalent, the chorus went the way of all things. Her attitude toward men is: "They figure you're a whore anyway, so you may just as well push the point and get paid and I'd rather take some old fat John's loot and be able to afford a handsome six-foot blond thing on my arm. You don't want him [the blond thing] too shabby so if he doesn't have any clothes, you buy them." She doesn't conceive of anyone liking her for no reason. Not counting Johns, she once said, "Men are great but they're always so darned expensive."

3. Interpersonal Relations

Because these girls did not know who they were, because they had such a poor sense of self, it was very difficult for them, as it would be for anyone in such a situation, to achieve any kind of satisfactory relationships with other people. To some extent all of us have had the experience of being in unfamiliar surroundings and in unfamiliar circumstances, not quite knowing what is expected of us or how we are supposed to behave. These girls found themselves in such circumstances constantly. Whatever relationships they could establish were frequently endangered by their over-aggressive attempts at over-dependency. The individuals with whom they tended to establish relations were apt to be equally unstable. In addition, since these girls feared and mistrusted other people, they were shy and awkward in any relationship except a commercial one. However, they felt the need of relationships so deeply that they frequently put up with a great deal of mistreatment and brutality rather than break them.

Examples of the fundamental inability to relate follow. Stella wrote:

Anne has written a novel about her life and love affair with a wealthy man who is dying of an incurable ailment. She states that he is handsome, brilliant, virile, wealthy, madly in love with her. This novel, she says, is "a novel of deep, intense passion described with cold, deliberate, unfeeling descriptiveness." She says: "I'm sometimes afraid I have no feeling. I can just close people out of my life if necessary. For instance, once I know of his death I will just drop a curtain over his memory and close out his memory." In describing her life in the racket she states: "I'm making men pay now for the beatings I took as an innocent, young, warm girl."

Carla asked Marie during the interview:

What's this doctor need this information for? Not that it makes any difference. I hate men and unless I'm getting paid plenty I ain't putting up with one for more than five seconds. You know I'd do anything for you except put up with a man.

Similarly in describing how she got into the racket, she stated:

I convinced this traveling salesman to take me to Chicago, which he did. He got a room at some hotel and when he woke up the next morning I was gone and so was most of his money.

Both these cases show a lack of feeling for other people. In addition to being a mask for their anxiety, the over-toughness was a mechanism with which they tried to disguise their basic incapacity to establish warm relationships and the feeling that nobody could possibly be interested in them. Their lack of experience with stable relationships in childhood seemed to make it very difficult for them to know how to relate to others.

For a further example, Diane stated:

I was raised on a cross-country bus. First California, New Jersey, Florida; wherever mother's next husband lived. My second father was the one I liked. He was always buying things for me. A bookie, you know— still loaded with cash. I hope the bastard leaves me something in his will.

This was the man she mentioned having liked and yet the attachment was so tenuous that she had no difficulty speaking of him as being both the father she liked and hoping "the bastard leaves me something in his will." There was perhaps also a need to defend herself against experiencing any tender feeling.

In all of their interpersonal relations the girls shifted constantly between an obvious, surface type of ingratiating behavior and deeply hostile, aggressive behavior. With their lovers they attempted to ingratiate themselves by giving them large portions of their income. At the same time, they frequently acted in an aggressive, hostile manner, calling them pimps and trying to degrade them in other ways. The money itself was used as a symbol of degradation—as if they were saying: "This money that I have earned in this low, vile way I give to you and make you even lower than myself."

In their dealings with their clients, too, they vacillated between ingratiating seductivity and marked hostility. Fourteen of the subjects expressed hostility to men, while only six reported they liked men. The hostility expressed by the fourteen varied from open, naked hatred like Carla's to a kind of indifferent contempt. Karen expressed the latter attitude when she stated about her clients: "What perfect asses they are. He has all that money and he has to call me, who doesn't give a damn about him." The very choice of profession showed that same shift between aggressive and ingratiating behavior. K. R. Eissler stated:[1] "In the delinquencies, aggression is always directed toward the outside." What distinguishes the call girls' delinquencies from those of other delinquents is that rather than expressing pure aggression, the act of prostitution itself is an act of gratification of another person. The aggression is directed against society. Again the call girl manages simultaneously to act aggressively and ingratiatingly.

4. Pseudo-Conformity

All of the girls spoke of the loneliness they experienced because of their difficulties in establishing close relationships. Since they could not get any emotional support from such relationships they tended to reject the group norms of society at large and attempted to disguise the rejection by donning the mask of conformity over their real feelings of disappointment in human contacts. Their lack of genuine contact with people made it difficult for them to understand how to conform, with the result that the conformity was usually on a surface level based on external factors. In common with some of their more respectable sisters they cherished the external symbols of middle-class conformity: the mink coat, the expensive automobile and the right address on the East Side or Central

---

[1] Eissler, K.R., "General Problems of Delinquency." In Eissler, K.R., (Ed.), *Searchlights on Delinquency*. New York: International Universities Press, 1949, p. 9.

Park South. Marie, in the course of her interview, asked whether the investigator knew a church she could join. She also boasted of her membership in the United Daughters of the Confederacy and the Daughters of the American Revolution which she had joined in an effort to gain status by attempting to conform to the mores of her native town.

However, the girls had great difficulty in really maintaining conformity to most standards. The home life of those girls who had been married or had established a permanent domicile with a lover was a mockery of family life, with the wife or mistress constantly going out to entertain other men sexually.

Another area in which they made efforts at conformity was in their description to the interviewer of their romantic attachments. Even though fifteen of the twenty girls seemed to be of above average intelligence, in describing their various love affairs they usually employed the exaggerated cliché terms of a "true-romance" magazine, with little evidence of genuine feeling. These girls had so rarely experienced any feelings of closeness to another human being that they had to fall back on clichés in an effort to describe their affairs.

The inability to conform, to live up to the standards of society, caused the call girls to be angry with those who were conforming and, at the same time, to deny that anybody else actually was conforming. When Karen was asked how she explained society's attitude toward the girls in the racket, she answered:

Women are afraid of whores because they do what they would like to do themselves. Most married women have guys on the side who give them money. Men fear a woman who is bold. All women want to be bold; that's why they buy ridiculous hats. Women become call girls because friends get them into it and they want to show the world they don't care. They scoff at the world. I didn't want to be squashed working in Macy's. I wanted to be able to take a cab if I had to go some place.

A number of characteristics of their attempts at conformity are illustrated by this example. First, Karen's perception of the world was distorted by her projections. She felt that all women act the same as prostitutes. Second, she tried to justify being in the racket as a type of conformity by explaining that girls entered it "because friends get them into it." Third, there was an attempt to conform to what she saw as feminine standards because, as she stated, "All women want to be bold," and she spoke as if becoming a prostitute was not very different from buying a bold hat. Fourth, the emphasis on the earnings was, in itself, an attempt at pseudo-conformity, an attempt to make her occupational choice sound similar to the choice of any other well-paid work. Actually Karen could not conform to society's standards. She had been married to a man with a good income and had left him. Later, she had several other opportunities to marry wealthy men. She was unable to avail herself of these opportunities for a more socially acceptable way of achieving the economic security she claimed she was seeking.

5. Reality Adaptation

The girls studied seemed to have little capacity to establish stable relationships with the external world. Their perception of reality was distorted, inconsistent and frequently disorganized. Fifteen of the girls complained of having no interests. While many of these girls had creative abilities (one wrote songs, three wrote poetry, one designed hats, four painted, two tried to write books), they seemed incapable of utilizing these abilities consistently. They complained about having to go to night clubs with some of their dates and being bored by the shows. While they liked television, they had difficulty watching a program for any length of time. Everything seemed to bore them.

There was little evidence that any of the girls had any kind of life goals beyond the moment, beyond earning enough for gratification of immediate desires. While they knew that the call-girl profession was a limited one and they could not remain in it very long, they made no mention of this reality factor.

An outstanding example of their inability to recognize reality was in their relationships with the men in their lives. Those who had pimps spoke of their affairs as being "different" and that their men planned to marry them, even though the evidence was frequently against such an outcome. Others looked to their clients with unrealistic wishes.

Beverly wrote about Jane:
She builds false hopes on Johns. One in the East she has been waiting to come to the Coast is supposed to arrive this week. She has not heard from this man since Christmas and yet she feels sure that he's going to get a divorce and marry her. She was making plans for the home they would build. She got a letter yesterday that his wife is coming with him and they are going to settle here in California. This threw her into a depressed state.

Here is an example of transforming reality through wishful thinking when the facts seemed obvious.

In a follow-up on the above case Beverly wrote:
Jane got married to a man of substance, a charming, intelligent man who thinks she's a charming child. She's leaving him this week because she can't sit and look at four walls all day. At least the racket was exciting. She says he's in debt but that isn't her problem. "Janie is looking after Janie and nobody else." She told him she's going back to the racket and if and when he gets out of debt and has something ahead, she'll think about going back to him. She was at my apartment the other day and while she was here he called and urged me to try once more to have her see that it was the worst thing she could do to go back to the racket. I tried once more. I asked her, "Don't you think it's a little cheap and shoddy to ask him to look you up when he can afford to better pay for your time or love?" She got quite incensed and said, "I'm no cheaper or shoddier

doing things with him than with other people. At least I get paid with tricks."

The inability to see the difference between sexual relations with a series of clients and relations with her husband seems to indicate a damaged value system or distorted perception of reality.

6. Lack of Controls

Like most delinquents[1] the girls could not accept the values of our society and make them part of their own value system, but while there was little evidence of a consistent value system, all of the girls interviewed showed varying degrees of guilt feelings. They seemed unable to restrain themselves from impulsively "acting out"[2] in a manner that made them social outcasts. Becoming social outcasts only added to their feelings of isolation and intensified their feelings of guilt. This guilt, when internalized, was frequently the cause of intense depression.

Five of the girls, aside from their behavior as prostitutes, were engaged in other types of socially disapproved behavior. Three boasted about stealing from department stores, one worked as assistant in a gambling house and one assisted in a number of swindles. Fifteen used marijuana and six heroin. All drank, but none of those interviewed was a serious alcoholic.

Carla, discussing the racket, said:
I don't care what kind of a man I take on. Black, white, what difference does it make? I'd screw a zebra for fifty dollars; and anything new they can invent I'm all for. I'm here for one purpose and that's to enjoy my life to the hilt and live it the same way.

---

[1] Glueck, S. and E., *Delinquents in the Making*. New York: Harper & Brothers, 1952, p. 158.
[2] "Gratifying a repressed desire by social behavior which brings happiness and suffering." Harriman, P.L., *The New Dictionary of Psychology*. New York: Philosophical Library, 1947, p. 10.

Diane, in describing how she got into the racket, said:

It was really quite simple the way I got into the racket. I needed to get hold of some kind of change and this jerk was on the make so I said: "All right, doll, but you'll have to part with some *l'argent*," so that was it. Well why? Well, you know I'm lazy and, hell, all a man wants is to get into you so why not make it pay off? Instead of your boss and a lousy sixty dollars a week, get yourself a lot of bosses, work when you want, sleep till you want to get up, have everything a rich husband could give you without the aggravation of putting up with him, running a house, et cetera.

I have attempted to isolate individual emotional tendencies in describing the factors which made the girls susceptible to choosing their way of life. However, it should be emphasized again that these factors do not exist as isolated traits. They are constantly dynamically interrelated within the personality and thus some may appear to be contradictory. Perhaps the picture will be clearer as we see how the girls attempted to prevent themselves from recognizing their feelings of anxiety and how they tried to use their profession as part of their inadequate systems of defense against guilt and anxiety.

C. Defenses

In the two previous sections of this chapter I have tried to describe the early development and the consequent conflicts which predispose a girl to choose the profession of call girl. The combination of emotional predispositions and personality trends that have been described are not unique to the call girl. They exist in many delinquents engaged in other types of antisocial and asocial behavior.

All of the girls suffered intensely from feelings of isolation and worthlessness. Becoming a call girl appeared to offer a desperate hope of halting the deterioration of self, but rather than showing a way out of their conflicts, their choice of profession made these conflicts more intense and more self-destructive.

The average individual, even the average neurotic, has the ability to build up a whole system of defenses that prevent him from being overwhelmed by anxiety unless some real situation occurs in which the anxiety is so great that no psychic defense can operate against it. The defenses the girls used just did not seem to work for them and they desperately clutched at one defense after another, in their efforts to escape their feelings of guilt and anxiety.

1. Projection

The most common attempt to justify participation in "the life" and thus relieve guilt feelings was to assert that all other women behaved in the same way they did. This defense is usually described in psychological terminology as projection—one projects onto others one's own feelings, attitudes, or experiences.

Diane, when asked about the attitude of respectable people toward prostitution, replied:

> What do you mean so-called respectable members of society? they're the worst freaks [perverts] of all. The more respectable they are, the freakier they are. Take that professor, I've got to beat him with a whip, and sit on his face and get him a black fag [homosexual]. It's the only way he can get his kicks. I'd love to see that society dame's face he's married to. Then she's most likely as freaky as he is. You know, those respectable women give me a pain in the ass. They look down on us and yet they're the biggest whores of all. When they think they've been pursued enough they condescend to go to bed with their husbands. Poor husband really feels good. Boy, did they get lucky. They made it with their wife.
>
> Let the poor bum figure up how many times a year she lets him have her, divide it by what he gives her, and she'd see if she's not the higher-priced whore. No wonder men step out. They like to feel human, wanted and loved even if they have to pay for it. And nine out

of ten of these women are trying their friends' husbands along with trying other men too.

This attempt to rationalize her own behavior by proclaiming that the rest of the world was worse, was characteristic of the manner in which all of these girls use projection.

The girls tended to see all men as predatory animals who have contempt for women. In part, this may have represented a projection of their own feelings about themselves as women.

When Beverly asked Helen how she felt about men, the reply was:

I like them but I wish they would or could be a little more idealistic and a little less physical.

In answering how she felt about getting old, Helen said:

I think it's wonderful getting older. Just think when I'm old and fat and ugly no one will want me for my body any longer and they'll just want me for myself.

The girls felt that their attitude about respectable society and about men was justified by the facts and by their observations even before they became prostitutes. It is true that only too frequently their early experiences were of a nature to create and reinforce these attitudes. However, because of their poor perception of reality they had difficulty in distinguishing between the behavior of individuals they knew in their early experiences and people they saw in their adult life.

2. Denial

"Denial," as used here, means the attempt to repress from consciousness those characteristics which are unwanted. One way in which this was done by the girls was through acting out the opposite.

An example of this denial was given by Marie:

I finally decided that prostitution was a business and I might as well stop kidding myself. I will play it like any other business, joke with the clients and not get upset about it. After all it's not sex; it's like I'm a wastebasket for a man to dump his passion in. Often when I'm with a man, I felt as if I was sitting on a mantel watching two strangers. When I go out, it's not really me, it's somebody else. The type of person a man wants just isn't me. I can't use four-letter words. I have no desire to put on a mask and submerge myself in a tub of water or hit him with a whip.

Here Marie attempted to deny the difference between prostitution and any other business. She was also denying her guilt feelings about sex by stating that she was not really engaged in sex. By imagining that she was watching herself from the mantel she even attempted to deny that she participated in sexual activity.

An example of denial used to protect a girl from her own feelings of worthlessness was given by Beverly when she described Frankie:

Formed attachments only with people that were inferior to her. With her brilliant mind, she'd take an immature mind and deplore having nothing in common and never finding anyone she could reason with. Deliberately, completely mismatched herself with people mentally, economically and chronologically her inferiors, even with Johns. One fellow she went with was a hunchback and bandylegged, only about three feet tall. When I asked her what her reaction was to people staring at the two of them, she said, "I never thought about Dick being small." He came to about the middle of her thigh. He kept her for six months or so at which time she saw no one else.

Apparently she had to deny Dick's shortness and malformation in order to deny the feelings of worthlessness which had made her choose such an inappropriate lover.

In using the mechanism of denial, poor perception of reality frequently led to strange attempts at rationalization. A rather bizarre example of this denial was given by Marie when she explained her reason for not leaving the racket:

> After all I have to pay off my debts. I wasn't raised to be dishonest.

When it was pointed out to her that she preferred being a prostitute to having unpaid debts, she replied:

> Nobody ever told me about not being a prostitute, but they did tell me that I shouldn't run up debts.

3. Reaction Formation

One of the defenses that the girls frequently employed was an attempt to express in overt behavior the exaggerated opposite of their original impulses. Being homosexual, they tried to act heterosexually; suffering from depressions, they tried to act cheerfully and happily; being dependent and passive, they tried to act independently and aggressively. This type of defense is called reaction formation. One tries to act out the exact opposite in order to deny the original impulse. However, because the defenses of the girls were so weak and spotty, one would frequently find reaction formations existing side by side with the direct expression of the impulse they were designed to suppress. The girl who tried heterosexual promiscuity in an effort to overcome homosexual drives often found it did not work and remained both homosexual and promiscuous.

The role of the call girl is rich in possibilities for a wide variety of reaction formations. The very exaggeration of their heterosexuality in their work, in their clothes, in their overly seductive manner, was in part an attempt to deny their homosexual components. Half of the girls were totally frigid and in their relationships with customers, eighteen of the twenty were completely without sexual feeling. They denied this frigidity by feigning all the transports of uninhibited orgasms many times nightly. Similarly, their inability to establish close personal relationships produced constant and indiscriminate sexual relationships, as if they were attempting to substitute quantity for the quality of close personal relationships.

4. Self-Abasement

One of the most tragic transformations that took place in the inner life of the girls was in respect of the wish for love. Having frequently suffered rejection, they seemed to have lost the capacity to believe in or to expect any genuine, unselfish affection. The ten who occasionally were able to respond sexually with lovers (not clients) seemed to be able to find gratification only in a relationship which they twisted—that is, one in which they experienced pain and degradation.

> Anne, in describing her sexual life, stated:
> I can only be excited by a man who despises me. I don't mean that he has to hit me or beat me because I don't like to be hurt. I have to feel that deep down he has nothing but contempt for me. With such a man I get very excited and passionate.

Brutalizing relationships were used as another defensive function to help justify poor interpersonal operations. Such relationships seemed to prove that the "fault" was not theirs, but lent credence to their projection that all men were brutal, worthless, seeking only to degrade the woman. They could then find external reasons for their suffering—it was because of someone else's actions rather than self-inflicted.

> Karen in talking about love and sex with lovers, said:
> I have the warmest feeling with the other person. I usually have an orgasm but I have to love the other person to be able to enjoy it. I often think of being completely dominated by a man and fighting it. He doesn't see me and punishes me in certain ways. He has a cellar with people he keeps there and I turn over men

who don't please me to him. Two or three different men are having sex with me and he comes in and out of the picture. Eventually I am no longer his equal and then he takes me. I frequently put myself to sleep thinking of this scene. In the cellar girls will undress me and play with me and caress me and things like that. Also they would use various machines like a table with a mechanical penis over it that could have intercourse for hours.

In the first two sentences of this passage Karen made an attempt to imitate feminine attitudes. The bizarre and exaggerated nature of the imitation became clear in the latter portions of the quotation when her controls over the situation broke down and she described the extreme nature of her fantasies. She seems to have felt such need to be degraded that she went to great lengths to debase herself in her fantasy. Even in fantasy, she could only experience sexual feeling when punished and debased.

One phenomenon that was mentioned frequently was the number of call girls who live with or marry Negroes. However, I believe this phenomenon has received undue attention. Part of the reasons for this exaggerated attention to Negro pimps lies in the tendency of law enforcement personnel to be more vigorous in their prosecution of Negro pimps and white girls living with Negroes. Also the girls were influenced by the attitude of those sections of our society which hold that relations between a Negro man and a white woman are an act of degradation of the woman. Their need for degradation and wish to break the taboos[1] caused the call girls themselves to overemphasize the Negro-white aspect.

Evelyn advanced the following explanation:
Most girls they get so jaded after a while they have to take dope and they hear about this Negro kick. Now Negroes is one thing that my husband being a Southern

---

[1] See Dollard, J., *Caste and Class in a Southern Town*, New York: Harper & Brothers, 1949, for a description of the taboos against sexual relations between white women and Negro men.

boy says, "Any girl going with a Negro boy it's the end of her." I couldn't help but feel that if I ever went with a Negro, that was the end of me because he feels that's the end. However, I've heard men say that the reason a girl is ruined if she ever goes with a Negro is that she's never satisfied by a white man. So this thought after a while gets very exciting. We're getting at my inhibitions now. So after a while this gets extremely exciting. What is it so great that they have to offer? What am I missing? And then when someone like Billy Daniels comes along and sings "That Old Black Magic," and then you see colored guys with girls sitting around and girls with colored guys around and it all seems very exciting, and then you go to low-down jazz joints and you hear this mad music, and you see those wild colored men and everything—man, it seems terrific. So you start thinking about it and then you hear all kinds of stories. One of the most famous and beautiful call girls I ever knew was being kept by a prince and he'd love to see her being made love to by a Negro.

So this sounds so exciting and a famous movie star has this all-white room with a mirror on the ceiling and all-white furniture and has a big, black guy. You hear these stories. And how another movie star loves to be beaten up and thrown down the stairs by colored men. You keep hearing these goddam stories, and eventually if you're thinking about sex twenty-four hours a day, and that's the thing you've got to keep thinking about because you've got to stimulate yourself to go out on dates, you keep talking and hearing and doing nothing but sex—if all this drive is concentrated on one thing, that's all I'm thinking of, that's all I'm concentrating on, it's a big thing. It started being very exciting to me.

Being a masochist, I would imagine myself going up to Harlem and being attacked or something and actually this is as low as I can go. I know it's not low, but in society's eyes it's low, so I want to degrade myself. I think that's why the average girl does, the average whore. So many whores end up with Negroes because they hate themselves so. They feel so degraded. They feel as though they deserve the worst. They want what they deserve so they feel that this is what society thinks is the worst. This is what they deserve. Also the Negroes themselves—many of these Negro pimps will have colored wives but white girls working for them. They, themselves, have no respect for these white girls, but they have great respect for their own wives. These white girls know this and this is why it's so degrading for them because the Negroes have no respect for them and certainly the rest of society has no respect for them. They hate themselves and they feel this is it. This is what they deserve.

In this passage a number of things are involved, including the search for degradation and punishment and the sexual excitation aroused by the contemplation of this degradation. (Degradation is necessary to many women of all classes in order for them to experience sexual excitation because they have been taught that good girls don't like sex and they have accepted this attitude.)

Speaking of her husband, Evelyn stated:
This was part of my masochistic drive, my staying with my husband, because I knew he was using me. . . . I didn't want him to be mean to me mentally because he would hurt me so many times, but I would want him to be mean to me physically sometimes and he was. When I wasn't in the mood he would make me go on dates and make me have sex, anyway, but he wasn't quite mean enough to satisfy me. I mean he never beat me or anything. . . .

At another point she stated:
I used to wish that I would lose a leg. This sounds terrible but because I felt so desperately ill and miserable and nobody ever took me seriously or believed me, that I would wish I would really have something to show them and that's the only way I would be taken seriously because I've been miserable for so many years.
I see my girl friend's problem. Her husband is having such a hard time of it. Still she's not the one that has to go out and wonder why the rent's not coming in.

I see that she's depressed and I think how I did it and I used to wish that I had a physical disability then and I wouldn't have to go out.

Even before that I would wish that I had a physical disability, then I could forget about my body. I could forget about this sex bit. I could go on to something else because I felt sex was holding me back. I used to wish that I could lose a leg or something so I wouldn't be able to think about sex.

The wish for actual bodily maiming seemed to represent a wish to be deprived of the ability to engage in the activities which caused her so much guilt and self-hate, as well as the hope that if she were maimed her dependency needs would be met.

5. Depression

Only five of the twenty girls interviewed did not report having made an attempt at suicide. The other fifteen had all made such attempts.[1] Of the fifteen, six made one attempt; seven two attempts; one made three attempts and one made six attempts. Beverly had the following to say about the girl Frankie, who made the six attempts:

Got into the racket through a smooth-talking guy who told her to go to work until they had a little money together and he would put up the same amount so that they could go into business together. The day after she turned her first trick, she attempted suicide for the first time by turning the gas on, following by at least six subsequent attempts, the last of which was successful.

Most of these attempts at suicide were made by taking sleeping pills. One girl tried to jump out of a window.

---

[1] The rate of actual suicides in the United States is 15.52 per 100,000 of adult population. World Health Organization, *Vital Statistics and Causes of Death,* Geneva, 1951. Unfortunately there are no accurate figures available on the rate of attempted suicides.

Another girl drank chloroform. Another one swallowed three boxes of aspirin and another one attempted to inhale illuminating gas. Another self-damaging attempt to deal with depression was the use of drugs. The girls who had used narcotics stated that no matter how worthless their lives were, no matter how debased and degraded they felt, the drug would help them forget these feelings temporarily.

6. Displacement

Displacement is a defense mechanism which attempts to express an originally forbidden impulse in a partial or disguised form. For example, a homosexual dress designer who might like to dress as a woman displaces his wish so to dress into designing clothes for women and dressing them. The profession of call girl was frequently used for disguised expression of forbidden impulses.

One of the explanations of prostitution that psychoanalysts have given (T. Agoston)[1] is that it is an attempt to act out incest fantasies. The case of Georgia seemed to give evidence of this motivation:

> One early sex experience at age twelve was when mother and fifth and last husband were traveling in car with mother driving and subject was in back seat with stepfather. Subject was awakened by stepfather fondling her. He attempted to have intercourse with her. Mother became aware of the situation and eventually divorced him.

Here was a symbolic incest attempt. While the man was not Georgia's biological father he was her mother's husband, and to a child of that age this would evoke the same feeling as incest. In her fantasies she often saw herself in a harem where she was the newest addition; she wanted desperately to please the sultan so that he would prefer

---

[1] Agoston, T., *Op cit.*

her to the others. Another of her fantasies was to be taken sexually against her will.

In the framework of the earlier quasi-incestual experience, the fantasy may be interpreted as a displaced wish-fulfillment. In a harem one man can have a number of wives; thus Georgia could share the father figure with her mother and not feel guilty. Similarly, if she were taken against her will the guilt would not be hers. The problem was to find the relationship between the first incestual approach, the fantasy and her career as call girl. In discussing her real father with Beverly she said, "I wonder if my father would trick me."

She was asked, "Wouldn't you feel strange having an affair with your father?"

She answered, "No, I think he wants to, and his money is as good as anyone's."

The triptych was complete. Being a call girl, she seemed to say, gave her permission to have incestuous relations with her father. This fantasy also explains one of the unconscious functions of the fee. By obtaining a fee, she seemed to feel that she had transformed the pleasurable relationship to a work relationship.

Thus far in this chapter I have devoted myself to the discussion of the early development of the call girls and the symptoms and defenses that grew out of such development. While my chief emphasis is on these internal factors, I want also to consider some of the external social forces that interacted with internal factors. The external forces helped originally to mold the personalities of the call girls and continued to exert certain influences on their expression.

D. SOCIAL FACTORS

1. Economic

In the past, many students of prostitution have attempted to explain the problem solely as a reaction to dire economic need. These writers felt that women were driven into prostitution by the need of money for food, clothing and shelter. Prostitutes themselves have frequently encouraged this belief by explaining their choice of profession in similar terms. It is quite remarkable, therefore, that not one of the girls I interviewed attempted to explain her choice of profession in terms of desperate economic need.

It is true that some of the girls mentioned economic factors. Several of them spoke of becoming call girls because it was an easy way of making a great deal of money. Marie explained her need to get out of debt. Carla saw it as a means of securing diamonds and minks, but not one said that she chose the profession in order to escape dire poverty.

It is true that none of them had skills to earn twenty to thirty thousand dollars a year in any other way. However, eighteen of the twenty girls reported that they had had chances either to marry or become the mistresses of wealthy men who could have made them financially secure but that they were unwilling or unable to avail themselves of these socially more acceptable solutions. Thus more is involved than an immediate economic problem. Two of the girls did become mistresses for periods of time but reported that they could not stand the monotony of the existence. They found living with one man in any kind of relationship boring and unendurable. Irene was the only girl who reported a relationship with a wealthy man that lasted for a period of several years. This was possible chiefly because he traveled for long periods of time, and even when he was in the United States they did not spend much time together since business and family commitments occupied him a great deal. During part of their relationship her lover arranged a convenient marriage for Irene to someone else so that he did not have to maintain a residence with her and she did not have to stay with him constantly.

While economic factors, such as the wish for a high income, may have had some influence on the girls' decisions to become call girls, these factors were apparently more useful to them as a way of rationalizing their choice.

They could deny the emotional problems that led them to becoming call girls by asserting that it was just for money.

In point of fact, however, the economic factors actually played a larger part in their lives than the immediate one of causing the choice of profession. Economic factors helped to mold the entire society, the family structure, and therefore the very personalities of these girls. We live in a society that places great emphasis on material success and on that demonstration of material success which Veblen called "conspicuous consumption." These girls were both the pawns and the beneficiaries of conspicuous consumption. They were able to obtain high fees for their services because it was important for many of their clients to be able to say, "I can afford a hundred dollars. This is further proof that I have arrived." In turn, the girls were caught up in the worship of material success and in the need to display the trophies of such success—the mink coats, the Cadillac convertibles and the expensive apartments.

2. Conforming Sexual Behavior

Another social factor that was important in their choice of profession was the emphasis that our society places on monogamous, conforming sexual behavior. Because of their special problems, most of these girls had not been able to adhere to the pattern of sexual conformity necessary to membership in most social groups. Most women avoid friendship with girls who participate constantly in promiscuous sexual relations. Therefore these girls, to have any friends as they grew up and as they began to participate in promiscuous sexual behavior, had to find groups of people like themselves, to whom their sexually deviant behavior was acceptable. Such associations are formed in that gray area situated halfway between respectable society and full criminals—an area where drug addicts, shady businessmen of various kinds, bookmakers and large numbers of other people who seem to have lost their attachments to normal society form a society of their own. It was within this world that the girls made their first contacts with other call girls. None of the girls interviewed decided to become a call girl without having someone make the suggestion to her. By becoming call girls, they gave themselves some sense of belonging—in this gray world.

The typical pattern was something like this: A girl was living in a small town and found that she could not get along with the people there. Usually she had been promiscuous since puberty. Also usually she came from a family that was socially deviant because it was a broken family, or a family in which there was such extraordinary quarreling or drinking or other abnormal behavior that she was unacceptable to her own community.

Finding life in her community unpleasant, she would leave it and drift to a large city. In a large city, because of her promiscuity and attractiveness, she soon found herself in the kind of society that centers in night clubs, bars and after-hours spots, filled with people with problems similar to hers. In this group she would find call girls, pimps and madams. While she was sleeping with people in this group, someone would say, "What's the sense of giving it away, baby, when you could make so much money out of it?" Once she became a call girl she no longer felt like an outsider in this group; she felt as if she belonged; she had a place. She would usually find a man to support in this way and this would be the first time in her life that she found herself accepted in any group.

3. Importance of Female Attractiveness

Movies, television, popular literature and, particularly, advertising make it seem that the cardinal sin a woman can commit is to be unattractive. The advertisements of bras and aphrodisiac perfumes are quite explicit in defining attractiveness as the ability to arouse men sexually. The call girls, plagued with uncertainty about their acceptability as human beings, sought evidence of their feminine desirability in their occupation. This occupation gave them the opportunity to demonstrate to the world and particularly to themselves that men not only desired them but were willing to give financial proof of their desires.

4. Attitude toward Work

Erich Fromm,[1] in discussing the meaning of work in our society, has the following to say:

> The alienated and profoundly unsatisfactory character of work results in two reactions: one, the ideal of complete laziness; the other, a deep-seated though often unconscious hostility toward work and everything and everybody connected with it.

Both of these attitudes were expressed by the interviewees. They expressed their overt hatred of routine, confining jobs. Also the unsatisfactory character of so many jobs in our culture, particularly for these girls, who had very limited tolerance of frustration, made the occupation of the call girl seem like a life of effortless luxury.

A question that remains unanswered is why these girls become call girls rather than streetwalkers. While I have had little opportunity of studying the streetwalker, it does seem to me that there are some possible explanations.

One reason is immediately obvious. The call girls tend to be more attractive than streetwalkers and can therefore automatically command a higher fee. In addition, the call girls are usually better educated and more intelligent. It should be noted that one does not become a call girl by working one's way up the economic ladder of prostitution. Call girls usually start at that level; here the factor of personal contacts comes into play. The call girls are usually recruited into the profession by other call girls or by men connected with call-girl circles.

Class origin also seems to play an important part. As has been indicated previously, most of the call girls came from middle- and upper-class families. It is easier for girls

---

[1] Fromm, E., *The Sane Society*. New York: Rinehart & Company, Inc., 1955.

with such backgrounds to associate with clients who are also middle- and upper-class.

Girls from these classes are usually more willing than others to provide the variety of sexual activities frequently required by middle- and upper-class males. Kinsey and his collaborators declared (speaking of prostitutes in general):[1]

> There are a few who are better educated, with high school or even college background; and there are some who are physically energetic, mentally alert and intelligent. They more readily accept and provide the variety of techniques which the upper-level males find most satisfactory. . . .

As regards the relationship between personality trends and choice of occupation I do not mean to imply that every girl with the particular constellation of personality trends shown above elects to become a call girl. Girls possessing the same kinds of personalities might choose other types of socially disapproved behavior. However, in the majority of call girls studied, these trends were present. It should be remembered that any extreme form of behavior, like turning to prostitution, is determined by many factors. Obviously, however, even a girl showing all of the personality tendencies described above could not possibly become a call girl if our society did not make such an occupation possible. Consequently I have also shown some of the social phenomena that aided in molding the girls' personalities and in providing the special expression that they chose.

In the next part we shall examine in detail those with whom the call girls have most to do, socially and professionally—the men in their lives.

---

[1] Kinsey, A. C., *et al.*, *Sexual Behavior in the Human Male.* Philadelphia: W.B. Saunders Company, 1953, p. 604.

PART FOUR

The Men in Their Lives

9. THE PIMPS

THE PIMP IS FREQUENTLY CONFUSED with the procurer or panderer—one who sells the prostitute to her clients. I shall be using the word in a different way. The pimp as he exists in the world of the call girl rarely performs any sales function. He is generally only a paid companion, a kept man, to whom the call girl gives her earnings voluntarily, not because he supplies her with clients. The chief relationship between the pimp and the call girl seems to be an emotional one.

Call girls, in common with many people who "deal with the public," and more so than most, are subject to great feelings of loneliness. The sales clerk in a store is frequently lonely for people to whom he doesn't relate on a purely merchandising level. This can sometimes be a matter of great annoyance to shoppers when they find sales clerks clustering in bunches and avoiding customers. The call girl, despite her frequent and intimate relations with clients, does not thus solve her problems of loneliness. The pimp performs that function in part. After the day's, or rather the night's, work is over, the call girls who have pimps have somebody to go home to; somebody to meet in the restaurant for a late cup of coffee, a drink, or a sandwich; somebody with whom to talk about the night's work; somebody with whom there is a relationship other than the purely commercial ones that they have with their customers.

A common myth is that the pimp is selected by the call girl because of his superior sexual prowess. The myth is based on the old belief that prostitutes in general are over-sexed and that when they find a man who can fill their sexual needs, as their clients cannot, they are willing to shower on him all the money they earn in gratitude for his great sexual potency. There seems to be very little basis in fact for this myth. While it is true that the call girls frequently found themselves able to have more satisfactory or, at least, less unsatisfactory physical relationships, with pimps than with clients, few of them spoke of their pimps as being great lovers. As a matter of fact, the relationship usually was not one of normal sexual relations but tended frequently to be limited to oral sex.

One point that all my informants were not happy to discuss was the amount of money they gave their pimps. However, in some cases it ran as high as five to six hundred dollars per week. Now while the basic contribution that the pimp made to the call girl was of a psycholog-ical nature, there were other aspects to his contribution. For example, a call girl with a pimp who was connected with the underworld would feel more secure from robbery and holdup. Call girls are frequent prey to petty thieves who feel that they are safe in stealing from a call girl because of her hesitation to call the police. If the pimp was well connected in the underworld, he could protect his girl from depredations by anyone but himself. Also, if there was an arrest or threat of an arrest, the pimp sometimes had the necessary political or police connections to make arrangements for the payment of graft so that the girl would not be sentenced to a jail term. One of the reasons that he had this ability was that he had a greater amount of time available to him than the call girl, who was working or had to stand by the telephone for calls, and he could spend that time in making the necessary contacts.

Pimps are usually people who are connected with the underworld or with the gray world. They generally have other subsidiary occupations; some are bookmakers (not successful bookmakers, who usually do not need such supplementary income), confidence men, and some are outright criminals. Occasionally police plain-clothes men who had first made contacts with girls through their professional activity had become pimps.

Drug addiction is quite common among pimps, in fact, more so than among call girls. They usually dress extremely well, because, as has been previously stated, this is important to the call girl herself.

One factor that must be mentioned is that the call girl is not necessarily the unwilling victim of the rapaciousness of the pimp. Often when a girl breaks off with a pimp because of frequent quarreling, it is she who takes the first step to repair the break.

Perhaps it will be easier to understand the pimp and his relationship to the call girl if we examine the life history of one such man, Henry.

10. HENRY: THE CASE HISTORY OF A PIMP

FINDING AND INTERVIEWING a pimp was much more difficult than interviewing a call girl. Three of the girls made efforts to provide one for me to interview. On several occasions they thought they had the agreement of a man, but it did not work out. Then Marie took me on a tour of restaurants and night clubs which a number of pimps frequented, in the hope that if we met one without preparation and if we had some drinks together, it would be possible for me to get some information. At three o'clock in the morning, when I felt as if I couldn't keep my eyes open much longer, we did, in an East Side bar, run into a friend of hers who was living off the earnings of a call girl at that time.

Marie invited him to our table. In appearance, Henry was not particularly remarkable. When he sat down with us, she introduced me to him as "her psychoanalyst" (which I was not). He immediately showed a great deal of interest in the fact that I was a psychologist and began to question me about many things in the field. His questions, though, soon narrowed down to one area. He told me that he had done a great deal of research on the question of sexual stimulation of women. Apparently he had read a number of handbooks which stress sex play and had made great efforts to be satisfactory to women.

It soon became clear that Henry enjoyed the conversation because he seemed starved for someone with whom he could discuss what he thought of as "intellectual matters." Henry was a self-educated intellectual. He asked me to call him in two or three days so that we could get together and have a longer talk. By now it was four-thirty in the morning and it was difficult for me, interested though I was, to continue talking to him, so I agreed to call him.

It was not easy to get in touch with Henry again, but eventually I reached him at the restaurant where he had asked me to call him. When he got on the telephone he said without preamble, "You know, what I really wanted to talk to you about was that I think I need some help. Would you take me as a patient?"

I told him then that I would have to know what his problems were before I could decide whether I could be helpful to him. We made an appointment and he came to my office. When he arrived he was not nearly as self-possessed and smooth as he had been when we had met in the bar in the early hours of the morning. He had great difficulty in speaking, like many persons coming to an analyst's office for the first time. However, he did tell me his story.

It will come as no great surprise that Henry's story was the male counterpart of the typical call-girl story. His experiences were very similar to the experiences of the girls'. Henry's father and mother had separated when he was three years old. He was not sure whether his father and mother had ever been married and doubted that they had been, even though his father's name was on the birth certificate. From early childhood Henry had seen a steady parade of men moving in and out of the house, sometimes men whom he saw only once, and sometimes men who would stay for weeks and months. His mother was, at that time, a vaudeville dancer, and until Henry was of school age he traveled with her, often spending long hours alone in a hotel room while she went out. Sometimes she would take him with her to wait backstage while she performed.

Many nights she would take him back to the hotel, put him to bed, then go out and come back hours later reeking of liquor.

On several occasions he woke up to see and hear his mother and a man having sexual intercourse. He remembered how he hated those scenes and that often he would lie in his bed in terror and loathing, afraid to give any indication that he was awake.

At six, Henry was put into a boarding school, apparently a very poor one where he was frequently beaten because he was incorrigible, or at least so the brothers who were in charge of the school said. His one saving grace in their eyes was that he was considered a bright student and won many prizes for scholastic ability. Even though he had difficulty paying attention, his mind was so agile that he was able to surpass most of his classmates. Also he spent a great deal of time reading, which made it easier for him to keep at the head of his classes. However, at the age of fourteen he left school because he hated the restrictions placed on his liberty.

From his experiences backstage and from his visits with his mother, he had learned to dance and was accomplished enough to become a member of a group of dancers who worked in night clubs and vaudeville. He felt too far above this kind of work to take it seriously, so he never studied further, although he knew that he should have had more training in dancing. He felt that it wasn't worth it to him, he just wasn't interested enough.

His sex life had been as precocious as his work life. At fourteen he went to live with his mother after leaving school and before going on the road as a dancer. One afternoon one of her women friends came to visit while his mother was away and sat down opposite him with her skirts lifted in a provocative way. She carefully watched him to see whether there was any reaction. Henry was uncomfortable and squirmed and his mother's friend stared at him and said, "What's the matter, afraid you'll see something? Don't be afraid of me; it won't hurt you. It's good for you." She led him into bed and encouraged him to have intercourse with her.

He was frightened by this experience and begged her not to tell his mother. She laughed at him and said, "Who do you think put me up to this? Your old lady is afraid you're going to grow up to be a fairy, and so she wanted me to give you a taste of woman so that you shouldn't go for boys if you're going to be a dancer."

As Henry grew older his experience and his comparative indifference to women made him extremely attractive to the kinds of women who make up the ranks of the society of the unattached, from which the call girl and other delinquents are recruited. He stated that he was never in want of a woman. One of the girls, Toy, with whom he took up at the age of eighteen, was working as a call girl and started to buy him things. At this time he was dancing, not making very much money, and had a love of good clothes which he could not afford. This girl started to give him clothes and he liked it and appreciated it. Sometimes when struck by fits of remorse she would say, "I don't know why I'm doing this to you. This is bad for you and I shouldn't do it." But she continued to do it. Soon Henry learned that when he wanted something that Toy didn't want to give him, all he had to do was threaten to go out with another girl and she would give him anything he asked for.

After a while he found Toy boring and too demanding; he left her when he was twenty and took up with Fay. She was three years older than he, an experienced call girl who was earning about thirty thousand dollars a year. She showered him with even more gifts than Toy had given him. By now Henry knew how to make the most of the situation. Within six months he was driving a Cadillac convertible, was dressing exceedingly well and had given up all pretense of earning his own living. At first, he had spent his afternoons reading at the public library and in front of the library arguing with a group of similar self-educated intellectuals who spent a great deal of time at the library doing research in order to win arguments from one another. This activity soon palled on Henry and he found himself frequently overwhelmed by boredom. Often he was depressed and felt empty and apathetic; it was during this period that he first tried marijuana. He had been exposed to it before, had tried it on several occasions, but had never been very much interested. Now, during this period of boredom, he found it his only source of release.

Through Fay he met other pimps and began to mingle in their society. He felt different from the others. He was never a flashy dresser; he dressed, even before it became widely popular, in "Ivy League" clothes, smoked a pipe, wore horn-rimmed glasses, had a crew cut and gave up the Cadillac for a Jaguar. In general he conducted himself more like a Madison Avenue advertising intellectual than a flashy pimp. However, the nature of Fay's profession made it necessary for him to associate with pimps. Frequently she would call him and ask him to meet her at a restaurant where she was with two or three other call girls who had worked with her on some especially important job. They would meet their men there and in that way he was introduced to the other pimps and became friendly with them. The hours at which they met their women were so similar that it was easy for him to spend time with them. He found that there were certain social patterns and requirements among pimps. For example, if one of the girls was arrested, her "old man" would go to the other pimps, if necessary, and ask them for money to use for lawyer's fees, for bail and for bribery. Requests of this kind were rarely turned down because any of them might get into the same difficulty and need help at some time.

Another reason for associating with the pimps, in addition to mutual aid, was the fact that Henry found it increasingly difficult to explain to other people what he was doing. People who met him at bars and restaurants and saw him well dressed and affluent, would frequently ask him what work he did and he usually felt that they were asking this question just to see him squirm. He felt that they knew what he was doing, that they knew he was in the life and that therefore they were just laughing at him.

At one point he decided that he would like to go to Europe. Fay and he had very little money saved because his tastes in liquor and clothes were expensive. In addition he was collecting first editions of books, which were also expensive. When he first broached the matter to Fay she was furious, saying that she wasn't going to work while he was off in Europe having a good time. She refused outright, but he kept insisting, and when she didn't want to give him the money he took up with an additional girl named Celeste. He now began to see Fay and Celeste on alternate nights and with both of them contributing it took only two months before he had enough saved for his European trip.

He stated that when he went to Europe he had hoped to come back with a different outlook and with plans, so that he could stop being a pimp. However, even in Europe, though he spent some time visiting the museums and behaving like most tourists, he found it difficult to mingle with other tourists because often he wondered, What if they knew what I was doing? These are different people; this is not my world. I can't stand them, they're so boring. Soon he fell in with the fast crowd in Paris and London, the two cities where he spent the most time, and found himself with almost the same kind of people he knew in the United States. Henry felt that both the French and English pimps he met were similar to the ones he knew at home.

He came back from Europe more dissatisfied than ever, and it was then that he took up the use of heroin. He had been on heroin for six months when he permitted himself to be arrested and pleaded guilty of possession—which carried a three-month sentence—so that he would be cured of the habit. It was shortly after coming out of jail that he came to see me in the hope that psychotherapy would help him avoid returning to drug addiction. He was determined to leave the racket and find some other occupation. I didn't see Henry for long, because after a month of therapy he decided that Fay and he had enough money saved to make it possible for them to get out of the racket. They had been offered a partnership in a small night club in a midwestern city, so they left town.

Even in my relatively brief contact with Henry I found

many resemblances between his personality structure and those of the call girls. The early family history was again a story of deprivation, of an uncertain family background, of being ashamed of the background, of being outside the pale of normal relationships. He always felt that his mother was too busy for him, that she was more interested in her conquests of men. He had few positive memories of his father. All he remembered were scenes of his father coming home drunk and beating his mother, or both getting drunk and becoming involved in drunken brawls. From the age of three, he had been exposed to a steady succession of other men with his mother. It was impossible for him to find any useful model for establishing his own sense of identity. His relationships had been so transitory that he, too, found it difficult to know how to establish close relationships; the only ones he had were based on mutual interest with other pimps, or were exploitative ones with the girls.

The factors that distinguished him in his group were his high intelligence and his intellectual interests. They were in part a by-product of the long, lonely hours he had spent in hotel rooms, in railroad trains and buses, reading because there was no other way of spending time.

Henry was constantly threatened with anxiety, always self-conscious, thinking that people knew what he was doing and deeply ashamed of the kind of life he was leading. He was constantly plagued by guilt feelings and recognized that a pimp was considered even lower than a prostitute. He stated that the other men in the racket were crude and didn't have his sensitivity. He felt they were better off than he because they didn't share his self-doubts. However, even in our short period of time together he came to recognize that the other pimps' addiction to drugs and alcohol (he said that every pimp he knew was either a drug addict or had been one) was in itself in part a reaction to their depression, owing to feelings of inadequacy and guilt. The drug made them feel temporarily adequate and free of guilt. Henry had never made any suicidal attempts and stated that he didn't know of any pimps who had done so.

On the question of confused sexual identity: Henry had had a number of homosexual experiences until he was twenty-one and then he had given it up, except for the three-month period when he was in prison, where he engaged in homosexual relations with one of his cellmates. This was an additional reason for coming into therapy; he feared that he was turning into a complete homosexual; he stated that he found heterosexual relations dull and boring. In order to have relations with Fay or with other women, he had to conjure up weird fantasies, fantasies of having relations with dead women (which was also true for three of the call girls), and fantasies of wild orgies in which men and women engaged in indiscriminate intercourse in a temple, like an ancient pagan bacchanalian revel. Also in addition to having such fantasies, he frequently would insist that Fay and her girl friend have homosexual relations while he watched, and then he would have intercourse with Fay.

On one occasion he got a male friend of his to go to bed with him and Fay and to have relations with Fay while he watched, and then he had relations with both of them. Henry felt that this acting-out was, as he put it, "all right," but he didn't expect me to understand.

Here too was role confusion, plus dependency, plus the inability for warm relations even in fantasy. His fantasies were of indiscriminate sexuality, without any hint of tenderness or warmth.

If we compare his personality with those of the call girls, there is a striking similarity. First, he too had an extremely confused self-image, alternating between wishing to be the dependent child, calling his woman "mommy," and trying to be the strong, brutal male, yet never really sure of which he was. (It is worth noting again that, so far from confirming the idea of the sexual prowess of the pimp, many of the girls commented that their pimps were frequently impotent. What was satisfactory in the pimps was their basic indifference, so that in having sex the pimp could act more as a technician of sex, rather than a real participant. To the girls, damaged as they were in their capacity for tender relationships, this kind of mechanical sexuality was less threatening than a truly intimate relationship.)

In his interpersonal relations Henry, too, was extremely damaged, finding it possible to relate, for the most part, only with people like himself. His reality adaptation showed a very similar defect to that shown by the girls. He was always planning large and improbable schemes that would take him out of this life, none of which reached fruition. Despite his real intellectual ability, the lack of controls that he shared with the girls made it impossible for him to apply himself to any kind of self-improvement schedule, to any kind of study pattern, which would have enabled him to establish himself in some other kind of work.

The defenses he chose against his anxiety and guilt were similar, also, to the girls'. He, too, protested that everybody was out "to get his, so why shouldn't I get mine?"

"What difference does it make," he asked, "if you live off the earnings of hundreds of women in a factory or if you live off the earnings of one woman?" He insisted that the psychoanalysts who are pleasant to their patients are really doing this in order to extract a fee and that therefore he and they were similar.

The role of pimp, like the role of call girl, is rich in possibilities for a whole variety of reaction formations. For example, the pimp is able to deny his homosexual drive by the fact that he is satisfying a woman who has so many other men. He proves himself a man in competition with the hundreds of Johns his woman sees. This very exaggeration of sexual potency is an attempt to deny the homosexual components which are frequently found in the pimp. Even the self-abasement that was typical of the girls was found in the pimp. In moments of bravado, for example, when someone asked Henry what he did, he would say, "I'm just a pimp. I get paid by a prostitute. I'm even lower than they." Apparently here, too, there was a need to debase himself in order to revenge himself on the mother whom he felt had caused him to behave this way. He would say bitterly, "Well, this is what my mother wanted. Now I'm just exactly what she made me."

In the formation of the pimp's personality there must also be taken into account the same social factors: the fact that for many people in our society the important goal is material success: to have clothes, an apartment in the right part of town, a high-powered automobile.

The pimp does not evince the suicidal tendencies characteristic of the call girl. The call girl turns her hostility inward upon herself, therefore experiences great depression and frequently tries to destroy herself. The pimp on the other hand, whose relationship with the call girl is aggressive in the extreme despite the fact that he is living on her earnings, has the ability to externalize his aggression; this apparently prevents him from feeling as self-destructive as does the call girl.

In the relationship between Henry and Fay, the neurotic interaction was a parody in an extreme form of the kind of interaction that one sees so frequently among couples in our culture. If Fay behaved possessively, Henry felt it necessary to "cool her off." He would retreat; he would find reasons for being away to intensify her need for him. If on the other hand, Henry was attentive, Fay would act coldly and indifferently.

Among many couples, every analyst has seen again and again that as the man approaches the woman and shows considerable interest in her particularly during the courtship period, the woman often finds it impossible to respond to this warm interest; she retreats from it, and acts "hard to get." In this case, we had an extreme of that kind of oscillation, between dependence and independence. I was struck by the similarity between this kind of oscillation and what one finds in infants. The infant who is fed on the demand schedule, who is fed when he is hungry, who is fed amply but not forcibly overfed, will, when he is satiated, stretch out, relax and go to sleep. The infant who is nurtured on a rigid schedule, who frequently finds that he has to cry lustily and angrily before he can be fed, will often thrust breast or bottle away angrily when he is replete. Henry thrust Fay's feeding of him away angrily when he was replete. Essentially, in both Henry and in the case of the call girl, we have individuals who feel unsure that there is anyone to feed them, who feel that they have to demand and grab; and when they have surfeited themselves, they thrust the source away angrily.

It is hard to believe that it is accidental that Henry found oral sex most gratifying and that he used this almost exclusively in satisfying Fay. He made a study of how to give pleasure most satisfactorily to a woman with oral sex. It served three functions for Henry. First, he had fears about his potency, fears that he would not be satisfactory in ordinary sexual relations; second, he felt less involved in an oral relationship, that is, he didn't have to be as close to the woman, the two bodies didn't have to touch—as he put it, he didn't have to be enveloped by her "disgusting softness"—and third, he was able thus to express the deep, instinctive suckling needs which apparently had not been satisfied in him.

11. THE JOHNS

IN ORDER TO UNDERSTAND the call girl better it is necessary to understand her clients and her relationships with them. The word usually used by call girls speaking among themselves to describe a client is "John." Who are these Johns? What kind of men are willing to pay large sums for the impersonal sexual release that a call girl provides?

While it is difficult to get an exact statistical breakdown of the kinds of men who are Johns, they can be divided into three main types, with some overlap among the three: the occasional, the habitual and the compulsive.

Perhaps fifty to seventy-five per cent of the call girl's clientele consists of occasional Johns. These are men who may be in town for a sales meeting or convention, and who at home usually lead staid and respectable lives but who, when they are away from home and in a large city, consider the trip incomplete without the services of a call girl. Others, alone in a strange city, missing their wives, try to find some surcease from their loneliness by paying for the services of a call girl. Occasional Johns may also be local businessmen who once in a while get the urge to kick over the traces or who sometimes join a customer they are entertaining, as it would seem ungracious to offer something to a guest in which they themselves are not willing to take part.

Habitual Johns are slightly different. They frequently tend to make a friend of one special girl, or several girls, and may establish a relationship in addition to the purely commercial one. Habitual Johns are frequently men who seem to crave not just the sexual release but also some form of friendship or social companionship. For example, one of my call-girl patients had a habitual John who was also in analysis, and they would often meet to discuss their experiences with their analysts. The John was greatly interested in psychoanalysis and psychoanalytic techniques, and he often questioned her about what had happened most recently in her analysis, comparing the techniques of his analyst with the techniques that I was employing.

I had the opportunity through one of my informants who was not a patient to meet one of these habitual Johns. She called me on one occasion and asked me to join her at a restaurant where she was with the president of a large firm. When I arrived she introduced the gentleman as Freddie, and then proceeded to spend the next two hours trying to convince Freddie that he should come to me for therapy. She wanted to be helpful to me by getting me additional clientele, but there was another motive. She felt that Freddie had a serious problem because, though he was anxious to go out with girls like her and was willing to spend large sums of money on their entertainment, he refused to part with any money as a direct fee.

Freddie, on the other hand, did not think that this was a sign of abnormality, but insisted that he would get no pleasure out of the relationship if he had to pay for it. During the few hours I spent with them on a tour of night clubs, Freddie spent several times over the fee that would have been required of him. They eventually compromised their difficulties when Freddie offered to buy the girl some object that she needed which was actually much more expensive than her fee would have been.

The compulsive Johns are quite different from the habitual Johns. These are men who cannot keep away from the call girls, men who frequently find that despite all kinds of resolutions, despite intense feelings of self-hatred, they are driven to seek the sexual company of call girls.

Barry, who will be described in the next chapter, is an example of the compulsive John.

Similar to the compulsive client is the man who can be sexually potent only with prostitutes. Frequently these are men who are married and find themselves completely impotent with their wives, or they may be unmarried men who find it impossible to consummate relationships with so-called "good" girls. These men feel they must resort to prostitutes.

A predominant type of client is the one whose craving for sexual variety is so great that he finds it difficult to satisfy it with any but a professional call girl. The varieties of sexual satisfaction required of the call girl are almost infinite. Most of the girls estimated that between seventy-five and ninety per cent of all their clients did not wish normal intercourse but preferred oral sex. They wished the call girl to address herself orally to them. Also a large percentage of men wished to give oral gratification to the call girl. Many of the call girls explained their attraction by stating that since the men could get normal intercourse at home, these Johns would come to them for deviant activities.

Another client is the one who comes to a call girl and does not require any physical contact at all but prefers, instead, to satisfy himself in the presence of the girl. Some of these men are pathological exhibitionists who thus find a comparatively safe outlet for their exhibitionism. A noted theatrical personality, who is a frequent client of several of the girls, would come armed with a magazine of "art poses" bought from the newsstand showing girls scantily clad in various positions. He would request the call girls to assume these positions and dress as shown in the magazine, and would auto-erotically reach orgasm while the girls assumed such positions.

The talkers are another group. Many of the talkers insist that the girls use obscene language during intercourse while others enjoy the freedom to use such language themselves (coprolalia). Stella had one special client who would call her up and engage her in detailed conversation about her sex life with men or women. Stella, who has a vivid imagination and a good descriptive style, would oblige by describing a variety of scenes with a great deal of emotion. Her client would occasionally interject additional excited questions. At the end of the telephone conversation he would thank her for the call and send her a check in the mail.

Sadists and masochists form a special section of the clientele of the call girls. Sadists, particularly, are so numerous that many of the girls wear dresses with belts because the men want to beat them and the girl prefers that her own cloth belt be used. Frequently the beating is purely symbolic and is not done to the point of pain. However, many of the girls mentioned men who had been carried away and had beaten the girls quite severely. In addition to beatings, some of the clients will demand the right to tie the girl up before administering the beating or before having intercourse.

Another type of client is the voyeur, who wishes to watch intercourse. Many men ask for and pay for the services of two girls who ostensibly have homosexual relations with each other. Such relations, when done in the presence of the client, are almost never (at least none of the girls ever reported them so) real sex. They are pseudo-sex in that the girls perform solely for the edification of the client. The client then has intercourse with either one or both of these girls. The usual explanation for this special kind of voyeurism is that unconscious homosexuality finds expression in the homosexual relations between the girls. This is the explanation given by Caprio[1] in his book *Sexual Deviations*. I believe that there is another possible explanation for this kind of deviation. Many men find it hard to believe that women are sexually aroused and they therefore wish to witness such arousal. The thought of observing normal heterosexual sex is unacceptable to them. Because of early childhood prohibitions or perhaps because there might be greater temptations to homosexual excitation at seeing the other male, they find

---

[1] Caprio, F. S., *Op. cit.*

it easier to witness the excitement of two females. However, there are cases where men will pay extra for the opportunity of watching their friends have intercourse with the girls.

Some men insist on going to bed with two girls at a time (troilism). In such cases they may caress one while having intercourse with the other, or they may merely require that one of the girls watch while they have intercourse with the other.

Another type of John is one who duplicates the tribal initiation rites practiced by more primitive peoples. This is the case where a young man is initiated into the mysteries of sex by his father who may be a habitual or occasional client, who brings him to the call girl so that he will "learn the facts of life," "lose his pimples," or "become a man." Some of these initiation rites end disastrously. Frequently in this situation the young man is impotent. Usually the professional call girl will come out before the other man or men who have brought the young man for the initiation and will give glowing praise to the young man for his sexual prowess rather than embarrass him in front of his friends. In other cases, fathers, fearful of homosexuality in their sons, take them to call girls hoping that this will cure them of homosexual or effeminate predilections by giving them a taste for women. The girls reported that this rarely works as a form of therapy in eradicating homosexuality.

There are also clients who require forms of sexual gratification more bizarre than those mentioned above. The object of many of these activities (such as urolagnia) seems to be the wish of these men to act out their need to degrade the woman before they can enjoy her. It is the necessity of catering to this wish to degrade that helps make the call girl's work so destructive to her personality. Those who argue for legalized prostitution or a laissez-faire attitude toward prostitution must recognize that a society which sanctions prostitution is thereby sanctioning this degradation of some of its members.

In addition to classification based on the frequency and the special circumstances under which they visit call girls, the socio-economic characteristics of the clients are interesting. The large majority of clients appear to be businessmen—both legitimate businessmen and men who are on the fringes of legitimate industry, such as former black marketers or people engaged in large-scale income-tax evasion. In another case, a large advertising account running into many millions of dollars each year was secured by an ingenious account executive who discovered the interest in plural sex of the president of a large manufacturing company and made provisions to provide such sex.

Surprisingly frequent visitors to call girls are well-known theatrical personalities. Some of these men are reputed to be the idols of young womanhood, causing swoons, screams and a variety of intense emotional disturbances in literally millions of young American females. Yet they are sometimes steady customers of call girls. The explanations for this are varied. For one thing, many of these men feel that it would be dangerous for them to indulge in sex with an "amateur" because of the danger of pregnancy, of being "shaken down" or of emotional involvements when they are already married or involved with somebody else. Another reason why they frequently resort to call girls is that being on tour so often, it is difficult for them to establish quickly the social contacts necessary for ordinary sexual experiences. In addition, being busy men, preoccupied with their careers and their own talents, they often do not have the time to pursue such contacts and find it much more economical both of time and money to avail themselves of commercial rather than usual sex.

Similar to these theatrical personalities are the prominent political figures who also avail themselves of the services of call girls. Here, too, the belief that the professional call girl will not use her knowledge for either blackmail or gossip makes them willing to avail themselves of sexual pleasures without the fear of exposure—which they would risk in any other illicit situation.

12. BARRY, A COMPULSIVE JOHN

QUITE DIFFERENT FROM THE occasional and even the habitual John is the compulsive John, the man who goes from prostitute to prostitute, who spends a great deal of his time, money and energy in searching for release with a prostitute. Barry, a highly articulate and intelligent man, was one such. He was referred to me by a psychiatrist he had been seeing for therapy previously. In the course of our talks Barry learned about my research into the problems of the call girl and volunteered to write up some of his experiences with prostitutes. Fortunately he writes quite well and, as a matter of fact, has writing ambitions. An interesting sidelight on his writing for me is the fact that he had been attempting to write a novel, largely autobiographical, and had found himself bogged down and unable to continue with it. After writing his experiences with prostitutes, Barry reported a renewed ability to work on his novel. He explained this by stating that he realized that one of the obstacles he had been unable to overcome was a fear of exposing too much about his interest in prostitutes, but because of the opportunity to express it in the writing he did for me, it was now possible for him to continue his work on his novel without further fear of self-exposure.

Barry is blond, slim, attractive, highly articulate and

intelligent. He was a fine student at high school and won a state scholarship. However, he found it impossible to complete college successfully without the external restraints and discipline that he had been given in high school. After leaving college he drifted into different occupations, served in the Navy, got married, drifted again occupationally and finally became a bartender. When he first started therapy, he found it difficult even to discipline himself in the occupation of bartending. At the present time, though, he is near the top of his profession as a bartender, earning at least two hundred dollars a week.

Because of its length and the nature of some of the material that Barry contributed, it will be impossible to include the entire account. However, portions of it give us clues to some of the unconscious reasons for Barry's compulsive relationship with prostitutes. Early in his sexual life Barry had found it difficult to permit himself to have sexual relations with a "good" girl and began to search constantly for prostitutes. His whole story is a picture of compulsive searching for something that he could not find. In his pursuit of prostitutes there is an indication of his anger at his mother and the fact that he used the prostitutes as a method of punishing his mother. In going to prostitutes he said in effect: "Because you have been mean to me, this is what I'm going to do."

The first page of his account makes this quite graphic:

The first intercourse I ever had was with a prostitute a few months before my seventeenth birthday.

At the time I was a freshman at NYU, living at home, extremely unhappy because of two immediate situations. First, I had been betrayed by my mother who had promised me that I could go to Harvard if I won a state scholarship, which I did; and second (perhaps first) because the first girl I had told I had loved, who said she loved me also, had broken off with me some weeks before.

Peggy and I had met at summer camp and the weekend we returned she was alone in her mother's house. I wanted to have intercourse with her and she with me but I felt I "might hurt her"; "I did not want to do something which she might rue later and hate me for"; etc. We were necking late at night and for the first time she touched me and for the first time I touched her. We had agreed nothing "below the waist" previously. We never spoke of this after but I felt it was the cause of our breakup, for our relationship changed from that time although I think her main objection to me was described as my "wildness."

At college I almost instinctively found out the kindred spirits; the very bright, very young, very neurotic, interested in cards, pool, all kinds of gambling, sex, liquor.

I had my first orgasm shortly after I was twelve and had since and after masturbated (almost) daily; so frequently that I do not remember my first wet dream until I was in my late teens.

The bunch I hung out with used to play cards in the game room at college from 11 A.M. opening to 11 P.M. closing and then usually go to someone's room for poker or dice or go bowling or pub-crawling. I learned it was the custom to go to a whorehouse afterward but never joined in these group visits although two or three times several months after I did go; twice with one of my best friends and once with a fellow I had a tremendous contempt for; also once or twice with vague acquaintances.

This first time I went to a hotel in the Times Square area. I knew the price (three dollars), of which the whore got two and the pimps, bellboys, etc. split the other dollar. (This was in 1939, before inflation.) Although it was not necessary I found myself tipping the elevator boy who led me to the prostitute's room a dollar. Going up alone in the elevator with him I was shaking violently. When I was inside and the door closed, I noticed that the girl was eating a sandwich. She got up and started to undress. I told her to finish her sandwich but she said no. She had brownish blond hair and looked about thirty. Her skin was clear but kind of dull-looking. She wore no make-up. She lay down calmly and her pubic hair was darker than the hair on her head. She was virtually odorless and I did not touch her except her breasts briefly before I began intercourse. As soon as, if not before I began, I was terribly disappointed. I was surprised at the ease with which I entered. I was clumsy for a couple of seconds, but got the knack quickly. My orgasm was almost immediate. Even as I finished, I remember my tremendous disappointment and the feeling that I had wasted this irretrievable experience meaninglessly and could never recover my loss. (What I felt I had lost was the looked-forward-to fantastic happiness of the first consummation and I could never again have this *first* pleasure with someone I loved.)

Afterward my main feeling was this loss, disappointment and some self-disgust, with some rationalized pride that I was no longer a virgin and need not lie about it although I realized the cheapness of my "achievement."

Here we see two of the motivative factors mentioned: first, his anger at his mother for not having kept her promise, and second, his fear of hurting a good girl. Barry's description of his experience with a prostitute is typical of all his subsequent experiences. The feeling of emptiness he speaks of is reported by most men who are clients of prostitutes. Closely allied with the feeling of emptiness was the feeling of disgust which usually followed his visits to a prostitute.

After these experiences I was almost always overcome by disgust and revulsion. I would spit all the way home, gargle, take a hot shower, etc. I always washed immediately after, gargled soapy water and was very lucky I guess. Crabs was the worst I ever got. Sometimes instead of going home, if I had more money, I would have a few more drinks, hang around and get it again.

This was my pattern from the time I was almost seventeen until I got married. Until then my wife was the only woman I ever had intercourse with whom I did not pay.

Also close to this feeling of disgust was the feeling of guilt that intercourse with a prostitute caused him. Despite hundreds of experiences, he was never to get over this feeling of guilt.

It was important to me to prolong intercourse, for I knew before I began that immediately after the pleasure of the orgasm, the guilt, revulsion, fear, etc. would begin and I wanted to put this off as long as I could.

I was married in 1944 (June) after about five or six years of this kind of life, two weeks after I volunteered for the Navy.

The idea of having relations with anyone other than my wife was extremely distasteful to me from the first time of my marriage. However, on my wedding night I remember (with great guilt then, less now) the problem of my wife, our both being perhaps a little drunk; and prowling the halls of the hotel unsatisfied looking for someone, a whore.

Great as his feelings of guilt were about relations with prostitutes, apparently the feelings of guilt about a relationship with a "good woman," even with his wife, were even greater. On his wedding night he found his experience with his wife so unsatisfactory that he went searching for another woman. Barry fought this drive and used a variety of ways to try to prevent himself from engaging in relations with prostitutes.

I began drinking a lot after work, almost every night sometimes as if to spend my money in the bar so as not to spend it on whores. My wife got very little from me although I made up to a hundred and fifty dollars, some weeks through the hardest, tensest work I have ever done. (My tension made it this hard.) I drove myself in a frenzy.

Apparently Barry felt particularly guilty toward his wife for his relationships with the prostitutes because part of the reason Barry went to prostitutes was his wish to avenge himself on his wife, whom he had substituted for his un-giving mother.

After, I would always wash with soap and hot water in the hotel and again at home and go to bed. Lying next to my wife I was afraid to touch her, afraid she would awaken and want me to make love to her.

In addition to his wish to revenge himself, and his fear of "good" women, he was actually afraid of *all* women For example:

I went into a house and there were eight or nine girls in rompers, kimonos. The madam said, "One dollar; they are all French." I was very disturbed about making an open choice.

The fear of making an open choice indicated one of the problems Barry had with women. Another example of the same problem is given in an experience he had while working in the fur industry:

I used to walk around with thousands in furs and could not pay my own rent (about thirty-five bucks then). I once went to visit a brunette call girl. I had no cash. This was after they laid me off and I was half-heartedly trying to peddle furs on my own. I had a few fur stoles on consignment with me. I gave her one stole. She was supposed to have intercourse twice. She told me she had been sick and her vagina hurt. I thought of venereal disease. After the first time she said she heard someone at the door and made me leave. I felt cheated (which I was, of course) and called up several times to collect but she always refused. I felt she must realize my weakness and ineffectuality and wanted to force her to somehow but had the sense and fear not to.

Here, again, we have an example of Barry's fear and also a reason why he had relations only with women he paid, until the time of his marriage. By paying he apparently felt that he placated them and that they wouldn't be angry with him. However, he could not demand what he was entitled to, because of his fear, even when he was as obviously cheated as in this specific instance. So great was his fear of "good" women, that Barry rarely felt any conscious sexual attraction toward them.

When my wife was pregnant and left Norfolk, Virginia, where she had been visiting me I was desolate and desperate and filled with guilt; I had neglected her and had been gambling very heavily and somewhat profitably. My sexual feelings toward women I met socially or through the navy were almost entirely repressed and I hardly remember feeling: "I'd like to have her" toward any woman, with two exceptions about which I did nothing and one girl I approached in a boorish and unsuccessful manner.

In the following instance a hint of the cause of Barry's fear of non-prostitute women is given:

One night I picked up a fortyish woman in a bar. I got drunk; she had two beers and took me home without a word as if we both expected and knew what would happen. I did not kiss her once but I had relations with her five times as if in a frenzy and then left and went back to the hospital where I was now stationed. She asked me for my cigarette lighter, which had cost about a buck, but I refused because I did not want to pay even this.

In the case of this woman, Barry came close to recognizing the resemblance to his mother. She was close to his mother in age. In the course of his analysis Barry brought out many examples of the sexual seductiveness with which his mother treated him. Frequently when he was in the bathroom, up to the time he was eighteen, his mother would come in without any clothes on and take a bath. Often she would get into bed with him with very little clothing on and occasionally lean over him with her breasts touching his face.

Even as a young boy he felt a mixture of desire and anger; anger at his mother for so tempting him. The frenzy that he felt with the bar woman was the frenzy of fear. The refusal to give her anything, even the cigarette lighter, was the anger he felt against this woman for going to bed with him, the same that he had felt against his mother for acting seductively.

Another purpose of the relations with the prostitutes was that with them, Barry could overcome his feelings of inadequacy. When he was working for the fur merchant, for example, and found himself inadequate as a salesman, he intensified his visits to prostitutes.

In addition to spending more than he could afford, Barry frequently exposed himself to actual danger. For example:

Did I tell you this before? Once I was told by a young Negro man near 126th and Eighth to follow him, he had a good whore. Up two flights of stairs—I was in the middle; his accomplice came down with a switch-blade and they held me up. I considered my chances and decided I couldn't get away. They led me up the stairs to the roof. One in front, one behind me. Terror began to take over but I still remember every detail (from 1943). On the roof they made me drop my pants, searched me, stole my money and coat. I asked for and they left me my papers, draft card, navy reserve papers, etc. When I turned my head slightly the one behind me, with the knife, cuffed me and said, "Don't look." I was in terror and looked across the flat roof, which had no parapet. I determined if they tried to push me over to take one with me. They took my dough and coat and left, however, warning me not to follow. It was almost like the revenge I fantasied for taking their women and in this sense I felt no personal rage toward them. It was as if I asked for and got what I had because of my own foolishness and lack of wariness in this situation. I knew these things happened and had been wary of them, but at this particular time I was on my way to navy boot camp and in some way had been blind to the situation which was, I realize now, obvious.

I see now that the novel I wrote in many ways parallels what I am writing now, and it is as if I could not express my feelings to the analyst directly because of my fear and now I have broken through.

The reason I went with the whores was to show how willing I was to do literally anything to evoke love and at the same time degrade them, control them and gain a certain victory which I find hard to express concretely. This victory also involved efforts to make them have orgasms, which I knew they usually faked, and finally the only way to "win" seemed to be to get more for my money, to beat down their price, to take longer, to pay less than they asked. This was delicate to handle: to steal back my money was unethical, to refuse to pay also unethical. The technique was to bargain and then have my orgasm, taking as long as possible without enraging the whore. Of course I can see now the whores probably unconsciously recognized this technique and started their initial bargaining accordingly. It is as if there was almost a ritual and the few really satisfying experiences (in their warped way) consisted of situations where I had my way with the paying, who did what and when and how and the length (usually so for reasons of liquor, previous orgasms and control), the sexual act finally culminating in a strong orgasm.

Barry's need to placate and to control came from an earlier situation. His mother and father were divorced when he was five years old. His mother then dated several other men. Barry felt highly competitive with these men and wanted to keep his mother for himself. As a young child, he had no way of doing this and so he tried in every way possible to placate her. In the relationships with the prostitutes, he was reliving this effort to placate and please his mother. At the same time, he was making an effort to control her, to prevent her from leaving him by establishing dominance.

During the course of his analysis, a number of changes took place in Barry's relationships with women.

As my analysis progressed I began to understand in part the reasons for my behavior. As an interim adjustment I returned to the dance halls more often. I had fewer relations with whores and rationalized unconsciously by developing a compulsive fear of venereal disease which even led me to take a couple of Wassermanns when I was particularly anxious.

I had a few affairs. One with a call girl. The first time I paid her thirty-five dollars. She was studying singing opera and said she was in analysis. I said I liked her and would take her out but not pay her. After a couple of dates I realized she could not tolerate this arrangement.

Barry was now making an effort to change. He now seemed to have made an effort to find and establish a relationship. An interesting thing here, too, is that as Barry increased his own feeling of self-esteem he went up the social ladder of prostitution and began to have more affairs with call girls and dance-hall hostesses, rather than with the streetwalkers and house girls with whom he had previously had relations.

What had happened in the analysis? First, he had begun to recognize the mingling of fear and desire that he had had for his mother and the fact that because of this mingled fear and desire he had found it impossible to establish satisfactory relations with a "good" (that is, mother-like) woman. Second, he had realized that he had used prostitutes as a way of handling his anxiety, chiefly his feeling of inadequacy as a person and his doubts about his masculinity. In the course of therapy he lost some of the feeling of inadequacy and fear and therefore was now able to establish relations with his wife on a healthier basis. Not being afraid of her, he was able to express anger directly to her, and therefore he did not need to express it by running off to prostitutes or call girls. Feeling more adequate as a human being, he was able to improve his relationships with people in general, so that he did not feel that the only kind of relationship he could establish was one for which he paid.

There are interesting resemblances between Barry's personality characteristics when he first entered analysis and the personalities of the call girls: the anxiety, the lack of inner controls, the depressions, the inability to defer immediate gratification, the fear and the utilization of rebellion against society's dictates as a means of expressing his pent-up feelings of anger, which he could not express in any other way. Barry, again like the call girls, had vacillated with his partners between attitudes of ingratiation and hostility.

Even in becoming a bartender he chose an occupation in which he could ingratiate himself by serving drinks to the customers who deserved them and act out his hostility by expelling drunks.

I do not know how Barry resembles other compulsive Johns, but in one crucial aspect there seems to be considerable similarity. From what the call girls reported, the compulsive John is one who finds sexual relationships with women other than prostitutes unsatisfactory. This is usually due to an over-attachment to the mother and the consequent need to assure oneself that the sex partner is as much unlike the mother as possible.[1] In addition, prostitutes evoke the feeling of degradation in sex. Once as an adolescent, Barry had been in his mother's apartment with a young girl friend his own age. The apartment door was locked. Their activity had been limited to dancing, listening to records, kissing and necking. Suddenly his stepfather came home and yelled at him that Barry was turning his house into a house of prostitution. Barry felt that this experience was a factor in making him feel that sex was low and degrading and that therefore in order to enjoy sex, he had to feel low and degraded.

As a result of his earnest cooperation in his analysis Barry was finally able to overcome his need for degraded sex and instead to use his sexuality in achieving a more loving relationship with his wife. He stopped being a compulsive, or for that matter, any other kind of John.

---

[1] Freud, S., *Collected Papers, Vol. IV*. London: The Hogarth Press, 1950.

13. CONCLUSION

THIS BOOK WAS UNDERTAKEN in an effort to make some slight contribution to our knowledge of human beings by describing a specific group—the call girls and the men in their lives. I recognize fully that even in this limited area much more remains to be learned and I hope that others will be encouraged to explore further. Particularly urgent is the need for the scientific exploration of means of handling the problem of prostitution.

There are those who believe prostitution necessary and who argue for its regulation rather than abolition. It is hard for me to understand how an ethical society can condemn some of its members to the kind of degradation to which even the aristocrats of prostitution, the call girls, are subjected. In this connection it might be instructive to note that the French, who for many years were the chief proponents of regulated prostitution, abolished it in 1946.

For many centuries the chief attempt to deal with prostitution has been to punish the prostitute. More recently there have also been efforts to punish those who live on the earnings of prostitutes, the pimps and procurers. I know of no society that claims to have abolished prostitution by these methods.

Some who have contemplated the problem of prostitution have thought of a different approach. The radical

238

social reformers, Anarchists and Marxists, have charged our form of economy as the villain and have seen in the degradation of prostitution another reason for reorganization of our economy.

In another vein, in their book, *Cast the First Stone*,[1] Judge Murtagh and Sara Harris express another view:

> But the fundamental answers to the problem are to be found primarily in an improved society, a society that will give greater recognition to its dependence on God and will more adequately provide for the humblest of His children.

While it is difficult to differ with this hope, I do not believe that we must sit by impotently waiting for this happy millennium. Beyond this hope I would suggest that the funds now used for trapping, arresting and imprisoning prostitutes be diverted to experimenting with alternative solutions to the problem. This is a study in which non-governmental organizations, too, such as foundations supporting research and social welfare groups, may be interested.

It seems to me that the clinical picture of the individual girls clearly indicates their need for some form of psychotherapy. In discussing this prospect with law enforcement officers, the problem of expense is inevitably brought to the fore. While it is true that individual therapy is often a highly expensive process, it need not be more expensive than the cost of arrest and imprisonment. To arrest one call girl generally requires the services of a number of highly trained men for many days and involves expensive wire-tapping equipment. The cost of therapy is no greater.

Fortunately, recent advances in the technique of group therapy make the cost of treatment less expensive, since one therapist can simultaneously treat six to ten patients. In addition, the group setting, by establishing a social situation in which the girls can experience some measure

---

[1] Murtagh, J. M. & Harris, Sara, *Cast the First Stone*. New York: McGraw-Hill Book Co., 1957.

of acceptance, may be helpful in dealing with their characteristic problems of "not belonging."

One important problem faces both therapeutic attempts, individual or group—the problem of motivation. It is extremely difficult to help people who do not wish to be helped. While it is frequently possible for a skilled therapist to motivate a reluctant patient, this is not always true. It might be helpful, therefore, to supply trained leadership for self-help groups of call girls similar to Alcoholics Anonymous.

Alcoholics Anonymous is led by ex-alcoholics who devote themselves to assisting alcoholics who wish to rid themselves of the problem of alcoholism. I have known a number of alcoholics who found this group approach helpful. With the call girls, I believe the effectiveness of this group effort might be increased through supplying individuals trained in group therapy or group leadership to assist in the formation and productive utilization of the group experience. It might also be possible to train former call girls to participate in the leadership.

The entire problem of the setting in which therapy takes place is of crucial importance. The fact that I had at least partial success in treating five out of six call girls was, I believe, owing in large measure to its being a voluntary arrangement on their part. They were not in jail: they were not coerced into the therapeutic relationship but entered into it of their own free will.

While it seems impossible to eliminate imprisonment for arrested prostitutes in the present climate of public opinion, it would certainly seem to be a worthwhile experiment to substitute for the present ineffective policy of punitive incarceration a therapeutic institutional community such as that suggested by Dr. Ralph Banay in *We Call Them Criminals*.[1] In this connection it should be mentioned that the Soviet Union has made such an effort with its prophylacteria. Much that is recorded with respect

---

[1] Banay, R. S., *We Call Them Criminals*. New York: Appleton-Century-Crofts, Inc., 1957.

to Russia will inevitably be suspect. However, several writers have attested to the efficiency of this approach.[1]

Included in such a therapeutic institutional community should be provision for vocational training and preparation for integration into normal society through some form of sponsorship into the community, preferably by non-official social or religious organizations.

In the Soviet prophylacteria the inmates (diseased prostitutes) had to maintain themselves by their work. They received training in some occupation, as well as a general education. In addition, efforts were made to provide facilities for creative expression through the encouragement of dramatic and music lessons, games and dances. After being gradually introduced to everyday life on the outside, the girls were discharged and sent to factories.

While it is important to experiment with efforts at the rehabilitation of presently practicing call girls, it is even more important that efforts be made to explore the possibilities of preventing the development of new generations of call girls. In the preventive attempts I would like to differentiate between relatively direct, immediate attacks on the problem and the long-range approach.

So far as the immediate approach is concerned, it seems to me that the focus of attention has to be on the special sub-culture from which call girls are recruited. As this is also the sub-culture in which drug addiction and other forms of social behavior flourish, it would seem to call for serious study by a number of cooperating agencies. In this approach perhaps valuable information could be obtained by applying methods similar to some employed by the New York State Youth Board. The essence of the method is

---

[1] Carter, D., *Sin and Science*. Toronto: Progress Books, 1945.
  Halle, F., *Women in the Soviet East*. London: Martin Secker & Warburg, Ltd., 1938.
  Bronner, V., *La Lutte contre La Prostitution en U.S.S.R.* Moscow, 1935.
  James, T. E., *Prostitution and the Law*. London: William Heinemann, Ltd., 1951.

that trained workers mingle with the groups in their own habitats for purposes both of study and of guiding them into more socially approved behavior. For example, Youth Board workers befriend street gangs and attempt to gain their trust. The youth workers make no attempt to act as law-enforcement officers, endeavoring instead to get at the causes of delinquent behavior. Similarly trained workers could perhaps gain entrance into the sub-culture from which call girls are recruited, to study it and develop ways of making the members of this sub-culture more socially useful.

The work of such groups as Synanon and Daytop where former addicts do most of the treatment in a therapeutic community is most impressive as most of the female members of this community have been prostitutes.

Since many of the tendencies which lead to the choice of the call-girl profession appear early in youth, it would be helpful for teachers, parents and social workers to be aware of the nature of these tendencies and to take appropriate steps to prevent their flowering into full-scale professionalism. Referral to proper treatment centers, such as mental-hygiene clinics, of both the pre-delinquent child and her family would seem to be the most appropriate action here. Also the growing field of family life education might be helpful in this context.

Long-range preventive planning requires careful assessment of the fundamental causal factors that develop the kind of personality which make it possible for a girl to choose the prostitute's profession. While I have tried to indicate throughout this book that I do not believe there is one simple factor that is enough to determine the choice, I do think there is a situation which makes it impossible for a girl to drift into the profession. Put as simply as possible, it is this: *the girl who is tied to her family with bonds of love and affection does not become a call girl.*

The fundamental preventive task, then, becomes strengthening the family as a source of love and growth. The forces of social disintegration which abound in our society are the chief enemies of rewarding family life. These forces include the sanctioning of exploitative relationships in order to achieve material success; the failure to integrate large sections of our population into our culture, chiefly the Negro and the foreign-born; and the lack of a unifying, constructive philosophy or system of ideals.

Essentially, then, while much can be done that might be of great assistance to the individual girls and to the men in their lives—the pimps and Johns without whom prostitution could not exist—our patient is society.

The treatment of the patient, society, should also be dependent on accurate diagnoses and skilled techniques. Although our knowledge of individual diagnosis and therapy is incomplete it is infinitely advanced over our knowledge of social diagnoses and therapy. It is imperative that social scientists address themselves to this therapeutic task as the next order of business. However, it is a task too great for any handful of specialists; it is a task that also calls for an aroused, interested and informed population.

Essentially, however, this is a book about the call girl herself, her problems and their possible solution. I can think of no fitter conclusion than a letter I received as I was writing this last chapter. While the writer of the letter, Beverly (who also wrote the letter quoted at the start of the book), praised me unduly for her improvement (she had two additional therapists and was endowed with a fine intelligence and wish for growth), I am quoting her letter to show how one human being was able to fight her way to health and happiness. When one considers her problems, this letter becomes a tribute to the human being's capacity for change.

Dear Harold:
I am so unbelievably happy that I have to pinch myself every hour on the hour. Although it was a painful blind groping for a long time, like learning shorthand, it's just confusion until one day all the pieces fit together and it makes sense, and the memory of the tedious practice hours forgotten.
I had such a long way to grow and with what seemed

the almost insurmountable obstacle of myself, that looking back it seems incredible.

I'm ecstatic, exuberant, hilarious and jubilant most of the time; the rest of the time I'm just happy. I maintain a serenic *sang-froid*, which practically amounts to emotional vacuity, with the exception of debatably neurotic lapses as an occasional tear of compassion for the mentally enmeshed.

I have taken up with religion (the mark of an unsuccessful analysis be damned); not the "pie in the sky," deathbed confessional type, but possibly the golden rule, love your fellowman variety, the fatherhood of God and the brotherhood of man.

I have found me a mate beyond all expectations and life is a thing of beauty and a daily joy.

This probably smacks of euphorism to you, but is not a perpetual state of euphoria to be envied?

I'm no longer fighting with my Mother (note capital letter), I have finally absorbed her. I dreamed of her not long ago, the first time that I haven't substituted a symbol for her. She was trying to get me to stay with her. I was in the car with Jack (my ever-lovin') and my bags were packed and we were about to drive off. She entreated me to stay saying, "You can't leave me!" I told her I had to go with Jack and we drove off. (If they had had analysis in her day, I wouldn't have needed you. But then of course she wouldn't have gone.)

All associations of the past have disappeared as you predicted, and although I disbelieved you at the time, it has become a matter of preference, not discipline, just as you said it would be.

What a service analysts render and yet with all the rewards how difficult it must be to be objective and have the required patience to have your hands tied while trying to make the blind see. I met a sculptress recently who would like to do creative things, but is making [prosthetic] noses, ears, fingers, etc. There is no one else here doing this sort of thing and the existing people in the country who are, do very garish work. She feels a moral responsibility to continue her work, and yet she feels stifled by the influx of the maimed. I asked her if it wasn't gratifying making people whole again as it were. She agreed that it was but that she was weary of the stream of negativity involved. I thought of you analysts making people whole again, and remembering when I asked you if patients didn't take a little piece of you away with them.

I've become "square" to a positively fanatical degree. Whereas "Forgive them for they know not what they do" was a fine stay of execution at one time, I now have been given the privilege of knowing better, and it is mandatory that there isn't the slightest infraction, with the result that with the police courts, front pages, etc. out of my life, it seems wonderfully uneventful. I no longer find it compulsive to be scintillating.

I remember one session we had and you tapped the ashes out of your pipe, characteristically, and said, "You mean you don't think there's a little good in everyone?" I thought you were pretty unprotected with that square attitude. The picture has changed, and I'm going through my "white" period now. I do still think that the good might possibly be a little more obscured in some than others; however, the Talmud says that man is given goodness in his heart at birth, the evilness he creates himself.

With comparative rapidity I've seen my previous associations fail to resolve their problems—Frankie's suicide; Sylvia's curettement and subsequent death; the "princess" serving one to ten in the state penitentiary for possession of "H" [heroin]. Sunny's just got out of jail after serving a ten-month sentence for possession of marijuana; Lester (he's the one that used to write me under the name of MRS. Chas. Addams when I was in N.Y.) was murdered a few months ago; and last week Stevie—a lez and racket girl—shot herself through the head while talking to her current butch. She was a remarkably beautiful girl (as was Sylvia), who looked like Lili St. Cyr, only prettier. Such a waste! Tom, who told the police (not cops any more) that the tea (marijuana) he was growing in the backyard was Chinese marigolds and won the title of the "Chinese Marigold Queen" thereby, was killed in an auto accident a few weeks ago.

Not one of them would have wound up in the scrap

heap if they had been able to straighten themselves out of the mire.

And so by the grace of God and psychoanalysis I have a brand-new wonderful life.

In closing this tome, I want to quote to you from Dane Rudhyar, under whom I have studied, a little excerpt from one of his books on spiritual growth called the *Age of Plentitude:*

"To all those who are struggling toward that dawn, psychology offers its guiding light. It is a light which often at first makes the night seem darker, which attracts to the searcher after plenitude monstrous shapes of the dark. It is a light for strong hands to hold and great hearts that know no fear. But no one has reached the Mount of Transfiguration who has not faced utter emptiness and, facing it, pressed on and through, in personal courage and faith with the love of Man burning at the core of his silence and his ever-repeated deaths."

Much love,
Betty

APPENDIX

THE FOLLOWING ARE EXCERPTS from the case histories of the twenty call girls who were interviewed for the social psychological portion of this book. To avoid repetition, many of those portions of the histories that have been quoted or summarized in the text have been omitted here. It was also necessary to omit other portions of the case histories in order to eliminate as much as possible any identifiable material. Also while the book proper emphasized the similarities to be found among the girls, in this section the emphasis is more on some of the individual differences.

In both the histories gathered by the volunteer interviewers and by the author, the material is presented in the language of the girls themselves as much a possible. As indicated at the head of each excerpt, ten of these interviews were conducted by myself, and ten by the girls described earlier. Thus there are variations in the commentators' styles.

ANNE A.

Age:	29
Years of Schooling:	9
Marriages:	2
Previous Occupation: Waitress	
Years as Call Girl:	10

Interviewed by Stella

247

ANNE: My father? Why he was a common laborer. He worked on a farm. All his life he wanted to own his farm but he wouldn't take anything from Kennedy. Kennedy offered to buy him one and make him independent but he refused. My father is *very* honorable. My mother was the mercenary one. My father was religious and always tried to make me see the error of my ways.

Kennedy gave me *everything*! I had a fifty-thousand-dollar home, jewels, clothes, money to spend like water. When my family used to visit me, I'd always give my mother a fifty-dollar bill. Why I gave them at least a hundred dollars a week. My father was very proud and we had to cover up and hide where the money I gave mother came from. My father wouldn't be obligated to anyone. He wanted to make it on his own. I had a terrible quarrel with him about his refusing Kennedy's offer. I told him that he was in no position to refuse Kennedy's offer and what's more he had no right. How could he send his wife out into the fields to work and let his other daughter grow up in poverty with nothing and no chance of making a decent life for herself? I'm a lot like my father but I'm more practical. I told him you can't throw away opportunity unless you don't need it but he couldn't see it. He begged me to leave Kennedy and give up everything. I told my father terrible things about himself but I couldn't help it. They were all true. Afterward I felt awful. Then I told Kennedy some equally horrible things. Oh I hurt that man so deep. I told them both off but it was just as terrible for me. I just couldn't help what I was saying to them.

It was my father who finally talked me into giving everything back to Kennedy and running away with O'Brien. My father wanted me to get married and live a quiet, decent life. The happiest day of his life was when I threw away fifty thousand dollars, leaving myself with nothing but O'Brien and my two children. It was worth it. It wasn't as if I could never make it again, but my father could never make it and I knew it. He had no chance at all. It was worth it to make him happy even if it did turn out so badly, but I've never told him so. I send money all the time but they don't know for sure where I get it. They've stopped asking questions. They're glad enough to get it but my father is a very righteous and religious man.

When did I first start getting paid by men?

The first time was when I was a waitress in Santa Fe. I was only sixteen. You wouldn't believe it. It's too fantastic. I used to let customers drive me home—then lay them and get ten dollars or so. But then I had that awful experience with that man I told you I can't remember about and I was so bitter, I decided I was going to get even with *all* men. I'd make them pay and pay and pay. I'd pick guys up in a bar and take them to my hotel (in Santa Fe) and soon a smart bell boy propositioned me (he had noticed the guys I'd bring in) and he used to send them up one after the other but I had to give him one-third. Why I'd see as many as fifteen men in a day.

That was before I met Kennedy. Now I know you get more from one guy sometimes than knowing fifty the other way. Having a "cushion" is very important—your bank books are your cushion but you need at least one good man that knows he is responsible for everything, or almost, in reserve as well. Not that I would pass up any "fifties" when they're available, though I don't need them. I used to paint, too, for money. At first I did pictures for tourists of horses and fields and then I did some portraits. I painted Kennedy four times and I've done portraits of almost every one I ever really liked.

The first portrait I did when I was nineteen. I loved that man so. Oh but I did! I would have done anything in the world for him. He had a wife and children, but I didn't know. I was so dumb then. He used to travel and he'd take me with him. He'd check into hotels under another name, not his own. When I told him I was pregnant he sat and looked at me as if he hated me. I'll never forget the look in his eyes. Then he tried to kill me. He got up and walked toward the window of the hotel room and opened it. When he turned around and came at me I knew what he was going to do. I don't know how I knew. I just knew. He pulled me across the room to the window and tried to throw me out. I fought him and screamed. I got away. He chased me around the room saying the most horrible things. I still can't bear to remember the things he was saying then. I had really thought he loved me. I couldn't believe what was happening. I don't remember how I got away. I think he was frightened at the noise I made. He couldn't risk being exposed as the father of my child.

It was after that that I tried to kill myself. I didn't want to live and remember those awful things he had said and done to me. I loved him so much. I was still so innocent about men. They found me half-dead and I woke up in jail somewhere in Texas. I don't even know how I got there. They got his name. I was babbling deliriously when I came to, I guess. It was the last thing in the world I wanted—for him to find out, especially if it didn't work. I was in that jail for a month and I had no way to kill myself. There was nothing I could do. I stayed there and heard his voice shouting those dreadful things in my head till I thought I'd go crazy. When I got out a month later, I had decided what I was going to do. I was going to have the baby. But I had a miscarriage at five months back in my own home in Santa Fe. The baby was born dead. I was alone with my mother when it happened. My family had stood by me and were going to keep the baby for me. But all I got was the disgrace and the baby was born dead. He was killed overseas and I wasn't even sorry. I still can't think about him without crying. I loved that man so and I was so innocent.

BETTY B.

Age:	31
Years of Schooling:	12
Marriages:	1
Previous Occupation:	Office worker
Years as Call Girl:	1

Interviewed by Marie

BETTY: Baby, you won't get me to talk to that kind of a doctor. I was under treatment by one for over a year and I never want to talk to another one. But I'll talk with you and, gal, I'm holding you responsible.

Schools—always went to private schools even a private kindergarter. Ritzy—no? And that's what my baby is going to do. Uncle Fred and Aunt Helen sent me. Mother married a good man. She thought he had money but he was poor and always sick. I never remember him being full of vim and vigor. My only recollection of him is either in bed or on the couch. Always sick.

I suppose I was what you would call an average student. I got C's and B's. I had no favorite studies. I sort of felt that since it had to be done, let's get it over with. I didn't go to college. You knew that I went to work for Uncle Fred. I was so sick of receiving charity from all the family relatives and shortly thereafter I met Doug.[1] Lord, I'll never forget the look on your face at our wedding. In your eyes I would have been

---

[1] Doug was a Negro; Betty was white.

better off marrying a leper. Did I ever thank you for coming? I always meant to. Now where were we? Oh, yes, I remember. Doug and I were happy as long as we were alone. His friends disliked me and my so-called friends treated him like the janitor of their building or worse. But since Doug had plenty of money and his practice was good, we got along fine with his friends. Then after a while they began to accept me into their society. They even asked me to work with the local chapter of the Society for the Advancement of Colored People. Since the family had completely disowned me, I did it. But every once in a while I'd get lonely for my own kind. Remember I'd call you and get you to drive me over to Cincinnati so we could lunch and take in the Saturday matinee?

You felt so sorry for me, the sick one, and you tried so hard not to show it. Sometimes I don't think you've changed at all and then at other times you'd have me puzzled. Well I've been living here now for almost a year. It became unbearable when I couldn't get a reservation in any decent hospital to have my baby. First I tried to put myself to sleep for good with pills, then I made Doug get me an apartment here and believe me I'm staying here. Doug has me on an allowance but, hell, it's not enough. This apartment needs four or five thousand dollars' worth of work done on it and I want all of the baby's memories to be pleasant ones.

The men—I have no feelings at all about. I'm just lucky they feel about sex the way they do and are willing to pay for it. I certainly couldn't make the kind of money I need any other way.

Did I ever have a woman—did I? She was terrific. It was the physical-education teacher in school. My first experience of any kind. I almost climbed up the wall. It was in the gym. After that we must have had a ball at least once a week until I graduated. Oh it was two or three years, I don't remember. It's been so long ago.

I can't talk about my family or being with them. I was always away at school or summer camp or visiting relatives so how could I talk about them or any of my relatives? I was never with any of them long enough to form any attachment.

CARLA C.

Age:	27
Years of Schooling:	10
Marriages:	None

Previous Occupation: Strip-Teaser
Years as Call Girl: 10

Interviewed by Marie

CARLA: You gorgeous thing. When are you going to let me make you? I'm serious. What's this doctor need the info for? Not that it makes any difference. Why don't you quit men and go for me? No worries and all sorts of fun. Let's go on a ball tonight. How could you be so old-fashioned?

How I got this way? Well I'm a twin and this is a funny bit—I go for girls and Bill goes for boys. Guess we were just born different. Who knows? But do we have fun. Hold on, my drink needs redoing. Now what can I tell you, my little one? All about the birds and bees. Ask me and I'll answer, maybe.

My family—I never knew Pop, and Mom never had time for us. So I was overdeveloped for my age and I convinced this traveling salesman to take me to Chicago when I was seventeen, which he did. He got a room at some hotel and when he woke up the next morning I was gone and so was most of his money. I then got a job at a club as a stripper but, hell, I saw all those broads wearing minks and diamonds. Six weeks later so was I.

How'd I start? Two guys were keeping a fat old bastard and his wife. The only way he could get his kicks was to watch me with his wife and boy did she get her kicks. When he wasn't around we had a ball. Sure when I was young and innocent I loved men. It's only been since I've been with Gussie that I've given up men. When she gets through there's nothing left for them. I could be made love to by a man for hours upon hours and nothing happens and no man can really stay long enough to please me. No man actually knows enough about a woman's body to do it well.

Black, white, what difference does it make? I'd screw a zebra for fifty dollars; and anything new they can invent I'm all for. I'm here for one purpose and that's to enjoy my life to the hilt and live it the same way. Oh call me another time —Gussie just came in.

MARIE: Shortly after Carla said this she tried to commit suicide when she found Gussie with another girl. Carla has been supporting Gussie for the last three years. She states that she and her brother grew up with very little attention from their mother (Carla's father left when the twins were born), and that her brother and she raised themselves, although her mother had a maid to take care of the house while the mother was operating a used-car lot, in the small Ohio town where they lived.

DIANE D.

Age:	27
Years of Schooling:	9
Marriages:	1
Previous Occupation: Wife	
Years as Call Girl:	11

Interviewed by Marie

DIANE: I quit school in first-year high. Some of those teachers were so damn stupid. I got out, found a soldier ready to be shipped over and married him. Got myself a nice allotment and started to live. But he would get himself injured and get shipped home so puff went my allotment. He found out I was living with Johnnie and I came East. Johnnie went to work as a bartender and after I started working he steered all the suckers my way. Men are all suckers so I say take them for every mother's cent you can get and if they don't give, take it anyhow if you can get away with it.

It was really quite simple the way I got into the racket. I needed to get hold of some kind of change and this jerk was on the make so I said, "All right, doll, but you'll have to part with some *l'argent*," so that was it. Well why? Well you know I'm lazy and, hell, all a man wants is to get into you so why not make it pay off? Instead of your boss and a lousy sixty dollars a week, get yourself a lot of bosses, work when you want and sleep till you want to get up. Have everything a rich husband could give you without the aggravation of putting up with him; running a house, et cetera.

I was raised on a cross-country bus; first California, New Jersey, Florida; wherever mother's next husband lived. My second father was the one I liked. He was always buying things for me. A bookie, you know—still loaded with cash. I hope the bastard leaves me something in his will.

Everything's a gamble. Oh, hell, I don't like to talk about the past. I told you all I'm going to tell you for your doctor. If he wants to know more, let him shop in my store. Well, love, if you run across any rich ones give mother a call. Nothing like money, unless it's more money.

MARIE: I've known Diane for over a year. She's been in the business since 1944 and during this time, according to the stories both she and her mother have told me, she's gone from one man to another either spending her money on them or giving it to them. Her mother tried to get her away. She is at present living with her mother and accepting an allowance of seventy-five dollars a week from her mother. Her father is and has been since she was two years old in a state insane asylum. Her mother got a divorce and married a bookmaker. They were divorced because of religious differences. Since then her mother has been working as a stenographer down on Wall Street. Diane made one suicide attempt with sleeping pills and reported having early sex relations with her stepfather at the age of eight. In addition, she has had occasional homosexual experiences.

ETHEL E.

Age:	28
Years of Schooling:	12
Marriages:	2
Years as Call Girl:	2

H.G.: Ethel is the daughter of a high-ranking executive in a large corporation. As a young girl she rarely saw her father who was usually away on business. Her mother suffered from extreme depression and frequently locked herself in her room for weeks, letting Ethel fend for herself. She found she could get her mother to snap out of her mood by engaging in some piece of outrageous behavior. Often she brought boys back to the house and had wild drunken parties until her mother emerged from her seclusion. Once she bathed nude in the creek that ran through the center of the small Connecticut town where she grew up. After finishing high school she came to New York, was married and divorced twice and started to live with a social worker with whom she had four children. When she found out her husband was having an affair with their 15-year-old-baby-sitter she started to go out with other men. One of the men she met was a powerfully built commercial artist, who had formerly been a boxer. It was to help him solve his financial problems that she became a call girl.

ETHEL: You don't know what it means for a plain girl like me to have men give me hundreds of dollars every week just to go to bed with me. My legal husbands and my common-law husband, all three of them made me feel unattractive and undesirable while these men are convincing me otherwise. One of them sends me boxes of 100 ten-dollar bills as a surprise if he finds our sessions exciting. It is true that I give all this money to Gene but its worth it to me. Gene saved me from a life of meaningless drudgery in the suburbs growing pepper plants. Now I associate with some of the most exciting people in New York. Last week a world famous artist painted my picture in the nude while he masturbated and made delightful conversation. Johns have taken me on trips to Bermuda, Jamaica, London and Cairo. We stay at the best hotels, I wear clothes I could never afford, I drive a new Jaguar and all I have to do is go to bed with some men. They all tell me how great I am and I probably would go to bed with them anyway if I met them socially and get nothing in return. For the first time in my life I am really happy.

STELLA: A week after Ethel told me the above, she took an overdose of pills and landed in Bellevue.

FRANKIE F.

Age: 37
Years of Schooling: Tutors, privately educated
Marriages: 1
Previous Occupation: Wife and mistress
Years as Call Girl: 17

Interviewed by Beverly

BEVERLY: Frankie was born in London, England. Went to India with father and mother. Was illegitimate. This used to weigh on subject's mind to an extent. Identified herself with and romanticized grandmother, who was also illegitimate. Father was in the service of the Crown. Economic factor different than here. Subject had personal amah and tutor and the family had many household servants. In India where poverty is prevalent, they would have been on a high economic scale by comparison. Did not have formal schooling, but was taught by mother, who was well educated in England, and by tutors.

When mother died she took her inheritance, about fifteen hundred dollars our money, and went to London, where eventually she met and married an American soldier, who brought her to this country.

Sex fantasies were priests in flowing robes or monks with erections showing among the robes. Also fancied herself with a man as being brothers and having sex together. Would have man tell her that he was her older brother. Lived with and had an affair with a Lesbian for about a year at one time, but eventually returned to heterosexual relationships. In her attitude regarding men she was always questing for perfection. "There must be someone who is right for me somewhere." Very critical of men but desired the approbation of men and was lavish with gifts and money. She hated being in the racket and would only see someone when finances made it imperative. There was a period of about two years when she quit and was kept by only one man. He gave her around one thousand dollars a month. At the culmination of this, his wife had interceded and he himself had a nervous breakdown and was committed to a sanitarium. She went back to the racket for about two years before her suicide.

Got into the racket through a smooth-talking guy who told her to go to work until they had a little money together and he would put up the same amount so that they could go into business together. The day after she turned her first trick, she attempted suicide for the first time by turning the gas on, followed by at least six subsequent attempts, the last of which was successful. She died about three months ago.

GEORGIA G.

Age:	35
Years of Schooling:	12
Marriages:	None
Previous Occupation:	Chorus girl
Years as Call Girl:	15

Interviewed by Beverly

BEVERLY: Subject lived with her father until about nine years old. Mother, preceding this time, took subject to California and then returned to Texas where father resided. Put subject in convent and private schools until she left the father, taking subject with her to California. Got a divorce and remarried six weeks later. Told subject the reason she left father was because of subject's asthma and that Houston was not climatically advantageous for her. The following marriages of subject's mother (five in all) were to ne'er-do-wells.

Father is upper middle-class and has repeatedly helped subject and mother financially through the years. Mother is ineffectual and dependent. Subject fiercely protective and masochistic regarding mother. Contributes to support of mother from proceeds of racket. Subject desperately afraid of marriage. When marriage is discussed, mother intervenes with: "What will I do?" Subject feels she cannot support herself and mother also, if she quits the racket. Is going through a situation now with a fellow who insists she quit and they get married. However the fellow has no visible means of support or potentialities and is six years younger than she and the mother is making tearful pleas not to leave her, so it is most doubtful subject will give up racket at this time.

Mother is a most attractive woman, who was only in her thirties when subject went into the racket, and she found and still finds various excuses for not seeking employment. Mother has not worked in sixteen years and is an alcoholic with such neurotic tendencies that an ultimate breakdown is a possibility.

Georgia is a complete extrovert, gregarious, indefatigable. Has a defensive attitude and is witty, caustic, thoughtless of others and completely self-centered. Has always had a pimp. Is terrified or refuses to be alone at any time. She is the most confused person I know and really needs help but has such a closed mind she couldn't conceive of needing anything from anybody.

In regard to the father, subject once said, "I wonder if my father would trick with me?" When asked, "Wouldn't you feel strange having an affair with your father?" she answered, "No, I think he wants to and his money's as good as anyone's." Knowing subject, I personally am of the opinion that she most likely misconstrued the father's affection and that it would not be feasible to her that any man could be affectionate to her for herself alone.

One early sex experience at age twelve was when mother and fifth and last husband were traveling in car with mother driving and subject was in back seat with stepfather. Subject was awakened by stepfather fondling her. He attempted to have intercourse with her. Mother became aware of the situation and eventually divorced him.

Sex fantasies are being in a harem and she is the newest addition. She wants desperately to please the sultan so that he will prefer her to the others. Another is to be taken by force and against her will.

Had first intercourse at seventeen. However, this was preceded by three months of oral copulation. The specific step into the racket was when she and another dancer were working in the chorus in San Francisco. A couple of men asked them to go out after the show. She was tired of men always making passes so she told them, "Sure we'll go to bed with you but it'll cost you a hundred dollars." When they acquiesced it seemed pretty easy and so stage-door Johnnies became stage door Johns. As the Johns became more prevalent, the chorus went the way of all things.

The only prostitute I know of who has *not* attempted suicide (except daily) and the *only* one who likes the racket. Says it's a challenge to make men like her. Thinks she is most attractive and has a blustering self-confidence that if it ever shatters or she faces reality, could be devastating to her.

HELEN H.

Age:	32
Years of Schooling:	12
Marriages:	2
Supplementary Occupation:	Astrologist
Years as Call Girl:	2

Interviewed by Beverly

BEVERLY: Subject of lower-middle-class parentage, Russian ancestry. Lived in Maryland with father and mother until the age of two. Father and mother divorced at that time. Didn't have much contact with father after that time. Subject was placed with family until she was eight years old at which time mother took her to live with her. Lived with mother until eighteen years old. Mother was employed as white-collar worker. Made an adequate salary to support self and subject. Also had outside money from alimony.

Subject only child of this marriage. Half brothers by mother's previous marriage very cool toward subject due to fact that mother ran away with Helen's father, deserting their father and them. Subject also has great antipathy toward mother.

Mother predatory and aggressive. Very interested in social work, women's organizations, etc. Subject introverted, shy, self-effacing, introspective, studious, well-informed. Finished high school and went to trade school, where she took telegraphy and a business course.

First sexual experience in basement with man who may have been gas man or electric meter man at about five years. Man attempted to put something metal under her dress. Next experience was at fourteen when subject first had intercourse.

Had girl friend who was a prostitute. After a suicide attempt with sleeping pills, went to girl and told her she was down and out. Girl friend introduced her into the racket. Has been in racket ever since. Hates the racket. "Doesn't everybody?" Is making every effort to get out. "Isn't everybody?" Has almost accomplished same. She only sees two people at this time. Is bringing eight-year-old daughter to live with her in June, an impossibility before, due to the racket. Has finally managed the financial possibility to quit. Receives social security from her second husband, who died. Is doing astrological charts to augment income. Has been studying astrology for the past three years with this in mind. Has saved enough money for a backlog and will see one or the other present tricks before retiring.

Said her fantasies are having sex with animals, namely, apes, gorillas, etc.

IRENE I.

Age:	30
Years of Schooling:	12
Marriages:	2
Previous Occupation: Mistress	
Years as a Call Girl:	4

Interviewed by Beverly

BEVERLY: Subject born in North Dakota. Came to California and was schooled here. Both parents still live together and subject lived with them until first marriage at seventeen. Subject reports parents entirely indifferent to her.

Subject's own first marriage culminated in divorce. Subject went to New York City and met a man who became interested in her. She traveled extensively with him and he spent most of his time in Europe. Due to the comment about the liaison he finally prevailed upon her to marry a seventy-year-old prince. The prince being impoverished, was put on the payroll and after his marriage to Irene he accompanied them on their travels for the sake of propriety. Subject went to Rome, Paris, Cannes, Switzerland, etc., living from place to place still with the same man. Eventually she became homesick and she came back to New York, where she lived for several years. The man came from Europe periodically to visit her and provided her with funds. From the environment of the low-class family background to the champagne-

and-caviar existence was not as much of a hurdle as the road back.

The money that was sent her was not commensurate with the life she had been leading. So when opportunity presented itself in the form of available men she immediately availed herself. At first it would be only for a bracelet or fur or such, and then cash and then less and less cash. She started to take cash about age twenty-two.

Built a complete fantasy about self. Alludes to: "When I was married to the Prince" frequently and has woven a romantic background for herself. When asked her name invariably says "Princess ————" with all the various names of the Prince. She has been Lesbian since late teens. Has not had an affair with a man for other than financial reasons since that time. Visited her family, which she keeps in the background and never refers to. Returned to New York with another Lesbian that she met in California, who had a background of heroin. It was only a short time before Irene was goofing with the needle. She got so badly hooked that she made an appeal to her European friend and he gave her money to go to a private sanitarium and take the cure. After being released she stayed off the stuff for a while but got back on it. She got so bad that time that she finally committed herself to Lexington. After being pronounced cured she returned to California.

She attempted blackmail of the European by threatening to expose him on the grounds that he had driven her to dope and thus ruined her life. He made a settlement and completely washed his hands of her. She went through the money in a short period of time and being back on the needle needed funds. At this time even as a low-priced call girl it was difficult because of her appearance. She is six-feet-two and down to around a hundred and twenty pounds. Her body is so thin and so scarred from needle marks. On the West Coast she got her weight back. When an addict gets off the needle they usually zoom up in weight.

She moved in with a family and was trying to rehabilitate. It was not long, only a month, before she was back on the needle. She got arrested for marijuana and for some reason or another they didn't detect the marks. However, it was a mixed-up situation. The fellow with whom she was picked up was wanted in the West for attempted murder and by the time they found it out here he had already bailed out and jumped his bail. They were so interested in finding him that they let her go. She told them she was a princess and didn't know this fellow except casually and that's what you get for getting mixed up with the wrong people. In view of the fact that she didn't have a record and the Lexington thing didn't come out, they released her.

Next time she was picked up for peddling narcotics. Police called her and told her that they were a friend of a friend and she had them come up in a cab and honk twice. She threw the key out of the window to them and when they came in had the H ready for them. The police also found a quantity of heroin in the apartment. She was so covered with marks that there is not a doubt in the world that she will go to prison. The fantasy of the title value has been destroyed and the publicity of her arrest has removed her defenses. The trial is coming up in a week and she has been unable to break her habit, which means that she would have to break it in jail, which is a pretty depressing thought. So a week ago she took a whole bottle of sleeping pills. But her father found her and called an ambulance and they "saved" her.

This subject was particularly aware of an extreme cruelty in her personality. She would pick out some unassuming little person and needle them without them being aware of it. She would get someone to sing who obviously had no voice at all and encourage them to get up in front of others. There was no limit to which she would not go to make a production out of a completely unnecessary situation. She would round up a group of people and get them to applaud the person singing and they would all join in on her private joke. It delighted her to see others making fools of themselves. When I would ask her why she would answer, "It amuses me. They are so—nothing." Then she informed me that they had no background. Irene's father was a milkman. I think she was convinced that she was royalty and "these nothings" were her inferiors. As long as she could humiliate them it seemed to make her feel more secure.

In her sex life she is essentially the femme but has gone a little the other way in the last year. Because of her size it is difficult to be the feminine counterpart. Also she is sadistic in her sex as well as in general. Girls that make it with her frequently show up with black eyes and the like.[1]

---

[1] Later Beverly notified me that Irene had gone to trial on the heroin charge and was sentenced to a term of one to ten years in prison.

JANE J.

Age:	43
Years of Schooling:	12
Marriages:	None
Previous Occupation:	Waitress, restaurant proprietor
Years as Call Girl:	13

Interviewed by Beverly

BEVERLY: Subject's father left the mother at a very early age. Subject doesn't remember him as child. Feels that possibly mother became pregnant and father married to avoid illegitimacy. Almost an over-attachment to mother. While mother was living and subject not living with her, subject wrote a letter to the mother every day. Great antipathy for the father. He has contacted subject but she refuses to have anything to do with him, feeling that he deserted the mother and that any need he might have of her is a little late in materializing. It pleases her that he is rather old and alone at this time. She feels that it is retribution. Mother died at eighteen, that is when subject was eighteen. Subject finished high school and had various jobs before entering the racket. Was a waitress for a while and then had her own restaurant.

Sexual experiences at an early age consisted mostly of intimacies with girls while in boarding school. Went with one girl for several years until the other girl graduated. Forgot about this after school years and fell in love with a boy when she was about seventeen. He came from a bourgeois blue-blood family. The boy's mother looked down on Jane and blocked the marriage. She had normal sex relations with this boy. The boy was apparently dominated by the mother and was torn between the two conflicting elements. He finally committed suicide by shooting himself.

Sexual fantasies consist primarily simply of envisaging a man and a woman co-habiting. I would say definitely homosexual inclinations, if I may presume to probably bark up the wrong tree. Subject has voiced a strong desire to try out a Lesbian. Tried with one but the sex scene for one reason or another never transpired. I've tried to discourage subject from this pursuit but she is at a restless period and since the natural inclination is latent it would be a vulnerable period to experiment. Fellow she has been going with—who is married and the father of four children—and she quarreled and she is feeling sort of lost and lonely.

She had a most unpleasant experience a few years ago just preceding her entry into the racket. She got mixed up with a man (married), and went to Miami with him. He was a check artist. He forged checks and when they picked him up she went too. She almost went to prison and it was a very bad period for her. This was the first liaison since the first boy committed suicide. And this time she felt betrayed. She has overcome this experience pretty well with the exception that she went into the racket. At the time of the trouble she was given probation. A doctor came along and helped her. He finally started keeping her, although she did work in his office as his nurse. At the conclusion of this she felt she would just as soon see several men as have her time completely usurped by the doctor, who was a bit of a bore. Hence, the racket.

Although fairly well adjusted, everything considered, she has quite a bit of hostility when her defenses are down, mainly when she is drinking. She gets hostile and makes a scene and then later cries and feels guilt. After clearing the air she'll be fine for another period until it builds up pressure again and it becomes necessary to get drunk again, to unload. Some people get loaded, she gets unloaded.

Her attitude about men? She'd like one. She'd like to settle down, but not with anyone who would infringe on her freedom or rather her way of life. She would not look for love but for financial security. However, she could probably talk herself into it.

She enjoys sex (not with Johns) but it is not a paramount interest to her. She has a few promiscuous affairs.[1] Feels that being used to someone is important. Fellow she just broke up with was very appealing to her sexually. "Believe me, in my opinion it must have been great because he didn't have anything else to offer."

Subject made one attempt at suicide with sleeping pills. Started in the racket at age thirty.

BEVERLY [a later report]: Jane is now forty-three. She got married two months ago to a man of substance. He is charming, intelligent, a man of the world. He met her as a trick. He worships her and thinks she is a wonderful, charming

---

[1] Non-commercial affairs.

child. She is a child all right. But the charming is a little debatable. Since the marriage she has started drinking much more heavily than before. Behaves like a fishwife by having tantrums and really terrible scenes in public, which has been going on for years. Cussing up a storm in front of waiters and patrons of restaurants, etc. She is leaving him this week as she "can't sit and look at four walls all day and at least the racket was exciting." She says he is in debt.

I asked her to get competent help and told her that in my opinion it is all a part of her self-destruction guilt thing, and that she just can't let herself be happy until she gets at the underlying causes and that time she said, "I don't need any help."

I answered, "Neither did Frankie" [who committed suicide]. She burst into tears and fled the table. We were at a restaurant having dinner. She was complaining of at least getting paid in the racket. This conversation went on. She said, "Do you think I want to sit for the next ten years waiting for a mink coat?"

I lost my head, so I almost cuffed out by saying, "Do you think you are going to earn a mink by yourself? You deserve to leave him. It's the best thing you can do for him. I think you should be a whore. That's the only answer for you. Fifty-year-old whores are in real demand these days."

KAREN K.

Age:	26
Years of Schooling:	11
Marriages:	1
Previous Occupation:	Model, Actress
Years as Call Girl:	8

Interviewed by H. G.

H. G.: Karen is a slim, intense, neatly dressed, attractive young lady. She was born in a large Southern city and came to New York at age sixteen to attend modeling school. Her present ambition is to be a successful actress. She started studying for the theatre after she got married. Her husband "loved the fact that she was good at acting but hated the fact that it took so much time." She would leave the house at 6:30 and not come home until 11:00 P.M. He resented it.

"I have very few interests. I like people. But not events

like basketball or football. I had an appendix operation and they did something which prevents me from ever being pregnant. I feel this is a real favor."

KAREN: My way of life was very different from my husband's. I wanted fame and fortune. He wanted me to love him. I became bored with him but I still respected him. I respect him because he is not selfish. It makes me feel sad to think that most people are so selfish. It's more than sad; I feel very annoyed, like the feelers on a spider's leg. I came to New York and modeled. I always felt I had to come to New York and find glamour. I didn't want to stay in the South and go to work and get married. I spent six years looking around for what I needed to make myself complete. It always seemed to me there was something lacking in my life and I was depressed. I kept bad company with people who didn't know how to open the door. I fell in love with an intelligent man who had a goal and was working toward it. In the company of this man I was always scared of saying the wrong thing and so I couldn't get this man. It became an unhealthy relationship. We couldn't resist seeing each other but when we saw each other we quarreled all the time. He knew how to reach all my weaknesses and hurt me. Once he hurt me so badly I tried to take my life.

Mother married six times but we were always very close. She always discussed her marriages with me and asked my permission. It was great, great love between Mother and me.[1] Mother divorced father when I was five years old but he never remarried and he always continued to be close to help Mother and me. When I was a little girl Mother was beautiful and I liked her very much. She became a sister to me rather than a mother. Mother tried to have me understand her rather than to understand me.

I started to take heroin when in New York. This man introduced me to it. He felt that he was not part of life and therefore he did not feel that anything was evil or wrong. He occasionally showed me some little signs of affection which made me very happy. Everything we do away from the golden path we are paid back. Fred, my husband, made lots of money but he could get no security out of it so he fell in

---

[1] Stella, who arranged for me to interview Karen told me that she never saw Karen with her mother when they weren't quarreling, usually bitterly and often violently.

love with me out of his need to help someone else. It was his compassion that attracted him to me. I started to study and I kicked the habit. [Gave up the use of heroin.]

While I was married I received a note from the intelligent man that I have loved. I memorized every word of it. "I wish I could glance at the stairs and see a pair of unforgettable legs. They would turn, and I would follow." I started to think of him and then I got a divorce and I tried to reach him.

When in a group I can talk and act friendly but when I am alone with him I can't talk. After kicking the habit once I received a call from Danny and again started to take heroin.

As a child I was dying to grow up and Mother allowed me to do whatever I wanted to do. At ten I went to live with my aunt. She was very strict. She made me act like her two younger children. She'd put us in bed at eight and I would lie there for hours unable to sleep and couldn't understand why she put us to bed. Also my aunt would question me about my parents and then discuss it with other people.

At four a friend of my father's took me in his car to teach me how to drive. I was sitting in his lap steering and he did something nasty. That evening he aked me to go for a ride again. He took off my panties and played with me. I thought as I looked at the clock in the dashboard of his car: It's almost time to go home. I'll be home soon. Finally he stopped. I thought I could not show fear or shock. I felt I had to move slowly. He told me I mustn't talk and I said, "Of course not." Years later I saw this man playing with another little child. It may have even been his own child.

How do I feel about sex now? I have the warmest feelings for the other person. I usually have an orgasm but I have to love the other person to be able to enjoy it. I often think of being completely dominated and fighting it.

At a party if I look well, I feel good. I try to look my best. First I decide what I am going to wear, according to what kind of people are going to be there—you know, what response I want from men. I want a friendly, relaxed, warm, relationship emphasized by the feeling that you are something special. The thing I look for is honesty. To be able to say what comes to your mind. I'd like to knew that the man really, really loves me. I like to feel that sexually we satisfy each other. Like conversation. I can't stand to go to bed without conversation. One fellow used to say that he would like me to be with other men in front of him. The thought did not interest me, although he attracted me very much. I liked his sadistic talk: "I like to whip your little ass." He used to slap my fanny, pull my hair, slap my face and ask me to tell him that I wanted this. I didn't encourage him because I didn't want him to beat me up too much. I like to be held. I like to be played with. I like to have my breast stroked, but I want a man who understands why he does these things, not to do them mechanically.

As a little girl I played with little girls. I had no desire to play with little boys. At fourteen I went out with a man who had a convertible. One time we went out with another couple. They were necking in back. We got out of the car and went around behind it. He put me on the rear fender and started to ————— me.

He kept going with me and I couldn't break up the relationship although I didn't care for him. I was afraid he would tell my girl friends. Finally I stood him up one time when we had a date and I went to a dance with another man, he walked in and told everybody that I had given him a disease. Then he took me out of the dance and we had sex.

At twelve I started to play around with a girl friend. Once I had a friendship with a girl who later proposed that we have sex. We did and I was the female. Another time I had an affair with a girl and I was the doer. I had another affair with another very dear girl friend of mine and enjoyed it tremendously. It was really a physical thing. This girl made me very passionate. She told me I must obey her and do what she wanted me to do. Once she got me very excited and then made me stop to go to school and then come back to her. I could never fall in love with a woman. I want a man to take care of me. This affair was during marriage. I only repeated this once. I later repeated and she was the aggressor, but only once.

I left New York and went home, where I met an older man about fifty-five who gave me a great deal of money. I left him because of boredom and came back to New York. I came back to New York with very little money. An old girl friend of mine who became a call girl called me and asked me to visit her. I went over to see her. She had a suite at a Park Avenue Hotel and she suggested that I become a call girl too. I took a suite and began to live very well. This lasted two or three years. A rich young man who knew what I was doing fell in love with me and wanted to marry me. I started to use heroin and continued for two years. For a period I supported a man because I was lonely and I needed someone to go on errands. He was the woman and I was the man. I couldn't give him any money because I paid three hundred dollars for rent and a great deal of money for heroin.

LAURA L.

Age:	24
Years of Schooling:	12
Marriages:	None
Previous Occupation:	None
Years as Call Girl:	6

Interviewed by H. G.

H. G.: Laura was born and raised in a small town in southern New Jersey. She was illegitimate. Her mother met a man at a church picnic and had relations with him. When Laura's mother realized that she was going to have a child, she told her mother. They found out who the man was, and eventually located him, which took some time, since he was a stranger in town. By the time they located him, Laura was born. However, the man married Laura's mother, lived with her for three months and then disappeared. Laura was raised by her grandmother while her mother went to New York, where she worked as a stenographer and occasionally sent part of her earnings home to take care of the child.

At school one of the children once said to her, "You don't even have a father." Laura replied, "Of course I do." The other child insisted, "You don't have a father and you're a bastard. I heard my father say it."

Laura went home indignant, certain that the little girl was wrong and asked her grandmother, who said, "That's right. You don't have a father and I don't want you to grow up like your mother." Laura doesn't remember much about her mother, whom she would see occasionally when she came home for a visit, frequently bringing presents. Her mother did not like to be seen in town where everyone knew about her, and would frequently come after dark and leave before morning. In addition to her grandmother, her grandfather, whom Laura liked very much, and her uncle Eddie also lived in the house where Laura grew up.

When Laura was about nine years old she was passing the open door of Eddie's bedroom and saw him standing nude masturbating. She didn't remember ever seeing a man nude before and she stopped and looked. He called her into the bedroom and encouraged her to do the masturbating for him. He then told her that if she didn't mention this to anyone he would give her candy and toys and be nice to her. They continued this relationship for about a year until they were discovered by the grandmother, who drove Eddie, her own son, out of the house and started to be much stricter with Laura. Laura's mother came home at about this time to visit and told her, "Don't worry about Grandma. I know you didn't mean anything wrong. You won't do such a thing again." Her mother went away and shortly thereafter Laura was informed by her grandmother that her mother had died. For a while the family suffered financially.

After her grandfather died they discovered that he had left substantial savings and Laura was able to go to high school. Her art teacher at high school encouraged her to continue with her drawing, which she had been doing at home. As far as her other school work was concerned, she wasn't interested, had trouble paying attention and would miss classes very often. On the recommendation of the art teacher her grandmother consented to let Laura leave for a New York art school when she was seventeen years old.

She registered at art school, went a few times and then stopped. Since she was now living in New York, she began to hang around restaurants and bars where she started to pick up men, with whom she had affairs, because she said she didn't like being alone nights. Two or three of the men whom she met at a particular bar used to take her to the home of a woman who would rent rooms specifically for such purpose.

The woman spoke to Laura one day and told her, "You're being very foolish, kid. You're not getting anything out of all this. You're a good-looking girl and men would pay you plenty. How about going into business with me? I'll get the boy friends for you, tell you what you're supposed to do and how to do it and you'll give me fifty per cent of what you make."

Laura felt that this was some kind of opportunity for her. She was very much attracted to one man, Fred, who was a racetrack tout, didn't have money, and had told her that he would like to take her out and see her more often, but he just couldn't afford it. On the allowance she was getting from her grandmother Laura couldn't possibly take him out. She felt that she would now be able to be closer to Fred on the basis of her new opportunity.

The woman introduced her to a number of men who paid her from twenty to fifty dollars. Soon a number of the men asked Laura if they could contact her directly. She didn't have any place to receive such calls (she lived at a girls' residence club), so she asked the men for their phone numbers and when she had a substantial list of such numbers she joined another girl, Phyllis, and they both rented an apartment in a hotel.

One of the Johns that Laura met fell in love with her, took her out of the apartment and moved her to a more exclusive hotel, paying all expenses. Laura soon tired of him and whenever he came to New York from Chicago she would instruct her answering service to say she was out and to take a message. She would see him the absolute minimum necessary to keep him paying all expenses. At this time he was married and was attempting to get a divorce so that he could marry Laura. He would be in town for two- or three-day visits and she would spend one night of these visits with him at the hotel suite. As soon as he left she would call Fred who would move back in. In addition to being a racetrack tout, Fred also became a dope pusher and would supply Laura and her friends with heroin, morphine and marijuana.

Laura continued to work with Phyllis and found it advisable to keep two apartments, one for professional purposes and the other to be paid for by the man from Chicago. Laura's day would begin at about 2:00 P.M. The afternoon Johns usually paid twenty or thirty dollars and would sometimes come in groups of three or four to her two-room suite. An afternoon's work often totaled a hundred dollars each for Phyllis and Laura. Evening dates were frequently for dinner and the evening. The minimum for an evening was fifty dollars. At the end of a night's work ending anywhere from 11:00 P.M. to 2:00 A.M., the girls would go home, call their friends, get high and go off to the bebop clubs until four. When Freddie wasn't with them they would sometimes pick up someone else, take him back to the hotel or go to his place to get higher and ball (have sex).

Laura began to spend more and more time high, lost interest in the Johns and hated spending any time out of her own world of illusion. Frequently she would fall asleep and burn herself and her clothes while sitting in a chair or reclining in bed. She lost weight and grew very pale.

After a while Fred left her and she took an overdose of sleeping pills. Later she found another man, named Arthur.

Arthur and she lived together, both taking dope, and she now began to do all her business at home. In the meantime she lost the John who had been paying for the hotel suite because she finally refused to see him altogether. Her business consisted mostly of quick twenties at home. When a John was expected Arthur would go for a walk or to the grocer. Laura seldom got out of bed, except for bathing or dressing. This last year she spent chiefly in this way.

MARIE M.

Age:	32
Years of Schooling:	14
Marriages:	2
Previous Occupation: Secretary	
Years as Call Girl:	5

Interviewed by H. G.

H. G.: Marie is a tall, Junoesque blonde about thirty-two years old, who still speaks with a slight midwestern drawl. She had been told about this study by a friend, became very interested in it and called me up to volunteer herself as a subject.

She made an appointment over the telephone to see me. I went to her apartment, a very pleasant place on the East Side of Manhattan in the lower Sixties. Three rooms: a living room which was well stocked with expensive antique furniture, a second living room where the furniture was simpler and a good deal more comfortable (this room also contained a large library of popular fiction), and a bedroom. She spoke without too much feeling about the things she told me.

Marie was raised by her grandfather, who was a federal judge, and by her grandmother, who was a concert pianist. Her father and mother were never married and her father left her mother after living with her only a few months. They had met when her mother, who was a concert singer, was on tour. Marie knew her father and later learned that he had married seven times. He acknowledged her as his daughter and introduced her to her four half brothers and her half sister. Her mother never married, but continued to travel as a singer. Her grandfather was very much interested in Marie, and having by this time retired, he spent a great deal of his time with her. Her grandparents, and her mother—on the rare occasions when she was at home—were a little disturbed by the girl's tomboyishness and decided to send her to a private school.

While Marie was in her senior year at high school her grandfather died. The grandmother was bedridden and to Marie the thought of going back to the small town and spending her time with the old lady seemed simply impossible. Marie had met a man at a local ice-cream parlor, where many of the girls congregated. He was twenty years older than she, an airplane pilot, a romantic, dashing figure who had flown with the Flying Tigers. She fell in love with him and they were married. She said he was very domineering and ruled her completely: told her when to get up; what to eat; what to wear; what to read. He was, in addition, insanely jealous.

For a time they lived in Mexico, where her husband engaged in some kind of smuggling activity for a foreign power and was constantly being looked for by the police and by federal authorities. She found this and his long absences highly upsetting. She stated that after he had been gone from home for a long period he would question her as to what she had been doing and she couldn't stand his jealousy. She found the relationship with him very uninteresting sexually but submitted because he wanted her.

She divorced him and went to Washington, D.C., where she worked as a private secretary for a number of legislators and diplomats. At home, she had always had enough money while her grandfather lived; and in her married life her husband's illegal activities had been very profitable, so she found her secretarial earnings insufficient to support her in the style she liked. She worked at night as a waitress for a time to supplement her salary, then left the government service to take a job as a bookkeeper with part of the big "Syndicate," a group of gamblers who then controlled the gambling world in Florida. She worked there for several months. At one point she asked one of the big racketeers how she could make more money, and he suggested that she become a call girl. She didn't like the idea, but he said they were closing their Florida operation, as they were due for one of their periodic check-ups, and he advised her to go up North and look up a friend of his, Larry D.

Marie went to New York and tried to find a job, without success. She called up Larry D., who asked her to meet him in a night club. He made it obvious that he was interested in her and told her that she was the kind of girl he was looking for and would take good care of. He kept plying her with drinks until she was quite drunk. Then he took her home to his suite in the penthouse of a large apartment building on the East Side. This, she said, was the first time she had ever had relations with anybody but her husband. In the morning she found a thousand-dollar bill under her pillow.

For the next six weeks she never stopped drinking, and in a kind of alcoholic haze went from one to another of Larry's friends and contacts, never getting less than one hundred dollars. Finally she decided: This is a business and I might as well stop kidding myself. She decided to treat it like any other business—joke with the clients and not get so upset about it. "That was after I tried to kill myself by turning on the gas jets in my room."

MARIE: Since I think it is a business I act very careful. I have health examinations every ten days and use a strong mouth wash. I'm willing to have oral sex with a man or a woman. Occasionally some of the men want an exhibition and so I'll do it, but I get no feeling out of it. In fact, I never got sexual satisfaction out of either man or woman. I was a virgin when I got married and I never had anything to do with any man other than my husband. With my husband, I got pleasure out of doing something that I recognized he liked but no physical sensation.

I've managed to keep my two lives separate. I still belong to the United Daughters of the Confederacy and to the Daughters of the American Revolution. And of course none of these people know what I do to earn a living. Two of the things which keep me going are religion and books. I don't care what kind of church it is or even a synogogue. If I pass one and I happen to feel low, I'll go in and I'll pray.

For reading I belong to the Book of the Month Club. I like to read popular fiction, historical novels and plays. Even in the racket I try to draw certain lines. Don't like to have anything to do with girls who go to bed with Negroes or who have pimps. I think any girl who is willing to do that is just so immature that there's no sense my having anything to do with her.

If there is any one reason why I'm in antisocial activity at this time, I think it is the FBI, who in one year questioned me one hundred and seventy-three times looking for missing people and other characters that my husband was supposed to know. I felt when they had come to question me that I had disgraced my grandfather's name who was, after all, a federal judge. Even to this day they'll question me about missing people, robberies and things of that kind. And when I had legitimate jobs they lost two or three of them for me by coming around to the offices where I worked.

I don't believe in displaying feelings. The only time I'll cry is in the movies when someone in the picture that I like dies. The only time I cried outside of that was when my grandfather died. I was on vacation and I went to visit some of the girls at the school I had attended. Five minutes to one as I was sleeping it seemed to me that a bell rang in my head. I jumped out of bed and ran home and discovered my grandfather had died at five minutes to one.

I felt so badly when my grandfather died that I determined never to love anyone enough so that they could hurt me so. The only other emotion that I display is that I have a violent temper. It makes me ill to lose my temper or I don't really remember what I do. I'd like to get more education and maybe you could help me pick out the courses that would be most helpful to me.

Being in the racket has made me more broad-minded. I think that now I could be a damned good wife. I approve a husband fooling around occasionally but not the wife because she could have children and women get more emotionally involved in affairs than men do.

Before I was in the racket I had a great deal of false modesty. I still like privacy. Now I think I'm more tolerant of other people but I still don't like moochers or laziness in others.

As a child I wore pants and did everything my grandfather wanted me to. He wanted a boy and I was it. I never cared for my grandmother or my mother. He was the only thing I had to love. He was probably the only person I ever loved.

I had some feeling for music but I resented studying the piano or voice because when I played the piano they said, "She'll never play like her grandmother" and when I sang they'd say, "She'll never sing like her mother."

I'm different from the other girls. I don't think I have any Lesbian tendencies because I don't have much sexual interest at all.

What is my attitude toward Johns? Some of those I like I try to make friends out of. I don't try to make it too cut-

and-dried a proposition. The majority of them come from the garment center and are very nice people. I keep up with their birthdays, send them birthday cards and Christmas cards, try to make them feel that I have an interest in them. If they have any intelligence I like to discuss different things with them but it is surprising how few of them have even as much intelligence as I do. One little fellow tried to steal my wallet. I turned him upside down and emptied his pockets. One man stole a camera from me at one time and I fixed him neatly. I çalled up and I told him I had syphilis. See, I can be mean. I learned this trick even in school. When a man would get me in a corner and there seemed to be no escape I would tell him I had syphilis.

After I left my first husband I got so tired of being pointed out as someone's former wife that I married another fellow just to get my name changed. My grandmother wound up psychotic. That isn't inherited, is it? My mother tries to devour me and I try to stay away from her. She is always questioning me as to what I'm doing. I've made a lot of good friends, good contacts out of my Johns. One of them was my agent when I wrote TV scripts. Through him I met two or three of the wives of my Johns socially. Now I understand why the men went out looking for call girls. Their wives were the kind that would never do the things for them that they want done.

NELLIE N.

Age:	22
Years of Schooling:	12½
Marriages:	1
Previous Occupation: Dancer	
Years as Call Girl:	2

Interviewed by H. G.

H. G.: Nellie is a tall, slim, dark, Latin-looking girl. She states that she is part Negro but often passes as white. She is twenty-two years old and occasionally works as a dancer. She was born in Detroit. Her mother died when she was three years old and after that she was taken care of by a succession of housekeepers, relatives and friends. Her father never remarried and was rarely home but provided for her from his civil service salary. In general, she felt he took pretty good care of her. She didn't see very much of her father or of any one person, because of the succession of housekeepers.

Nellie attended parochial and public elementary and high school and then went to the University of Tennessee. She didn't like going to the University and stayed there only six months. She had studied dancing in order to improve her posture and after the first semester was offered a job as a dancer during the summer vacation.

She came to New York and decided to stay, and then when she couldn't find any other work she drifted into "the life." Nellie has an older sister, who is now twenty-eight, and an adopted brother, who is nineteen. She doesn't see either of them and didn't have too much to do with them even when they were growing up because very often they would be divided among different friends and relatives who would take care of them during the day. Sometimes they would come home to sleep and sometimes not. Nellie says she never felt toward them the way most people feel toward brothers and sisters.

She feels she got along fairly well with her father, as they never had any trouble. She didn't make many friends. She used to spend a lot of time by herself daydreaming or going to the movies. The people who took care of her were only too happy to give her money so she would go to the movies and be out of their way. Finally, at high school she did make one close friend, a boy. At elementary school Nellie had one girl friend who was a pretty good friend of hers, but this girl had a habit of always taking other girl's boy friends away. The girl friend tried to do the same with Nellie's boy friend, but this didn't bother Nellie because she knew the kind of a girl her friend was. "I take these things in stride," says Nellie. "I don't get too excited. I'm not very emotional and I don't cry very much. I used to cry when I was younger but I don't cry any more."

NELLIE: Of course, I do get nervous when I'm in a scrape and then I keep thinking about it and thinking about it. Otherwise nothing much bothers me. I was married in 1952 to a gambler. I was nineteen then. I'd been going around with him occasionally. Nothing too much. I wasn't too interested in him, but I got sick for a while and had to stop dancing. I ran into him when I felt lonesome, staying home, nobody

around the house except my father once in a great while—
my sister was married by then and my brother didn't come
home very much—I didn't want to marry him but he kept
after me and after me.

After we got married we traveled all over the country
going from race track to race track and I got tired of that.
I wanted to settle down but he couldn't, so I stopped traveling with him and we drifted apart. Then because he wouldn't
settle down with me I finally got a divorce.

When I was in second year in high school I met a boy at
a masked ball and I went with him all through high school,
and at graduation we became engaged. When I went off to
college I missed him quite a bit. He was very jealous and he
made life difficult. He was very cruel, although I gave him no
reason to be jealous. We had several quarrels because of his
jealousy and my father wanted me to stop seeing him. After
a while he went off to Europe to go to medical school and
he wrote me a great deal but I never answered him. There
was another difficulty between us. He wanted to be a doctor
because it was so highly paid. Not to help people. I felt he
shouldn't be a doctor if he felt that way. This caused a great
many arguments. He thought I was dumb because I didn't
care about money.

When I started dancing I was in shows and we would go
to different towns all the time and there would be different
men at the stage door wanting to take me out. I found out
that the longer you stayed away from men, the more you get
from them. The more I held out—didn't do anything but
maybe hold their hands and give them a good-night kiss—
the more they would be willing to go for. In one town I met
a man who bought me a ninety-dollar bathing suit. It was a
beautiful bathing suit but I felt badly about it. After all, I
didn't think he should go for so much money. But the other
girls told me to see him plenty but no sex because otherwise
he wouldn't be interested in me. Well, when I refused to go
to bed with him he offered me money and the girls told me
that if he offered me enough money it was okay. Still I held
out for two months, and once when I wasn't working he sent
me money to come to New York to see him. After that we
started to have an affair. But he didn't want to marry me so
I broke off relations because I didn't or couldn't see any future in it. With my husband, I never had anything to do with

him sexually until we got married. He never made any attempt—I should have said before we got married.

Once when I was living in New York, in between shows, there was a man who supported me. Paid the rent, fed me. Through him I met another man with whom I became close friends. He helped me furnish my apartment and he gave me food and occasionally money. Then he had an accident and he lost all his money. When he lost his money, his wife threw him out. At that time he moved in with me. He was sick and he had been so nice to me, how could I let him down? So I took care of him. He was broke and I was broke. It was hard to get a job dancing and I told a girl who was in the life about it and she fixed me up and suggested I go out on dates. I did but only just enough to pay for the rent and light bills. One time he said to me, "What are you doing; where are you getting the money?" He was just trying to psychologize me. I felt this was an opportune time to tell him so I told him the truth.

I still go out, mostly just for the rent. Actually I should go out much more than I do. I have gone out and gotten enough money so I could dress well, be able to go to places that I like to go to, especially I like to go to see shows, go dancing or the ballet when it's in town. All of these things cost money and you have to look well. But I can't go out as much as I should—earn the kind of money I should—because, well for one thing, I can't call on the phone. I couldn't call up a John. I wouldn't know what to say. I don't have too much sexual feeling with most men. If it's somebody I like I will, or occasionally I'll have a clitoral orgasm. I only had a real orgasm about three times in my life. With a John, I have never had any sexual feeling at all.

Another thing that keeps me from getting really involved in the racket and going steady is the freakish things that different Johns want. That's one thing I couldn't do.

H.G.: Marie, who had introduced me to Nellie, told me that Nellie had been working as a call girl quite regularly until the time of our interview. Shortly after the interview Marie called me and asked what I had said to Nellie, because she refused to go out on dates. Several months later, Marie told me that Nellie was working as a dancer in a large night club in the metropolitan area and had quit the racket for good.

OLIVE O.

Age:	23
Years of Schooling:	8
Marriages:	None
Previous Occupation:	Laundry worker
Years as Call Girl:	6

Interviewed by H. G.

H. G.: Olive is a rather tall, twenty-three-year-old Negro girl—slim, dark and attractive. She was born in Pittsburgh. Father is unknown. She was illegitimate and her mother never publicly acknowledged that she was her child. She lived with her grandmother and an aunt who raised her, and would spend part of the time in Pittsburgh and part in Cleveland. She would travel back and forth from one place to the other never knowing when she was going to stay with her grandmother and when with her aunt. She went to school in both places, but because she moved so frequently she never formed any close relationships with any group either in Pittsburgh or Cleveland.

When Olive was fourteen years old she started to work in a laundry in Pittsburgh. The work was very hard but she liked it because there were other girls her age working there and she had fun. One of these girls invited her to go to a party with a whole gang. They had a lot of liquor to drink and then the party turned into an orgy. Olive had never been to such a party before: boys with girls, boys with boys and girls with girls. She found it quite exciting. She tried everything at this party and she said it was the first time that she actually had intercourse. She started going to a great many such parties.

Olive noticed that the girls at the laundry who knew how to get along well with the foreman and the boss had the easiest jobs and made the most money, so she decided that she would learn how to get along well with men. "I felt that if I would watch the faggots at parties I would know what to do to please men because the faggot is a man himself and he knows what other men like. I learned special tricks from them and I can do things with a man's organ that very few other women can do."

She continued working at the laundry and continued going to these parties for pleasure and amusement, and after a while she met a man named Joe at one party. Joe was very pleasant to her and she found out that he was a musician who had a job playing in Chicago with one of the bands. When Joe had to leave Pittsburgh he asked her to return to Chicago with him. She didn't feel that there was any real reason for her to remain in Pittsburgh, especially since Joe had promised to get her a good job in Chicago. When she went to Chicago she called Joe up and a woman answered the phone. Olive realized that Joe was married and she didn't know what to do. However, she knew the place where he was going to start work. She slept in railroad stations for two or three days until Joe started on his new job. She went there and Joe took her to a hotel room. While at the hotel room he asked her if she would see a friend of his. The friend was a white man and this was the first white man that she had ever known sexually. When the man left he gave her one hundred dollars. When Joe got back she said, "Gee that white fellow is a nice guy. He left me a hundred dollars and I really had a good time with him."

Joe said, "There's plenty more where that comes from," and took fifty of the hundred dollars.

Joe started to send men to her and took a percentage each time. There was one thing she insisted on. She didn't mind whether they were young or old but she said, "I don't want to go for money with any colored men—just with white men. This way when I go out for a good time, go into a bar where there's all colored, nobody can point at me and say I'm a whore."

OLIVE: One of the things I like with a man, and any man who can do this can have me any time, is I like him to take off all his clothes, get on his belly and come crawling to me like a snake; come crawling right through the kitchen, through the hall, into the living room and on into the bedroom. Any man who would do that really could get me excited. I don't care much about hitting or being hit. But this really gets me.

I don't mind girls either. In fact I like them sometimes. It's nice to have a change. I don't care, though, for girls who try to boss you around. I like them to be soft and pleasant.

One day while I was still going with Joe and giving him half of my money and more, I decided that this was too much. By this time I knew plenty of men who would call me up on their own and I really didn't need him any more. Besides it wasn't so good with him. His wife was always calling up and making a fuss and a bother. I didn't feel like taking him away from her any more so I just moved into another place and never saw him again. Two weeks ago I heard that he found out where I was living and was going to make some trouble, so I came to New York.

I just got to New York last week. I haven't really gotten located yet. I have a lot of friends, though, who I knew from Chicago, a lot of New York men who used to come to see me there, and I think I'm going to like New York okay.

PAULA P.

Age:	28
Years of Schooling:	10
Marriages:	2
Previous Occupation: Waitress	
Years as Call Girl:	11

Interviewed by H. G.

H. G.: Paula is short, has small features, and is the mother of two children. She was left on the doorstep of the mayor's house in a small town in Iowa. The mayor had three children of his own so he gave her to his childless brother-in-law to raise. The brother-in-law had a large farm and Paula felt that he and his wife were not interested in having a child except as help on the farm. They would buy her just the bare necessities, as far as clothing was concerned. When anyone spoke to them about "your daughter," referring to Paula, they would immediately deny that she was their daughter. When Paula was nine, the farmer fell off the tractor he was driving and was killed. His wife sold the farm and Paula was sent to an orphanage because the woman felt she would have enough trouble taking care of herself without the additional burden of providing for Paula.

When Paula was twelve years old and still in the orphanage, one of the boys came over to the girls' section to do some work. He took Paula into a closet and had relations with her. She didn't like the girls in her ward and felt that it was nice to have some one who seemed to like her. She saw this boy sporadically during the next six months. One day they were discovered in the closet by one of the matrons and were sent to separate institutions.

Paula felt very lonely in the new orphanage and when she

was fifteen she ran away from the asylum and went to Detroit, where she got a job in a restaurant because she looked older than her age. While working there, she met a man who came in every day to eat. He would talk to her and was quite friendly. One day he waited for her after work and took her to his apartment. She felt it was worth while staying with him in order to sleep overnight in such a pleasant place with plenty of room, instead of the little hall bedroom she had over the coffee pot where she worked. He asked her to move in and she did. After she had lived with him for a little while she noticed that sometimes he was nervous and jumpy and at other times seemed pleasant and happy. She wondered about this and when she asked him about it, he told her that he was using medicine. The medicine turned out to be heroin and he introduced her to it. Soon there wasn't enough money for both of them to take heroin and the pusher who sold it to them suggested that she could make a great deal more money by taking on men than by working in the coffee pot.

She didn't like the idea at first but drifted into it and started to see men without too much difficulty. She became pregnant after a short time and had to quit. She had no idea who the father was but she had the baby and decided to keep it. After the baby was born she went back into the racket on her own. The man she had been living with left her during her pregnancy; when he refused to return she tried to commit suicide. When she recovered she decided: No man is worth it.

After a few months in the racket she committed herself to the Federal Hospital at Lexington in order to take the cure because she felt that she didn't have enough money to raise her child properly since she was spending it all on heroin. She found the psychologist at Lexington helpful. She said, "He was so nice to me that ever since then anybody who says he's a psychologist I'm willing to tell anything to. Otherwise I'd never be speaking to you now."

When she came out of Lexington she got a job in an office, went to business school at night to learn shorthand and typing, and was soon promoted to private secretary. One day she met some old friends and they all went drinking. After they were drunk someone suggested that they go to somebody's house and take heroin. She joined them and got into the habit again. She soon found that her earnings as a secretary were not enough to pay for the heroin. She went back into the racket, worked at it for another three months, and became pregnant again.

PAULA: I don't understand it. I know from talking to the psychologist at Lexington that the first pregnancy had been a kind of punishment. The second time I became pregnant I knew who it was; I knew the man who was responsible, but I wouldn't go back to him. I wouldn't give him the satisfaction of knowing that he had done such a thing to me, so I went off by myself and had the baby. Now I've got two children to take care of and the habit.

H. G.: She came to New York in 1954 and moved into a hotel room for professional purposes. She took an apartment in the Bronx for the two children and had a woman whom she knew from Detroit take care of them. When she first came to New York she started to pick up men in the streets. She would stay on street corners in prosperous neighborhoods and bump into a man, then apologize, strike up a conversation, arrange a fee and take him to her hotel room. Every time she met a man she made an effort to be friendly and get his phone number. After a while she was able to build up a list of names in her address book and no longer had to work the street. She would call one of the men she knew and have him come to her hotel room.

Of all the girls interviewed, she was the only one who occasionally worked the street. When she felt that she needed a "fix" (narcotics) in a hurry, she didn't want to wait to call or wait until a man called, and she would then go out and pick up men.

For the last three years she has been completely homosexual as far as her own satisfactions are concerned. She had had occasional homosexual experiences previously, having had her first homosexual affair in the orphanage.

RHONDA R.

Age:	19
Years of Schooling:	10
Marriages:	None
Previous Occupation: Pianist	
Years as Call Girl:	1

Interviewed by H. G.

H.G.: Rhonda is short, blond, petite, nineteen years old. She is shy and hesitant in manner and speaks almost inaudibly.

She dresses very simply. She was raised in a medium-sized town in Ohio, where her father and mother had a dry-goods store. They were always busy in the store. She had no brothers or sisters. She was shy and had great difficulty making friends, so that after school she would come home and read a great deal. She started to take piano lessons and found it very interesting. She was willing to practice the piano for four and five hours at a time or play the radio and listen to the piano in the various orchestras and bands. At high school she was occasionally asked to play, but her marks were so poor that she could not often play in school. She found it very hard to concentrate at school and would sit in the classroom daydreaming.

When she was ten years old she went to a movie and became very interested in the man who was the chief character. She daydreamed that she married the man, that they had built a whole life. She took the whole imaginary family through two or three generations, and whenever she had a chance she would sit and think about this family and all the children and all the things that had happened to them. She would sometimes think about her imaginary children and wonder whether one of them who was going with a man should marry him or whether he was the right man for her or whether she should go with someone else.

RHONDA: Many times I think I would have gone crazy if I didn't have my family to think about, especially when I used to be at school and it was so boring, or when I'd come home and I couldn't practice the piano because it was Sunday and my folks didn't like me to play the piano on Sunday, or there was some other reason why I couldn't play. At such times I used to love to just sit down and think about my family, which is the way I think of them.

H. G.: The parents were so occupied with their business, which did quite well, that they never seemed to have any time for her.

RHONDA: I could understand my father—after all he was the man of the house—being so busy with the store. I couldn't understand why mother was always so occupied. In fact I think she was really the boss. She would run the store and tell my father what to do and he always agreed. Sometimes I would get so angry at him thinking, What kind of a man is my father to let a woman boss him? Often I wished that he would act like other men and take over control of his own house. Whenever I would be talking to my mother I would feel that she was a million miles away worrying about something that was going on in the store or about a sale that she was planning or about the help. She seemed much more interested in the girls who were working for her. They had ten girls working in the store by the time I was in high school. I asked her if I could work in the store just so that maybe she'd pay some attention to me, and she laughed and said, "Go play your piano; you don't have to work; we're doing well enough here."

H. G.: When Rhonda was seventeen, she left her home town and came to New York to study to be a concert pianist. Her family sent her money and visited her once or twice a year. Once when her mother was in New York she told Rhonda to change her teacher, because she didn't seem to be making very much progress. Rhonda was very much attached to her teacher and did not want to change to the one her mother had picked for her, so she refused. The mother said, "If you won't go to the teacher I picked for you, I won't send you any more money." Rhonda replied, "As you please."

The next day Rhonda went out and got herself a job playing the piano in a neighborhood bar. The pay wasn't much but it was enough for her piano lessons and the rent. She had her meals at the bar. She stopped writing to her parents even though they wrote to her, and she moved several times until they lost track of her. "I didn't think they cared. They were probably glad not to have to bother with me at all."

RHONDA: While at the club a number of men started to pay attention to me and take me out. I had never had much to do with boys at school because I was too shy. Besides, I was always too wound up in my thoughts and had never been very interested in boys. Back home, there had been two or three boys who had kissed me and I had also gone to a few dances while at high school, but nothing that really amounted to very much. I didn't really know what to say to boys. When these men at the club started to take me out, it was nice to have somebody to talk to. I would tell them different things and they would talk to me about my playing and it was nice rather than having to go home alone.

There was one fellow, Frank, who was pretty nice. One

day we got into a conversation and I told him about my imaginary family. He was the first person I ever told about it. He seemed very interested and told me that he used to think things like that himself one time and so we started going together. One day we were out in his car and he parked and started to make love to me. He was nice and I couldn't think of any reason not to do it because he seemed to want it so much and so I did. I didn't enjoy it very much but he seemed to enjoy it.

After a while Frank stopped coming around. I wondered what happened to him but I never found out. Well after him—I don't know what it is, maybe men can tell—but for the first time other men started trying to make love to me and usually I didn't know how to get out of it. I just didn't know how to say no. I didn't know how to refuse. I would find that I didn't have the words, so I would agree and pretty soon it seemed to me that every man I went out with wanted to make love to me and that I would let him.

I never found this very exciting and sometimes while they were carrying on and panting, I would be thinking about my imaginary family and sometimes I would make it that one of the people in my family was making love with her boy friend or her husband or something of that kind.

Then the bar closed down for the summer. I couldn't find any work. One of the fellows who had been coming around to the club and taking me out occasionally was talking to me one time and asked me what I was going to do. I told him that things looked tough. I had gone to the unemployment insurance, but found that I hadn't been working long enough to collect anything from them. I was telling him about this and saying what a shame it was because I needed the money so badly and he said, "That's all right, kid. I'll take care of you." He took me up to see a friend of his, a girl who lived in a beautiful apartment, and he said, "Here's a friend of mine who's in tough luck. Maybe you can help her out."

The girl told me she was a call girl and she would be glad to introduce me to some men who would be willing to give me money. I went out with one man once. He seemed very much like the other men I had gone with. The only difference was when he got through, he gave me a hundred dollars. Well, that money lasted two weeks and then I went back to this girl and she introduced me to another man. I guess it was about nine or ten weeks before I realized what I was and that I was a call girl myself.

I've been at it a year now and I think that about Christmas I should have enough money put away. I don't spend very much. I have a very small apartment and I don't spend too much on clothes. I usually go to the men's places and they pay for everything.

Oh I don't mind it too much. Some of the men, I guess, are kind of unpleasant, but I don't really think about them very much. I think about other things usually.

SALLY S.

Age:	26
Years of Schooling:	12
Marriages:	2
Previous Occupation:	Commercial artist
Years as Call Girl:	5

Interviewed by H. G.

H. G.: Sally is twenty-six, slim and dark, the mother of three children and has been working as a call girl for the last five years. She looks much younger than her years.

Sally was born in New York. Her mother is of Hungarian descent and says that she can trace her family back through ninety generations of nobility. Her father left her mother when Sally was six months old. Sally attended private school in New York City. Her mother had some money at the time and received regular contributions from the father, who was out on the West Coast but never came to see Sally or her older brother and sister.

Since she had always excelled at art, she started to do small commercial jobs even while she was at school. At eighteen she left school, got herself a job with an art agency, moved to Greenwich Village, made friends with a group of artists, painters and musicians and had a series of affairs. She asked, "If a man needs me, why shouldn't I give what I can give so much of without losing anything?"

It was at this time that she was introduced to heroin. She found the sensation very pleasant and felt that for once she was really "outside of herself." She took heroin sporadically for about two years and then decided that she didn't want to spend her own money on it and it wasn't fair to take it from other people who couldn't afford it very well.

Art work was hard for her because she didn't want to do all the ridiculous things that an agency required. She felt there was something wrong and despicable about trying to sell things with her art. When she met several girls who were working as call girls she joined them because it seemed to her a "much more honest way of living than selling your talents. A body isn't very important but talents are."

When she was young Sally's mother didn't want her to associate with other children because, her mother said, they would demoralize her and since she was a descendant of nobility it was wrong for her to associate with the ordinary children in the neighborhood. The first time she ever had any girl friends her own age was when she was thirteen. She was quite friendly with a number of girls until she overheard the mother of one of the girls at a party warning her to avoid Sally because she was bad. After that she avoided close relationships because her ideas were different from those of people her own age.

SALLY: One thing I can't abide by are the moral codes. To me they are meaningless. My mother would rather be dead than have the wrong silverware on the table. I know a lot of the attitudes about the moral code may be a rebellion against Mother, who always wanted us to be well-behaved and well-mannered above everything else. Maybe it started out as rebellion but now it's part of me. If I were to get married—I tried it twice—it would be such a waste of time to go around talking about the beauty parlor and the butchers, and that's what husbands seem to want from their wives.

H. G.: Sally was married for the first time when she was nineteen, had a child, left her husband and placed the child for adoption. She tried to visit the boy many times but finally he was adopted and although Sally tried to find out who the foster parents were she didn't succeed. Now she feels that it's better for the child not to know. She divorced her husband and a year later, unmarried, had another child. This time the child was taken from her at birth and she arranged for its adoption. She doesn't even know its sex. A year and a half ago she had a third child, who lives with her. An old woman helps to take care of the child while she is away.

SALLY: Even though I don't know where my older two children are, I don't think it really matters because life is a network and somehow through that network I am connected to them. Many times I'm motivated by things outside myself and then I feel as if I'm a vehicle of some other power. I have no will of my own at those times. I feel directed by this other force. Most people block these feelings within themselves. There is a universal intelligence and all people can contact this if they would only permit themselves. That's why I like to write poetry so I can bring other people in contact with this world of universal intelligence. Of course I've missed out on many opportunities in my life. I had an opportunity to publish some of my poetry, and never followed up on it. I had an opportunity to have a newspaper job and never followed up on that either. It doesn't matter to me very much. I can go without eating, but not without sleeping. If I have less than ten hours I feel the day is very difficult.

I don't really have many strong drives. Nothing moves me very much; nothing is really a matter of life or death. I can do many things, but no one thing very well. I used to write poetry and a lot of things, but I can't discipline myself very much. I'd rather dream about it than do it. I never have any interest in making a big effort. I think maybe it's because I don't have any fear of death. To me death is not an ugly thing. If I were to change my ideas about death and have the same ideas as other people, I would have to start to fear it. This would mean giving up a great deal. I would have to give up courage. I don't really believe that death is the end. I think that life and death are like a thread, both of which are connected. If I wanted to I could live like other people. I could disguise my feelings and live out what is expected of me. I don't believe in doing what society wants you to do. I don't believe in accepting society's ideas as my own.

When I was married I used to tell my husband to go to another woman. I don't know whether I loved my husband or whether it was gratitude. My mother often used gratitude as a whip. I could never be very intimate with her. I always felt that she wasn't too happy with me and that she held me responsible because she had lost her husband. It was difficult to see eye to eye with Mother, even when I was a young child. Mother was a phony and she always showed off. She'd show one face to the family and another face to the world. She tried to eliminate other children as my friends. She tried to devour me. When I got old enough so that I could do what I wanted to and leave home, I made a lot of unconventional friends who wouldn't go for the kind of phonyness that Mother believed in.

Why should I love a man? After all what is there in the relationship? Yes, I had orgasms with my husband more than ever before. When he told me about them, I began to have them, but it's meaningless. An orgasm is an anticlimax. It never measures up to the idea of it that you have. It's just a physical thrill, no more enjoyable than eating. I had a relationship with a man by the name of Norwin once. For two years we only had sex four times but we had something more important. We had knowledge. If I can have a relationship with a man where I can gain in knowledge, that's worth while.

One of the reasons I left my first husband was his attitude during pregnancy. He didn't want the child and even when the baby was three months old he still wanted to give him out for adoption or leave him on a doorstep. I don't think very much of men. I think that women are really the stronger ones. Oh I might like to have the physical strength that men have, but even that's not so much because women can take pain much better than men can. Man gets hurt a little and he runs to his mother's breast. Women, on the other hand, are used to pain. If women had had a voice long before this, a lot more progress would have been made.

While I was living with one man at a time I found that I had to repress myself for so long. Now that I'm on my own and can choose the men I want, I choose them on the basis of their paying me and taking care of my material needs. I feel I'm beginning to be free and that I can express myself. This way I can give myself to anyone who needs me.

There's another thing that must have led me into my present life. When I was young and I was good, Mother seemed to be unhappy with me and displeased with me. That's when I was good and compliant. But whenever I was mean it seemed to me that the meaner I was the more she liked me. Probably that's why I picked masochistic men. They must have fulfilled something like what I had with my mother. I guess I hadn't outgrown my need for her. Now that I don't need these kind of men around me, I think it shows that I have separated myself from her. Of course sometimes I've been pretty masochistic myself. I was punishing myself because I felt I had committed so many atrocities when I was taking heroin that I didn't care about anything—also when I tried to commit suicide once. This was another attempt to punish myself. But now I'm through with punishment for myself or others.

Toni T.

Age: 27
Years of Schooling: 12
Marriages: 1
Previous Occupation: Typist, singer
Years as Call Girl: 8

Interviewed by H. G.

H. G.: Toni is twenty-seven, dark, svelte, tall. She was born in the Bronx in New York, the younger of two children. When she was six months old her father and mother separated. She was raised by her mother. The parents made many attempts at reconciliation and for various periods did live together, but after two or three months would begin quarreling again and again separate. Toni went to elementary school, finished high school, and then started working as a typist.

While at school she was fat and unattractive and the children made fun of her. She remembers little boys following her home and calling her "fatso," "fat stuff" and "fat-ass Toni."

When she was twelve, her mother had a lover. He used to come to the house very often and spend the night. Many mornings Toni would find her mother in bed with her lover.

One time when her mother was away from the house the lover came in while Toni was in her slip and asked her to sit on his lap. Toni's breasts had just begun to develop and she felt a strange kind of excitement as he fondled her. She then looked for opportunities to have contact with boys. One time three of the boys who lived on her street asked her to go up on the roof with them. She did and they all had some kind of relations with her. Pretty soon she began to be known as "a girl who was willing to put out." She found that this made her quite popular with the boys, and the very boys who had formerly called her names were now eager to be her friends. Many of the girls would not associate with her, especially since their mothers warned them not to because "she did bad with the boys," but she laughed at them and felt that they would do the same if they had the opportunity or the courage.

When she was seventeen and finished high school, she

started to work as a typist in a large office. There were a number of salesmen working the office and several of them took her out and had affairs with her. As a result they always told the supervisor that she was the best stenographer in the office and she received increases. The other girls hated her for it but she didn't mind.

She was working for a toy firm at one time and a salesman asked her up to his hotel room during the toy show. She had a few drinks with him and he persuaded her to accommodate two of his customers. It was difficult for her to continue to work as a secretary and through her contacts she became a full-time call girl.

Two years ago one of her clients fell in love with her and asked her to marry him. She thought this was rather silly but he insisted, saying that he didn't care about her past and that he loved and wanted her very much. Toni said, "After all I'm a very sexy piece and I guess any man would be proud to be married to a woman like me." For a while she gave up being a call girl and settled with her husband in the Bronx, not far from where her mother still lived. However, she couldn't stand the boredom and monotony. She got so bored with this monotonous life that she would pick quarrels with her husband just for the excitement of it. Once he got so angry at her that he beat her and locked her in the bedroom. She swallowed about fifty aspirins, which she had in the room; her husband found her and rushed her to the hospital.

One day she called up some of the men she met when she was a call girl and went out on a few dates. Her husband found out, was furious, they had a quarrel and Toni moved out.

At the present time she is working as a call girl. Occasionally her husband catches up with her, begs her to come back to him. She sometimes goes back to live with him for a week or two but whenever they quarrel, she leaves.

URSULA U.

Age:	35
Years of Schooling:	10
Marriages:	3
Previous Occupation:	Waitress, gambling assistant, actress
Years as Call Girl:	18

Interviewed by H. G.

H. G.: Ursula is slim, dark and vivacious, with a hint of Southern accent.

She was born in a small town in South Carolina and was one of eleven children. Her father was a garage mechanic. When she was six the family left town and went to Birmingham, Alabama, where her mother ran a boarding house. She completed only the tenth grade, was uninterested in her school work but says she never caused her teachers any great trouble. She stayed away from school on numerous occasions but she states, "They were not too conscientious about checking up on my excuses for being absent."

After leaving school she worked for the telephone company. At the age of seventeen she met a young man in the small restaurant where she had lunch. They became friendly and one day he told her he was going to Chicago and invited her along. She had always wanted to go to a large Northern city and she agreed on the impulse of the moment.

When she arrived in Chicago she got a job first as a waitress and when that didn't work out, she found a job with a side show, working with the barker to attract crowds.

After the show closed she worked as an assistant in a large gambling house and met the fast Chicago crowd. She started to work in small night-club shows and when there was no work earned her living as a call girl.

A well-known writer was interested in her and publicized her so that she was offered a part in the movies. She appeared in several small parts, and at one point was sent to New York to help publicize a picture. In New York she managed to be seen frequently in the company of well-known figures in café society and thus came to the attention of the Broadway columnists, who gave her considerable publicity. She was frequently referred to as the heiress to a Texas ranch or as the owner of a Mississippi plantation. She broke her movie contract and was kept by two wealthy racketeers. She found it difficult to stay with any one man and drifted into being a call girl after she left the racketeers. She has been working as a call girl in New York for the last ten years and appeals especially to older men, who remember when she was a celebrity.

BIBLIOGRAPHY

1. Abraham, K., *Selected Papers on Psychoanalysis*. New York: Basic Books, Inc., 1953.
2. Ackerman, N. W. & Jahoda, M., *Anti-Semitism and Emotional Disorder*. New York: Harper & Brothers, 1950.
3. Adler, P., *A House Is Not a Home*. New York: Rinehart & Company, Inc., 1953.
4. Agoston, T., "Some Psychological Aspects of Prostitution—the Pseudo-Personality." *International Journal of Psychoanalysis*, 1945, No. 26, pp. 62-67.
5. Banay, R. S., *We Call Them Criminals*. New York: Appleton-Century-Crofts, Inc., 1957.
6. Bender, L. & Blau, A., "The Reaction of Children to Sexual Relations with Adults." *American Journal of Orthopsychiatry*, 1937, No. 7, pp. 500-518.
7. British Social Biology Council, *Women of the Streets* (ed. Rolph, C. H.). London: Martin Secker & Warburg, Ltd., 1955.
8. Bronner, V., *La Lutte contre La Prostitution en U.S.S.R.* Moscow, 1935.
9. Caprio, F. S., *Female Homosexuality*. New York: The Citadel Press, 1954.
10. Carter, D., *Sin and Science*. Toronto: Progress Books, 1945.
11. Curran, F. J. & Levine, M., "A Body Image Study of Prostitutes." *Journal of Criminal Psychopathology*, 1942, No. 4, pp. 93-116.
12. De Beauvoir, Simone, *The Second Sex*. New York: Alfred A. Knopf, Inc., 1953.
13. Deutsch, H., *The Psychology of Women*. New York: Grune & Stratton, Inc., 1945.
14. Dollard, J., *Caste and Class in a Southern Town*. New York: Harper & Brothers, 1949.
15. Durkheim, E., *La Suicide*. Paris: Felix Alcan, 1897.
16. Eissler, K. R., (Ed.), *Searchlights on Delinquency*. New York: International Universities Press, Inc., 1949.

17. Flexner, A., *Prostitution in Europe*. New York: The Century Co., 1914.
18. Ford, C. S. & Beach, F. A., *Patterns of Sexual Behavior*. New York: Harper & Brothers, 1951.
19. Freud, S., *Collected Papers*, Vol. IV, London: The Hogarth Press, 1950.
20. Freud, S., *Three Contributions to the Sexual Theory*. New York: Journal of Nervous & Mental Disease Publishing Co., 1910.
21. Fromm, E., *The Sane Society*. New York: Rinehart & Company, Inc., 1955.
22. Glover, E., "The Abnormality of Prostitution." In Krich, A. M. (Ed.), *Women*. New York: Dell Publishing Co., Inc., 1953.
23. Glueck, S. & E., *Delinquents in the Making*. New York: Harper & Brothers, 1952.
24. Glueck S. & E., *Later Criminal Careers*. New York: Oxford University Press, 1957.
25. Halle, F., *Women in the Soviet East*. London: Martin Secker & Warburg, Ltd., 1938.
26. Harriman, P. L., *The New Dictionary of Psychology*. New York: Philosophical Library, 1947.
27. Henderson, D. K., *Psychopathic States*. New York: W. W. Norton & Company, Inc., 1939.
28. James, T. E., *Prostitution and the Law*. London: William Heinemann, Ltd., 1951.
29. Jameson, T. A., "Psychological Factors Contributing to the Delinquency of Girls." *J. of Juv. Res.*, January, 1938, No. 22 (1), pp. 25-32.
30. Kemp, T., *Prostitution, an Investigation of Its Causes*. London: William Heinemann, Ltd., 1936.
31. Kinsey, A. C. *et al.*, *Sexual Behavior in the Human Male*. Philadelphia: W. B. Saunders Company, 1948.
32. Kinsey, A. C. *et al.*, *Sexual Behavior in the Human Female*. Philadelphia: W. B. Saunders Company, 1953.
33. Krafft-Ebing, R., *Psychopathia Sexualis*. New York: Physicians and Surgeons Book Co., 1922.
34. Kuhlen, R. G., *The Psychology of Adolescent Development*. New York: Harper & Brothers, 1952.
35. League of Nations, *Inquiry into Measures of Rehabilitation of Prostitutes*. League of Nations IV, 1938.
36. Lindsey, G. (Ed.), *Handbook of Social Psychology*. Cambridge, Mass.: Addison-Wesley Publishing Co., 1954.
37. London, L. S. & Caprio, F. S., *Sexual Deviations*. Washington, D.C.: The Linacre Press, 1950.
38. Mead, Margaret, *Male and Female*. New York: William Morrow & Co., Inc., 1949.
39. Murtagh, J. M. & Harris, Sara, *Cast the First Stone*. New York: McGraw-Hill Book Co., 1957.

40. Reckless, *Vice in Chicago*. Chicago: University of Chicago Press, 1933.
41. Reik, T., *Masochism in Modern Man*. New York: Farrar & Rinehart, 1941.
42. Riesman, D., Glazer, N., & Denny, R., *The Lonely Crowd*. Garden City, N. Y.: Doubleday & Company, Inc., 1953.
43. Super, D. E., "Vocational Interest and Vocational Choice." *Educational and Psychological Measurement*, 1947, No. 7, pp. 373-384.
44. Super, D. E., *Dynamics of Vocational Adjustment*. New York: Harper & Brothers, 1942.
45. Sutherland, E. H. (Ed.), *The Professional Thief, By a Professional Thief*. Chicago: University of Chicago Press, 1937.
46. Termon, L. M. & Miles, C. C. *Sexual Personality*. New York: McGraw-Hill Book Co., 1936.
47. Warner, W. L. & Lunt, P. S., *The Social Life of a Modern Community*. New Haven, Conn.: Yale University Press, 1941.
48. *Webster's Encyclopedic Dictionary*. New York: Columbia Educational Books, 1941.

INDEX